T0330428

Public Capital Expenditure in OECD Countries

To Juliane

Public Capital Expenditure in OECD Countries

The Causes and Impact of the Decline in Public Capital Spending

Jan-Egbert Sturm

University of Groningen
The Netherlands

Edward Elgar
Cheltenham, UK • Northampton, MA, USA

Published by
Edward Elgar Publishing Limited
8 Lansdown Place
Cheltenham
Glos GL50 2HU
UK

Edward Elgar Publishing, Inc.
6 Market Street
Northampton
Massachusetts 01060
USA

A catalogue record for this book
is available from the British Library

Library of Congress Cataloguing in Publication Data

Sturm, Jan-Egbert, 1969–
    Public capital expenditure in OECD countries: the causes and
  impact of the decline in public capital spending / Jan-Egbert Sturm.
    Includes bibliographical references and index.
      1. Expenditures, Public. 2. Expenditures, Public—OECD countries.
    3. Public investments. 4. Public investments—OECD countries.
    I. Title.
    HJ7461.S78 1998
    336.3'9—dc21   97–47519
                                                                              CIP

ISBN 1 85898 827 6

Printed and bound in Great Britain by
MPG Books Ltd, Bodmin, Cornwall

Contents

List of Tables

List of Figures

Acknowledgements

This book is the result of my research effort at the Department of Economics, University of Groningen over the past four years. Many people have directly or indirectly contributed to its completion, and although it is impossible to mention all, I would like to mention a few.

First of all, I would like to express my deepest gratitude to my direct supervisor, Jakob de Haan, whose 'to-the-point' approach kept me on the right track over the course of the project. His confidence in my abilities stimulated me during the up- and downturns in the project. Furthermore, parts of our joint research efforts are included in this book. I am also indebted to Flip de Kam for his participation during several phases of the project.

I am grateful to Casper van Ewijk, Matilde Mas, Elmer Sterken, Cees Sterks and Harrie Verbon for reading the entire manuscript and providing me with useful comments.

I thank Peter Groote, Jan Jacobs, Gerard Kuper, and Bernd Jan Sikken for conducting fruitful joint research projects and letting me use the outcomes in this book. To reflect this fact, I use the plural form throughout.

Furthermore, I would like to thank both Lans Bovenberg and Simon Kuipers for making my stay at the CPB Netherlands Bureau for Economic Policy Analysis possible and the members of Department I (model building and economic analysis) of the CPB Netherlands Bureau for Economic Policy Analysis, and in particular Nick Draper, Johan Graafland and Ton Manders, for their support during this stay. My research at this institute resulted in Chapter 6.

Apart from the editors and referees of *Applied Economic Letters*, *Economic Modelling*, *NEHA-jaarboek*, *Openbare Uitgaven*, *Weltwirtschaftliches Archiv*, *Tijdschrift voor Politieke Economie*, I would like to thank the participants of the workshops and congresses I have attended for their comments and suggestions on earlier versions of various chapters.

I am also indebted to Siep Kroonenberg for her help with LaTeX. Her efforts made it possible for me to meet the layout requirements.

I benefited much from being a member of the research group CCSO. Discussions with, and help and suggestions from, other members certainly improved the quality of this book.

Financial support is gratefully acknowledged from NWO, Shell and the graduate school SOM.

Several research projects conducted with, among others, Marianne van den Berg, Walter Fisher and Klaas Knot, which were not taken up in this book but took place during its development, made me enjoy this research project even more.

I thank my colleagues of the Department of Economics for creating a pleasant working environment. In this respect, a special mention goes to Peter Heijmans, Victoria Hoogenveen, Jan Kakes, Fieke van der Lecq and Marieke Rensman.

Finally, I wish to thank my relatives for their support and, of course, my wife Juliane for the many ways in which she has contributed to this book. In grateful acknowledgement I happily dedicate this book to her.

Jan-Egbert Sturm

1. Introduction

1.1 INTRODUCTION

Government can try to improve future living conditions in various ways: it can stimulate private (foreign) investment, spend more on education and health programmes in order to enhance human capital, preserve the environment, or it can add to the stock of public capital. The past few years have witnessed growing awareness that the stock of public capital especially has been neglected by many OECD governments.

Almost everyone has experienced the frustration and delay of congestion on overburdened motorways. In the United States (US) the deteriorating quality of roads, bridges, and sewer systems has already led to serious problems. No wonder then that the debate on macroeconomic consequences of the declining stock of public capital started there and became an important topic on the political agenda. Recently, the issue of inadequate public investment has come to the forefront in member countries of the European Union (EU).

The purpose of this book is twofold. First it aims at determining the causes of the decline in public capital spending that over the past quarter century occurred in most OECD countries. Second, this study tries to estimate the macroeconomic consequences of this decline in the Netherlands and in the US. To make the topic manageable, this book focuses on public investment in physical capital only. This should not be interpreted to mean that public investment in human capital is in any way less important.

We concentrate on public capital spending in a macroeconomic context. It is our contention that changes in the public capital budget can best be explained by national developments. Spillover effects from foreign public investment are not likely to play an important role in the analysis of the impact of public capital formation on economic growth, and we can therefore easily abstract from them in the second part of this book. Recent results and insights from spatial science concerning, for instance, location decisions and impacts of interregional trade flows—which are probably also related to public capital spending—are not discussed here. We refer to Rietveld (1989) for an excellent survey.[1]

In recent years some theoretical papers have been published on the effects of public capital.[2] Most of this theoretical work is based on Arrow and Kurz

Figure 1.1   Public investment as a share of GDP, means over 1970–75 versus 1987–92

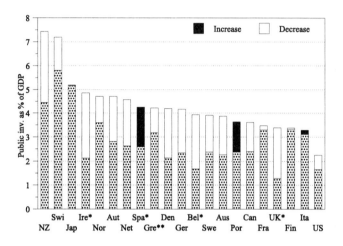

* Only data available until 1991.
**Only data available until 1989.
Source: OECD Annual National Accounts (1994).

(1970). In these studies it is mostly *assumed* that public capital is productive and therefore that it should be included in the production function. In the second part of this book we concentrate on the question of whether public capital is indeed productive and if so, to what extent. As this book will show, getting an accurate estimate of the output elasticity of public capital is not an easy task.

The remaining parts of this introductory chapter discuss both objectives in somewhat more detail. Section 1.2 elaborates on the objectives of the first part of this book, whereas the aims of the second part are the subject of section 1.3. Finally, section 1.4 provides an outline of the book.

1.2   EXPLAINING THE DECLINE

Figure 1.1 shows government investment (excluding residential buildings) as a share of Gross Domestic Product (GDP) for 18 OECD countries over the period 1970–92.[3] The figure shows that public capital spending as a share of GDP declined or remained stable in almost all countries between 1970 and 1992.

Figure 1.2   Public investment as a share of GDP and labour productivity growth in the Netherlands[a]

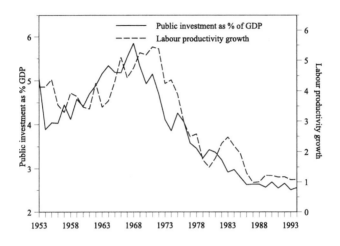

[a]Five years moving average labour productivity growth in the private sector.
Source: CPB Netherlands Bureau for Economic Policy Analysis.

Spain and Portugal were exceptions. In order to become more competitive within the EU, these countries undertook extensive programmes of upgrading their stock of public capital. A small rise occurred also in Italy. Another conclusion that can be drawn from figure 1.1 is that the level of government investment spending varied considerably across countries, ranging between 1.3 per cent of GDP for the United Kingdom (UK) and 5.8 per cent for Switzerland in 1992.

Economists disagree on what caused the downward trend in public capital spending. Many hypotheses have been put forward in the literature. For instance, it is generally believed that during the 1970s and 1980s many OECD countries offset increases in debt interest payments and rising social security transfers by winding back public investment. Also, demographic and politico-institutional explanations are often given.

The purpose of the first part of this book is to take stock of hypotheses that have been put forward to explain trends in public investment spending and to verify them empirically.

1.3   IMPACT

As figure 1.1 shows, public capital outlays have decreased dramatically in most OECD countries since the early 1970s. At approximately the same time productivity growth plummeted almost everywhere, including the Netherlands.

Figure 1.2 displays the five years moving average labour productivity growth in the private sector and the public investment/GDP ratio for the Netherlands between 1953 and 1993. This figure clearly suggests that the decline in public capital spending might explain a large part of the productivity slowdown experienced in the Netherlands since the early 1970s.

A similar pattern emerged in the US, Aschauer (1989a) was the first to notice it. Taking a Cobb–Douglas production function and using annual data for the 1949–85 period, this author found a strong positive relationship between productivity and the ratio of the public to the private capital stock in the US. On the basis of his results, a 10 per cent increase in the public capital stock would raise multifactor productivity by almost 4 per cent. Consequently, much of the decline in US productivity that occurred in the 1970s can be explained by lower public investment spending. The implications of these results for policymakers seem to be clear: public investment should go up to boost the economy.

The aim of the second part of this book is to summarize the stream of literature following the seminal work of Aschauer (1989a), and to extend three approaches to estimate the productivity effect of public capital. So far, only a few studies have been conducted for the Netherlands. Since figure 1.2 suggests that public capital might be very productive here, we concentrate on this country in the empirical part. However, some additional results for the US are also presented.

1.4   OUTLINE

The remainder of this book consists of eight chapters: the next two examine possible explanations for the trends in public capital spending, while Chapters 4 to 7 estimate the effect of public capital on economic growth. Chapter 8 summarizes our findings and offers a general discussion of what we have found.

By applying bivariate Granger-causality tests, Chapter 2 addresses the question why public capital spending decreased in the Netherlands over the last couple of decades. Before doing so, it describes the development of public capital spending in the Netherlands in greater detail. In Chapter 3 several hypotheses explaining the decline are tested, using a panel of 22 OECD countries covering the 1980s and early 1990s.

The second part of the book starts with an extensive summary of methods used to estimate the impact of public capital on output and productivity growth

(Chapter 4). The following chapters focus on three of these approaches. The so-called production function approach in which a (Cobb–Douglas) production function is extended with the stock of public capital will be used in Chapter 5. Such an enhanced production function is estimated for the Netherlands and the US using post-World War II data. By taking a cost function dual to the production function and deriving factor-demand equations from it, a more behavioural approach will be followed in Chapter 6. In that chapter we focus on Dutch sectoral data covering the period 1953–93. Finally, in Chapter 7 we apply Vector AutoRegression (VAR) analysis using data for the Netherlands in the second half of the nineteenth century.

NOTES

1. Recently, Van den Berg and Sturm (1997) have empirically investigated the relevance of several location factors at a regional level in some EU countries. They show that available infrastructure plays an important role in this.
2. Barro (1990), Barro and Sala–I–Martin (1992), Lee (1992), Futagami *et al.* (1993), Glomm and Ravikumar (1994), Futagami and Mino (1995), and Turnovsky (1996) are examples of this theoretical work.
3. The data relate to consolidated general government and have been taken from the Standardized National Accounts compiled and published by the OECD.

PART ONE

Development

2. Public Capital Spending in the Netherlands*

2.1 INTRODUCTION

Of late, the issue of public investment has been high on the political agenda in the Netherlands. In part, this may be explained by the marked decline in public outlays for investment. Government capital spending generally halved from on average 5.0 per cent of Gross Domestic Product (GDP) between 1960 and 1970 to a mere 2.4 per cent in the 1984–94 period. As we have seen in Chapter 1, this pattern is not unique to the Netherlands. In most OECD countries, government investment has decreased substantially during the last two decades. Economists disagree on the causes of this trend. It is often stated that the decline is due to policies of fiscal restraint (Roubini and Sachs, 1989a). The reasoning behind this view is that it is easier to cut back public capital spending than other categories of public outlays, since this can be achieved without much societal resistance as no strong pressure groups are associated with public capital spending. Moreover, the long-term consequences of reducing government investment spending are not felt in the short run. However, there are also other explanations why the level of public capital spending may have halved in the Netherlands. For instance, demographic developments— such as, lower population growth—might explain the decline of at least some components of public capital spending (school buildings).

   In this chapter we confront these and other theories concerning the development of public capital spending as put forward in the economic literature with Dutch data. The next chapter will analyze the development of public capital spending in an OECD context. Chapter 3 will also give a fairly comprehensive overview of the economic literature on this subject. In this chapter we will apply Granger-causality tests in a bivariate 'Vector AutoRegression' (VAR) framework to test various relevant hypotheses. Granger (1969) has defined a concept of causality which, under fairly suitable conditions, is easy to deal with in the context of VAR models. Therefore it has become quite popular in

*This chapter is based on Sturm and De Haan (1995b, 1998) and Sturm (1994).

recent years. To avoid unnecessary complexity in the estimation procedure as a result of the non-stationarity of the data, we follow the procedure as recently developed by Toda and Yamamoto (1995).

The remainder of this chapter is organized as follows. The hypotheses will be formulated in section 2.3. By looking at the data and using the concept of Granger causality, these hypotheses are tested in section 2.4. Before doing so, the next section will first trace the development of public capital spending in the Netherlands since World War II. The final section summarizes our findings.

2.2 DEVELOPMENT

Before describing trends in capital outlays of the Dutch government, it is necessary to define the concept. Statistics Netherlands (1995) defines *investments* as expenditures on goods intended to be used as a capital good in the production process. In general, this concerns goods with an expected lifespan of more than one year and involves new fixed capital formation as well as replacement investments. All expenditures on capital goods of the government are classified as *public* investment. The government is subdivided into central government, local government and social security funds. Local government consists of municipalities, provinces, and local administrative bodies. Transactions involving disability pensions, health insurance and public pensions are registered under the social security sector.

Because of this narrow definition, capital outlays of publicly-owned firms like, the Dutch railway company (NS) are not counted as part of public capital spending. Public utility firms concerned with electricity generation, gas distribution and water supply are likewise excluded. In the national accounts, all such firms come under the heading of the private sector.

Furthermore, investment in military equipment is classified as being for public consumption and therefore not captured by the definition of Statistics Netherlands. Although 'land' is often considered to be an indispensable factor of production and therefore regularly counted as part of the capital stock, public purchases of land are excluded by definition.

It could be argued that intuitively some of the above-mentioned expenditures should be included in public investment. For instance, Boot (1986) poses that essential features of public investment are that the government is the formal owner, finances a substantial part, and plays an important role in the decision process concerning spending levels. In particular, investment by firms such as, the Dutch railway company, the former publicly owned postal services (PTT), public utility firms and public transport firms should in this view be included in the class of public investment. However, implementing this broad definition raises questions as what to do when the state is not the sole shareholder—as is the case with the Royal Dutch Airlines (KLM)—or when its share changes over time, as happened when the postal services were privatized. As Boot's definition is hard to implement over a longer time period, we prefer the well-defined narrow definition used by Statistics Netherlands.

In the remainder of this chapter we will subdivide public investment into the following categories:

- public expenditures for the construction and renovation of government buildings (total buildings);
  - public expenditures for the construction and renovation of school buildings (schools);
  - public expenditures for the construction and renovation of other government buildings (buildings);
- public expenditures to carry out civil engineering works (infrastructure);
- public expenditures on office furniture and equipment, technical installations, transport equipment and other investment goods used by the public service sector (equipment);

Figure 2.1 shows that public investment increased practically every year until 1971. In that year it attained its maximum of almost 17 billion Dutch guilders at 1985 values. In 1987 public investment dropped by nearly 40 per cent and fell below its 1963 level of around 10 billion Dutch guilders (at 1985 values). Local government takes care of by far the largest amount of public investment (on average 73 per cent). As social security funds hardly invest at all, the remaining part consists of investment by the central government. Quite strikingly, the shares of the sectors remained roughly constant over time. Note, however, that the central government increasingly finances public capital spending by local government. Roemers and Roodenburg (1986) report that during 1969–72 approximately 27 per cent of all public investment of local governments was financed by central government. In 1983–84 this share had increased to around 44 per cent.

Figure 2.2 displays public investment as a percentage of GDP. It shows that the public investment share of GDP increased until 1968. Ever since, its share has dropped virtually continuously. Between 1960 and 1970 public investment was on average 5 per cent of GDP. During the 1984–94 period its share more than halved to nearly 2.4 per cent. Compared to the peak in 1968, public investment fell by more than 60 per cent to reach 2.2 per cent of GDP in 1993. This suggests that the diminution of infrastructure spending plays some role here. The decline in capital spending on streets, sewerage, bridges, canals, harbours and suchlike, and the expiration of large-scale projects—in particular

Figure 2.1   Public investment by different tiers of the public sector

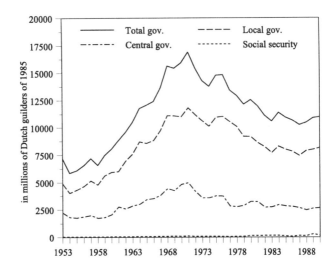

Source: Statistics Netherlands.

the *Deltawerken*—explain this considerable drop.[1] Furthermore, whereas in the post-war construction phase mainly new fixed capital formation took place, more recently the emphasis was on replacement investments. Although public investment in buildings has also declined, its decrease was less marked. Public investment in equipment is the only type to increase steadily over time. Its share in GDP amounted to 0.44 per cent by 1994.

Despite this severe drop, infrastructure spending is still by far the largest part of total public capital spending. Figure 2.3 shows that the relative shares of these three classes have changed over time. Infrastructure investments have definitely lost ground. Whereas this type of investment confiscated on average 67 per cent of the total public investment budget during the 1960–70 period, its share was reduced to 57.5 per cent during the 1984–94 period. Investment in equipment and transport mainly compensated for this loss; its share increased during the same periods from 5.4 per cent to 16 per cent. After an initial increase in the 1950s, investment in buildings as a percentage of total public investment hardly changed at all.

Figure 2.2 Public investment by type as a share of GDP

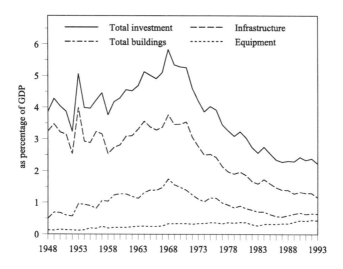

Source: CPB Netherlands Bureau for Economic Policy Analysis.

2.3 HYPOTHESES

Several authors, e.g. Buiter (1977), Aschauer (1989b) and Erenburg (1993), take the view that public and private capital spending are complementary. A decline in private investment might in turn allow the government to reduce its capital outlays. For instance, when private investment in building declines, public investment to develop building sites can also be reduced. However, the causality may also run the other way round. For instance, positive backward linkages of public investment might cause this complementary relationship to exist. Higher levels of public investment may also stimulate short-run demand and thus affect private investment. A third possible explanation for a complementary relationship is that a higher stock of public capital may raise the return of private investment projects. These forward linkages are primarily long-run effects and the main focus of recent literature on public capital spending.

On the other hand, public investment might also act as a substitute for private investment "...as the private sector utilizes the public capital for its required purposes rather than expand private capacity" (Aschauer, 1989b, p. 186). Alternatively, firms might for instance construct a road themselves thereby allowing the government to withhold from this investment. In this case higher private

Figure 2.3   Public investment shares by type

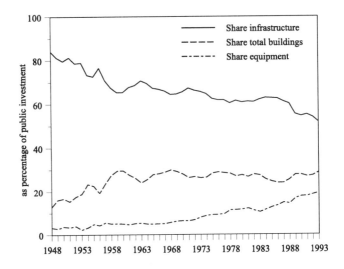

Source: CPB Netherlands Bureau for Economic Policy Analysis.

investment results in lower public capital spending.

Beforehand, the net effect is unclear. Still, there are good reasons to expect that public and private investment influence each other, which is our first hypothesis (hypothesis 1a). In general, it is held that private and public investment are complements. In particular, the forward linkages are supposed to be important. Especially, infrastructure investment is often believed to create a favourable environment for private investment (hypothesis 1b). Backward linkages are often considered important for private investment of the construction sector (hypothesis 1c).

Population growth might influence the level of public investment. For instance, a larger population leads to an increase in house building. In a regression for the 1962–80 period, the CPB Netherlands Bureau for Economic Policy Analysis (CPB) (1985) concludes that the number of residential buildings under construction influences infrastructure investment. Population growth might also influence other types of public investment (hypothesis 2a).

Hypothesis 2b is closely related to this. (Expected) school enrolment rates determine the required capacity and may therefore affect investment in schools. Zalm (1985) has advanced this argument in order to explain the reduced investment in school buildings. Indeed, estimation results presented by the CPB

Table 2.1   Formulated hypotheses

1 PRIVATE INVESTMENT
   a Public investment and private investment influence each other.
   b Public infrastructure investment affects private investment.
   c Public infrastructure investment affects private investmer.t in
      buildings.

2 DEMOGRAPHIC AND SOCIAL DEVELOPMENTS
   a Population growth affects public investment.
   b The growth in the number of schoolchildren affects investment in
      schools.
   c The size of the civil service affects public investment in buildings and
      equipment.

3 MOBILITY
   Public infrastructure investment and the growth of the number of
   vehicles influence each other.

4 GOVERNMENT BUDGET
   a The increased interest burden crowds public investment out of the
      budget.
   b Expenditure cuts severely affect public investment.

5 PRIVATE PRODUCTION
   a Private production and public investment influence each other.
   b Private production of the construction sector and public infrastructure
      investment influence each other.

(1985) confirm this view.

Furthermore, Zalm (1985) poses a connection between the size of the civil service and public investment in government buildings (hypothesis 2c). In the 1980s the central government introduced various measures to reduce the (growth of) the number of civil servants (De Haan and De Kam, 1991). Hence, it might be expected that investment in governmental buildings has decreased over time. The CPB (1985) reports a marginally significant effect of the change in the size of the civil service on public investment in buildings. Their results relate to the 1961–82 period. For his model on Swedish public investment between 1950 and 1984, Henrekson (1988) also finds a significant effect of the size of the civil service on the level of government investment spending.

Hypothesis 3 is also based on Zalm (1985). As the fleet of cars expands, the demand for infrastructure investment will grow; a good road network is necessary to take care of the ever-increasing number of vehicles. However, the causality may run in the other direction if a better road infrastructure should attract additional cars.

At present, an overwhelming majority of politicians wants to increase public investment in the Netherlands. The chief concern is that the increased interest burden that the government faces has crowded public investment out of the budget (hypothesis 4a) and that during periods of fiscal restraint, the capital budget has been hit disproportionately hard (Bijl, 1983; Boorsma *et al.* 1987). In contrast to other categories of public expenditure, public capital spending is hardly supported by interest groups in society. Moreover, investments can be deleted or temporized on the basis of each individual project which makes it easier to implement spending cuts (Kamps, 1985). This results in our hypothesis that public capital spending will be reduced during periods with an increased pressure to reduce the level of total government outlays (hypothesis 4b).[2] This hypothesis has been tested by the CPB (1985). In their study the lagged value of the budget deficit was taken to proxy the need to redress public outlays. Only in the regression for public investment in equipment had this variable a significant influence. However, it is questionable whether the level of the deficit is a good indicator for fiscal restraint. Furthermore, no substantial drop in the budget deficit occurred during the short estimation period considered by the CPB (1985). In his model for Swedish public investment, Henrekson (1988) did find a significant effect of the budget deficit.

The above-described mechanisms probably result in a relationship between private production and public investment. Besides stimulating aggregate demand, public investment might raise productivity. For example, it is likely that a better road network increases the productivity of the transport sector. The causality might also run in the opposite direction. Owing to increased private activity, bottlenecks in the infrastructure network might show up, making public investment necessary (hypothesis 5a). Aggregate demand effects probably dominate when investigating the relationship between public infrastructure investment and the production of the construction sector (hypothesis 5b).

Table 2.1 summarizes the hypotheses.

2.4   CAUSALITY ANALYSIS

2.4.1 Methodology

We will use causality tests to investigate the above-formulated hypotheses. The idea behind causality analysis is that a cause cannot come after the effect. Thus, if a variable x affects a variable z, the former should help improving the predictions of the latter variable. Granger (1969) proposed a concept of 'causality' based upon prediction error:

> "x 'causes' z if and only if z_t is better predicted by using the past history of x than by not doing so with the past of z being used in either case." (Guilkey and Salemi, 1982, p. 669)

This interpretation of causality—henceforth called 'Granger causality'—is, of course, intuitively attractive. It has therefore become widely accepted, although some of its implications are still under debate.[3] It is important to note that this definition is of a purely statistical nature.

Several tests have been developed to put this concept of Granger causality into practice. Geweke *et al.* (1983) compare eight alternative causality tests and conclude that their modified version of a test originally proposed by Sims (1972) and a test proposed by Sargent (1976) outperform the other tests in Monte–Carlo experiments. Guilkey and Salemi (1982) show that—of these two—the causality test developed by Sargent (1976) is to be preferred where degrees of freedom are limited. As most of our series are only available on an annual basis from the early 1950s, it was decided to use Sargent's test.[4]

Simple Granger-causality analysis may be obstructed by simultaneity effects: one variable may Granger cause an other, while at the same time the reverse is also true. To avoid this problem, we analyze Granger causality in a bivariate VAR model. As several endogenous variables are considered together, VAR methodology resembles simultaneous-equation modelling. In a bivariate VAR each of the two variables is explained by its own lagged values and the lagged values of the other endogenous variable. An advantage of this solution to the simultaneity problem is that *a priori* no identifying conditions, to be derived from economic theory, are needed. Beforehand, the only decision that should be made concerns the variables to be included in the analysis, and not their causal relationship. If the direction of causality is unclear on *a priori* grounds, this is a clear advantage.

The Granger-causality test proposed by Sargent (1976) starts from the following VAR model of order p (VAR(p)):[5]

$$\begin{pmatrix} x_t \\ z_t \end{pmatrix} = \begin{bmatrix} \Psi_{11}(L) & \Psi_{12}(L) \\ \Psi_{21}(L) & \Psi_{22}(L) \end{bmatrix} \begin{pmatrix} x_t \\ z_t \end{pmatrix} + \begin{pmatrix} \varepsilon_{1t} \\ \varepsilon_{2t} \end{pmatrix}, \qquad (2.1)$$

where $\Psi_{ij}(L) = \left(\psi_{ij1}L + \psi_{ij2}L^2 + \ldots + \psi_{ijp}L^p \right)$, L is the lag operator such that $Lx_t = x_{t-1}$, and ε_{it} are zero mean white noise innovations with constant covariance matrix Σ.

In this two-equation model, x does not Granger cause z if and only if all the coefficients of $\Psi_{12}(L)$ are zero. Where the series are stationary, i.e. integrated of order 0 (I(0)), likelihood ratio statistics can be computed to test this hypothesis.[6] Stationarity ensures that this statistic is distributed asymptotically as a χ^2 random variable with degrees of freedom equal to the number of restrictions imposed.

However, if the variables are non-stationary, i.e. integrated (of a higher order), Park and Phillips (1989) and Sims *et al.* (1990) have shown that the conventional asymptotic theory is, in general, not applicable to hypothesis testing in a VAR. If economic variables were known to be, e.g. I(1) with no cointegration, then one could estimate a VAR in first-differences. Similarly, if the I(1) variables were known to be cointegrated, then one should specify a vector error correction model (VECM). But, in most applications, it is not known *a priori* which order of integration the variables are and whether they are cointegrated or not. Consequently, unit root and cointegration tests are usually required before estimating the VAR model, and the hypothesis analysis is therefore conditioned on these pre-tests. As the power of unit root tests is known to be very low and cointegration tests are not very reliable for small sample sizes, these pre-test biases might be severe.[7]

Toda and Yamamoto (1995) propose a simple way to overcome this problem. Their method is applicable whether the VAR is stationary (around a deterministic trend), integrated of an arbitrary order, or cointegrated. They first of all show that usual lag selection procedures can be applied to a possibly integrated or cointegrated VAR, as the standard asymptotic theory is still valid as long as the order of integration of the process does not exceed the true lag length (p) of the model. After having determined the lag length p, they propose to estimate a $(p+d)^{\text{th}}$-order VAR, where d is the maximal order of integration that we suspect might occur in the process. Toda and Yamamoto (1995) prove that in that case standard asymptotic theory still applies. Since the last d-lagged vectors in the model are regarded as zero, one can consequently test linear or nonlinear restrictions on the coefficients by applying, e.g. the likelihood ratio criterion on the first p coefficient matrices, paying little attention to the integration and cointegration properties of the time-series data at hand.

As we are not interested in the existence of unit roots or cointegrating relations themselves, we avoid the possible pre-test biases and apply the procedure developed by Toda and Yamamoto (1995). We use likelihood ratio tests to determine the lag length p and to investigate the hypotheses in table 2.1. As suggested by Sims (1980, p. 17), we correct the likelihood ratio tests in order to improve the small sample properties.[8] Augmented Dickey–Fuller (ADF) tests give us an idea of the maximal order of integration in our models.[9]

In general, the Granger-causality testing procedure does not give us an estimate of the sign of the overall effect. Therefore we cannot identify whether x has a positive or negative effect on z. If, for instance, the true lag length of a model is 2 and both lags of x in the z-equation are significant with similar coefficients but with opposite signs, then—by definition—x Granger causes z. However, probably no significant positive or negative overall effect of a permanent change in x on z will occur in this case. Therefore, we also calculate the sum of the lagged values of the explanatory variable and test whether it significantly differs from zero, i.e. whether $\sum_{k=1}^{p} \psi_{ijk} \neq 0$ for $i \neq j$. Following Zarnowitz (1992, pp. 365–379), we label this the neutrality test.

2.4.2 Results

We first take logarithms of all series and include a constant and a trend in the bivariate autoregressive model. The ADF tests indicate that most series are integrated of order one. Unless stated otherwise, we therefore set the maximal order of integration d in the Toda and Yamamoto (1995) procedure equal to one. The maximum number of lags p are set to five. In case the last lag is insignificant, we re-estimate the model using four lags. This procedure is repeated until the last lag is significant at a 10 per cent level.[10]

First of all we test the hypothesis concerning the relationship between total private and total public investment.[11] As the left panel of figure 2.4 shows, public and private investment shares of GDP moved in tandem until 1984. However, after 1984 private investment jumped whereas public investment continued its downward trend.

Table 2.2 shows the outcomes of the Granger-causality tests and indicates the sign of the sum of the lagged explanatory variables. As expected, we find a positive relationship between total public and total private investment. This suggests a complementary relationship between public and private investment. However, the χ^2-statistic indicates that this relationship is not significant in either direction. We do not therefore find a Granger-causal relationship. As figure 2.4 indicates this might be caused by the increasing share of private investment after 1984. Therefore, we re-estimated the model using the 1954–84 sample. Now, public investment does Granger cause private investment. Furthermore, we find a significant positive effect of public investment on private investment. There is no evidence that private investment affects public investment. Our result confirms the findings of Roodenburg (1984) and Roemers and Roodenburg (1986), who also reported a significant positive effect of total public investment on total private investment.

Almost the same conclusions prevail where public infrastructure investment is used. Again, only for the 1954–84 period, a significant positive effect of public infrastructure investment on private investment is found. This time, however, the Granger-causal relationship is not very significant.[12] Still, public infrastructure spending has a positive long-term effect on private investment.

The right-hand panel of figure 2.4 depicts the development of public infrastructure investment and private investment in total buildings (including residential buildings). It suggests a positive relationship which is confirmed by the estimation results as shown in table 2.3. Infrastructure investment by the public sector Granger causes private investment in buildings. This corroborates earlier results of the CPB (1985). In the reverse direction there is also evidence of a Granger-causal relationship. Note, however, that the aggregate sign is insignificantly negative. Splitting up private investment in buildings into private investment in residential buildings and non-residential buildings reveals that

Table 2.2   Hypothesis 1

PUBLIC INV.	⇄	OTHER VARIABLES	p^a	d^b	LR^c	EFFECT^d	SAMPLE
1a total	⇄	private investment	1	1	0.06 0.00	+ +	56–90
total	⇄	private investment	2	1	1.56 6.90*	– +**	57–84
1b infrastructure	⇄	private investment	1	1	0.02 0.00	– –	56–90
infrastructure	⇄	private investment	2	1	2.74 4.16	– +	57–84
1c infrastructure	⇄	private building	5	1	9.74† 10.46†	– +*	60–90
infrastructure	⇄	private non-residential building	5	1	7.88 5.74	– +†	60–90
infrastructure	⇄	private residential building	4	1	7.60 11.82*	– +**	59–90

^{a} Estimated order p of the bivariate VAR model using the corrected Likelihood Ratio (LR) statistic as proposed by Sims (1980) and applying a 10 per cent significance level.

^{b} Maximal order of integration d of the bivariate VAR model.

^{c} Granger-causality test. The corrected LR statistic indicates whether each of the p-lagged explanatory variables significantly differs from zero and is distributed asymptotically as a χ^2 random variable with degrees of freedom equal to the number of lags p. The upper corrected LR statistic tests whether the other variable Granger causes the public investment variable. The lower corrected LR statistic tests whether the public investment variable Granger causes the other variable.

^{d} Neutrality test. The sign of the effect indicates whether the sum of the p-lagged explanatory variables is positive or negative. The significance of the sum is determined by using a corrected LR test.

† Significant at a 10 per cent level.

* Significant at a 5 per cent level.

** Significant at a 1 per cent level.

Figure 2.4   Hypothesis 1

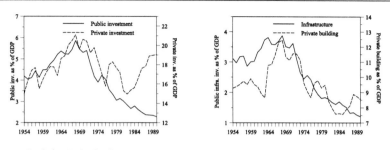

Source: Statistics Netherlands.

public infrastructure mainly influences the former.

Figure 2.5 shows the trend of the series used in testing hypotheses 2 and 3. As suggested by the upper-left panel of the figure, population growth shows a Granger-causal relationship with public investment.[13] Table 2.3 shows that an increasing (declining) rate of population growth raises (decreases) public investment. So hypothesis 2a is corroborated.[14] Taking only infrastructure investment does not alter this conclusion.

Hypothesis 2b is also supported by the data. The growth rate of the number of schoolchildren, which we labelled the school enrolment rate, positively Granger causes public investment in school buildings.[15] Taking the number of schoolchildren instead, gives virtually the same results. In planning the future construction of school buildings, the government apparently anticipates the future number of pupils.

A relationship between the growth in the number of civil servants and public investment in buildings used by the public service sector is somewhat harder to find.[16] Strikingly, the growth rate of government personnel does not affect the level of public investment in buildings. However, in the reverse direction the effect is significant at a 10 per cent level. Again this result can be explained if one assumes that the government takes the future size of the civil service into account when developing its building plans. Taking public investment in equipment leads to virtually the same result (not shown).

Despite the very clear relationship depicted in figure 2.5, no distinct Granger-causal relationship is found between (the growth in) the number of vehicles and public investment in infrastructure in the Netherlands.[17] The number of vehicles Granger causes public infrastructure investment at a 10 per cent level. However, as denoted by the neutrality test, its aggregated effect is insignificant. The growth in the number of vehicles also Granger causes public infrastructure investment. However, this time we find a positive effect, which is significant at a 10 per cent level. In the opposite direction we never find any evidence of

Table 2.3 Hypotheses 2 and 3

PUBLIC INV.	⇄	OTHER VARIABLES	p^a	d^b	LR^c	EFFECT^d	SAMPLE
2a total	⇄	population growth	5	1	13.30* 2.32	+** +	60–90
infrastructure	⇄	population growth	5	1	9.27† 1.21	+* +	60–90
2b schools	⇄	number of schoolchildren	2	2	7.25* 1.40	+* +	58–90
schools	⇄	school enrolment rate	2	1	10.41** 1.53	+** +	58–90
2c buildings	⇄	growth civil servants	1	1	0.00 3.49†	+ +†	60–90
3 infrastructure	⇄	vehicles	2	2	5.82† 3.58	– +	56–90
infrastructure	⇄	growth vehicles	1	1	3.25† 1.94	+† +	56–90

22

Figure 2.5   Hypotheses 2 and 3

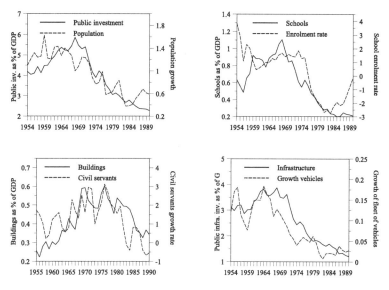

Source: Statistics Netherlands, CCSO.

a Granger-causal relationship. These findings make us reject the hypothesis that additional infrastructure opens the way for even more cars to hit the road. However, we are not able to reject the idea that—as suggested by figure 2.5— an accelerating growth in the number of vehicles forces the government to increase its infrastructure spending.

As shown in table 2.4, Granger-causality tests on interest payments of the central government and public investment of the central government results in no Granger-causal direction in either direction.[18] Whether we take the level of interest payments, or its growth rate, does not make any difference in this respect. A closer look at figure 2.6 confirms this finding. Only after 1980 do interest payments on government debt start rising. The diminution of public investment spending already started more than a decade earlier. Therefore, the increased interest burden cannot offer a significant explanation for falling public capital spending outlays in the Netherlands. These results do not change when we use public investment of total government (not shown).

To test hypothesis 4b several yardsticks for the pressure to cut public expenditures have been constructed based on the public budget deficit and the public debt.[19] Following CPB (1985), we first use the public budget deficit as proxy for the need to redress public outlays. As table 2.4 shows, we do not

Table 2.4 Hypotheses 4 and 5

PUBLIC INV.	⇄	OTHER VARIABLES	p^a	d^b	LR^c	EFFECT^d	SAMPLE
4a central government	⇄	interest payments	3	2	1.97 3.58	+ –	59–90
central government	⇄	growth interest payments	1	1	1.08 0.08	+ +	56–90
4b total	⇄	public deficit	1	1	0.56 0.15	+ +	56–90
4b total	⇄	Δ public debt	5	1	6.47 1.98	+ –	60–90
4b total	⇄	Δ² public debt	1	1	2.63 4.13*	+ –*	56–90
total	⇄	Δ public deficit	1	1	1.34 0.07	+ +	56–90
5a total	⇄	private production	3	1	7.35† 9.67*	–* +**	58–90
5b infrastructure	⇄	production construction sector	4	1	4.71 14.16**	– +**	58–90

^{a} Estimated order p of the bivariate VAR model using the corrected Likelihood Ratio (LR) statistic as proposed by Sims (1980) and applying a 10 per cent significance level.

^{b} Maximal order of integration d of the bivariate VAR model.

^{c} Granger-causality test. The corrected LR statistic indicates whether each of the p-lagged explanatory variables significantly differs from zero and is distributed asymptotically as a χ^2 random variable with degrees of freedom equal to the number of lags p. The upper corrected LR statistic tests whether the other variable Granger causes the public investment variable. The lower corrected LR statistic tests whether the public investment variable Granger causes the other variable.

^{d} Neutrality test. The sign of the effect indicates whether the sum of the p-lagged explanatory variables is positive or negative. The significance of the sum is determined by using a corrected LR test.

† Significant at a 10 per cent level.

* Significant at a 5 per cent level.

** Significant at a 1 per cent level.

24

Figure 2.6   Hypothesis 4

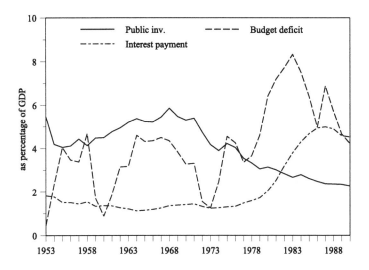

Source: Statistics Netherlands, CCSO and De Nederlandsche Bank.

find any evidence of a Granger-causal relationship between the public budget deficit and levels of public investment. Taking the growth in public debt as proxy does not alter these conclusions. In contrast to the CPB (1985), our conclusions furthermore do not change when we take separate categories—like public investment in equipments—into account.

It can be argued that the periods of restrictive fiscal policy and fiscal consolidation are better proxied by the change in the public budget deficit. A problem with the previous yardstick is that—at least in the short-run—a rising deficit makes it possible to increase expenditures. Therefore table 2.4 also shows the results where we took the first difference of the public budget deficit as yardstick. Still no evidence is found in favour of hypothesis 4b. Therefore, these Dutch data do not suggest that public investment has been crowded out in order to reduce the deficit.[20]

Table 2.4 finally reports the outcomes of testing hypotheses 5a and 5b. The production of the private sector and total public investment affect each other.[21] Both the negative effect of the production level of the private sector on public investment and the positive effect in the reverse direction are statistically significant. Therefore there exists a feedback mechanism between public investment and private production. It may be noted that the positive effect of public investment on private production dominates here. Taking only public infrastructure spending confirms this finding (not shown). Subdividing public investment in public infrastructure and private production of the construction sector shows that public infrastructure investment positively Granger causes the output level of the latter sector, as might be expected. The development of public infrastructure investment is not influenced by the output of the construction sector.

2.5 CONCLUSIONS

In the previous section we found empirical support for several hypotheses formulated in the economic literature to explain trends in the level of public investment. Both private investment and private output are related to public investment. Public infrastructure spending in particular has a highly significant positive effect on investment as well as production of the construction sector. Note, however, that for the private investment series these results are based upon a sample period ending in 1984. When we take the entire sample period into account no strong Granger-causal relationship between both investment classes is found. After 1984 public and private investment started drifting apart.

Changes in demographic variables influence public investment. A decreasing population growth rate limits government capital spending. The expected growth in the number of schoolchildren affects public investment in school buildings. The number of future civil servants affects investment in buildings. The number of cars affects infrastructure investments.

However, three important hypotheses are rejected. Our test results do not support the two hypotheses concerning the impact of government budgetary problems. Neither the increased interest burden nor a rising budget deficit seem to have crowded out public investment. Finally, no confirmation is found for the idea that additional infrastructure stimulates an increase in the number of vehicles in the Netherlands.

It is important to note that these results are only tentative. The approach of Toda and Yamamoto (1995) we have followed here is somewhat inefficient and suffers some loss of power since we deliberately over-fitted our bivariate VAR models in order to get around non-stationarity and cointegration issues. Furthermore, economic relationships between several variables—like private investment and private production—are not modelled at all. Still, we think that this chapter has specifically demonstrated that the effect of public investment on the private economy is pronounced in the Dutch data. The second part of this book will concentrate on this result. However, before turning to that issue, the next chapter will take a look at the development of public capital spending in the OECD area and will test hypotheses similar to those in this chapter, using a somewhat different approach.

NOTES

1. After a storm flood in 1953, in which almost the complete province of Zeeland was inundated, a large project—labelled the *Deltawerken*—was developed to prevent the coast provinces in the South-West from being flooded again. As the final touch to this project was only made in 1986, it had claimed large parts of the public investment budget for over 30 years.
2. It has been argued recently that the government should be allowed to borrow for public capital spending because of the redistributive effect over generations. In the Netherlands public investments are booked in the year in which they are conducted. This might also have enhanced the drop in public capital outlays (Vereniging Nederlandse Gemeenten, 1994, pp. 91–92).
3. Granger (1980) gives an early overview of pros and cons of Granger causality.
4. In order to keep the peak in public investment in 1953, caused by the flood disaster in that year, out of the analysis, we start our sample period in 1954. As most series are only available from 1952, this has a negligible effect on our degrees of freedom. Data limitations force us to end our sample period in 1990.
5. This VAR(p) model can be seen as the reduced form of a standard bivariate dynamic structural model.
6. To calculate a likelihood ratio statistic, first estimate the residual cross-product matrix (U) using the unconstrained model, and then estimate the cross-product matrix (C) using the constrained model. The likelihood ratio statistic then equals: $-T(\ln|U| - \ln|C|)$, where T is the number of observations and $|\cdot|$ is the determinant. See Appendix A for an explanation of stationarity.
7. For instance, Reimers (1992) and Toda (1995) discuss the sensitivity of Johansen (1988, 1991) type VECMs to nuisance parameters in finite samples.
8. Instead of calculating the likelihood ratio statistic as presented in note 6, Sims (1980, p. 17) recommends: $-(T-c)(\ln|U| - \ln|C|)$.
9. See appendix A for a description of the ADF test and the applied estimation procedure.
10. When a likelihood ratio test indicated that the fifth lag was significant, we also estimated a VAR(6) model and tested the significance of the last lag in order to assure that we did not underfit our model. At a 10 per cent level the sixth lag was never significant.
11. All public investment series were kindly provided by Statistics Netherlands. The private investment series are extracted from the data bank kept by the CCSO Centre for Economic Research (CCSO) of the Universities of Groningen and Twente. See Jongbloed *et al.* (1991) for a description.
12. The likelihood ratio statistic of 4.16 with 2 degrees of freedom reported in table 2.2 is significant at 12.5 per cent.
13. The population is defined as the total number of inhabitants which is taken from Statistics Netherlands (1989).
14. Neither total public investment nor public infrastructure investment has a Granger-causal relationship with the level—instead of the growth rate—of the Dutch population. This is in sharp contrast with the results of Van Dalen and Swank (1996). They include the population size in their model explaining government capital spending cycles and find a strong positive relationship.
15. The number of schoolchildren is the sum of the children attending primary education and those attending secondary education. Source: Statistics Netherlands (1989).
16. The number of civil servants are extracted from the database kept by the CCSO. See Jongbloed *et al.* (1991).
17. The number of vehicles represents the sum of company cars and privately owned cars. Source: Statistics Netherlands (1989).
18. Data on the interest payments of the central government are taken from Statistics Netherlands (1989, 1988).
19. Date on the budget deficit of the total government are taken from the databases kept by CCSO and De Nederlandsche Bank. Figures on the total government debt are taken from Statistics Netherlands (1989).
20. In the next chapter we will construct some other yardsticks and test this hypothesis in an

OECD context. As that chapter will show, taking a somewhat different approach we find evidence that governments did relatively easily cut back their public capital spending during the 1980s and early 1990s.

21. Private production series are extracted from the database kept by CCSO and equals gross value added of the private sector. See Jongbloed *et al.* (1991) for a description.

3.   Public Capital Spending in the OECD*

3.1   INTRODUCTION

During the 1980s, a clear break in the rate of change of government outlays relative to GDP occurred. Whereas on average that ratio rose steadily during the 1970s by around one percentage point each year, after 1982 it stabilized for a few years before declining slightly in most countries (Saunders, 1993). This reversal in the growth of government spending took place at various moments, but by the end of the 1980s outlays had fallen below their peak in most OECD countries. Exceptions included Greece, Spain and Italy, where the public sector further expanded during the whole decade. At the beginning of the 1990s a slight increase in the size of the public sector took place in many OECD countries, in part due to the recession at that time.

There are also some common patterns with respect to the structure of government expenditure. For instance, most countries have offset increases in debt interest payments and rising social security transfers by winding back public investment. According to Oxley and Martin (1991, p. 161) this pattern reflected "the political reality that it is easier to cut-back or postpone investment spending than it is to cut current expenditures".

Quite a number of empirical studies, such as Saunders and Klau (1985), Roubini and Sachs (1989b) and De Haan and Sturm (1994), have attempted to explain cross country variation in the growth of the share of total government expenditure in GDP.[1] There are, however, very few studies trying to explain cross country differences in specific categories of government outlays. An exception is Solano (1983), who distinguishes between domestic, defence, education and social security spending and concludes that institutional variables contribute substantially to explain differences in public expenditure levels among high-income democracies. Unfortunately, Solano (1983) does not single out government capital spending as a separate category.

This lack of analysis of determinants of public investment spending is quite surprising, as many authors have argued that government capital spending may have important effects. As we will see in Chapter 4, Aschauer (1989a) has

---

*This chapter is a revised version of De Haan et al. (1996) and De Haan and Sturm (1996).

29

*Figure 3.1   Public investment as a share of GDP, means
over 1980–83 versus 1989–92*

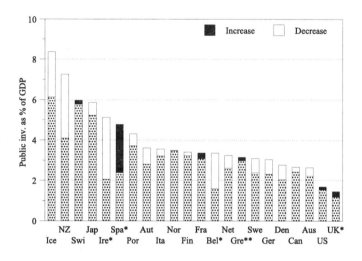

* Only data available until 1991.
**Only data available until 1989.
Source: OECD Annual National Accounts. (1994).

hypothesized that the decrease in productive government services in the United
States (US) may be crucial in explaining the general decline in productivity
growth in that country. His empirical results show a strong and positive relationship between productivity and public capital, which seems to confirm his
initial hypothesis and lead to a clear policy recommendation: public investment
should be raised to boost the economy. Indeed, in many countries, politicians
of various persuasions support such policies.[2]

Using panel data for 22 OECD countries for the period 1980–92, we test
various hypotheses that may explain the development of government capital
spending. As previous studies on total government spending have found that
institutional and political factors are of prime importance, we will focus here
upon politico-institutional explanations (Saunders and Klau, 1985).

The remainder of this chapter is organized as follows. Section 3.2 describes
the development of government investment in most OECD countries over the
period 1980–92. The third section reviews previous time-series studies on
determinants of public capital spending. Section 3.4 formulates the hypotheses
and describes our politico-institutional variables. The fifth section presents our
estimation results and the final section summarizes our findings.

Figure 3.2   Public investment as a share of total government outlays, means over 1980–83 versus 1989–92

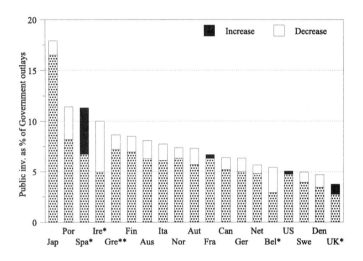

* Only data available until 1991.
**Only data available until 1989.
Source: OECD Annual National Accounts (1994), OECD Economic Outlook (1995).

3.2   DEVELOPMENT

Figure 3.1 compares average government investment—excluding residential buildings—as a share of GDP for 22 OECD countries between the periods 1980–83 and 1989–92. The data relate to consolidated general government and have been taken from the Standardized National Accounts (SNA) compiled and published by the OECD, in accordance with the United Nations guidelines. They represent the most reliable and consistent expenditure series available on a comparable basis for a broad range of industrialized countries. As follows from figure 3.1, public capital spending as a share of GDP declined or remained stable in almost all countries between 1980 and 1992. Spain, France and the United Kingdom (UK) were exceptions here. Small rises also occurred in Switzerland, Greece and the US. Another conclusion that can be drawn on the basis of figure 3.1 is that the level of government investment spending varies considerably across countries. Whereas the public capital spending-to-GDP-ratio in the US amounted to only 1.8 per cent of GDP in 1992, it stood at 5.9 per cent in Switzerland.[3]

Figure 3.2 presents government investment as a share of total government spending.[4] Again the 1980–82 period is compared with the 1989–92 period. It follows from figure 3.2 that government capital spending as a ratio of government outlays declined in most countries. Exceptions were Spain, France, the UK and the US. The share of capital outlays in total public spending varied between 2.9 per cent in Belgium and 16.3 per cent in Japan in 1991.

3.3   PREVIOUS STUDIES

As explained in the introduction, there are, to the best of our knowledge, no cross-section studies explaining government capital spending. However, various authors have estimated time-series models for government investment spending. Table 3.1 summarizes these time-series studies. They are all based upon various hypotheses put forward in the literature to explain government growth and well reviewed by Lybeck (1988). Unfortunately, the various studies are rather fragmented and cannot be combined into a coherent theory. At best, they allow us to derive a number of more or less conflicting hypotheses (Kirchgässner and Pommerehne, 1988).

According to Kirchgässner and Pommerehne (1988) the following sets of explanatory variables can be distinguished:

Economic variables: real GDP (Y) or its growth rate ($\dot{Y}$), ratio of median to mean income (Inc), GDP per capita (YCap), trade balance (Trade), unemployment (U), real interest rate (R), (real) wage rate (Wage), inflation (Π), relative prices of investment (and other categories of government spending) (RelPrice), indicator for government budget deficits (Def) and/or government debt (Debt);

Structural variables: population (Pop), share of older people (Old), share of younger people (Young), labour force participation rate (Part), female labour force participation rate (Fem), urbanization level (Urb);

Politico-institutional variables: degree of unionization (Union), fractionalization of political parties in parliament (Frac), interest groups (IntGr), share of government employees in employment (Empl), ideology (Ideol), coalition variables (Coal), share of taxes collected by central government (CenTax), electoral cycles (Elec), variables capturing enfranchisement (Vote), popularity of government (PopGov).

As follows from table 3.1, time-series studies on the determinants of government investment vary widely concerning the number and significance of explanatory variables. We will review the reasons given by various authors to include certain explanatory variables so as to determine whether they should be included in our panel data model.

Table 3.1   *Time-series studies of government investment*

STUDY	COUNTRY AND PERIOD	DEPENDENT VARIABLE	INCLUDED VARIABLES[a]
Henrekson (1988)	Sweden 1950–84	Government investment deflated by GDP deflator	Urb*, Y, Inc, Union, Def*, Empl*, U, Coal*, CenTax, Fem
Kirchgässner & Pommerehne (1988)	Germany, Switzerland 1961–83/84	Share of government investment in total government expenditures	RelPrice, Part, Debt, U, Old, Union, Elec, Ideol
Sørensen (1988)	Norway 1865–1985	Government investment deflated by public consumption price index	Vote, IntGroup, Union, Ideol, Frac, Ẏ*
	1963–86 (quarterly)		U, Trade, Wage, Π, PopGov, Ideol, Elec
Aubin *et al.* (1988)	France 1961–83	Growth rate of nominal government investment	Π, Wage, Inc, Pop*, RelPrice, U*, Elec*, Def*, R*
Van Dalen & Swank (1996)	Netherlands 1953–93	Government investment as percentage of GDP	YCap, RelPrice*, Pop*, Old, Young, U, Elec*, Ideol*

[a]See main text for explanation of abbreviations.
*Reported as a significant variable.

Inflation and unemployment are generally included to take cyclical factors into account. In the case of counter-cyclical policy one may expect public spending to be restrained when inflation accelerates and to be increased with rising unemployment levels (Aubin *et al.* 1988). Alternatively, the growth rate of real GDP can be used. Note that the reason for including GDP in this model differs from the conventional motivation, which is to test for Wagner's law, especially in the version that stresses the fact that many goods and services provided by government have a high income elasticity of demand.[5] Generally in that case, the level of GDP is employed (Henrekson, 1988). Given the short-term nature of our study, we will employ the growth rate of GDP, which is intended to reflect influences of the business cycle.

The inclusion of the ratio of median to mean income is generally based on income distribution considerations (Lybeck, 1988). Assuming that the median voter also has the median income in society, government popularity may be increased by redistributing disposable income from the mean towards the median. This variable is clearly not relevant in explaining government investment.

The government budget deficit is often included to test for fiscal illusion.

Again, problems of interpretation may arise in the case of government investment spending. For one thing, it is often stated that governments should be allowed to borrow for public capital spending because of the redistributive effect over generations. However, this policy is not officially pursued at the national level in any of the selected countries. Furthermore, high deficits (or high levels of government debt) may lead to restrictive fiscal policy measures. Therefore, we have decided to construct dummy variables to identify periods of fiscal stringency (see below for further details).

Relative prices are often included to take Baumol's disease into account.[6] However, as pointed out by Lybeck (1988), relative prices will also have an effect through demand. Relative prices are included in our model.

Most of the so-called structural variables are included to test for Wagner's law, especially in the version that stresses the transformation from traditional to industrialized society, with its accompanying shift of services like education and health from the family to the public sector.[7] Given the short- to medium-term nature of our analysis these variables are excluded from our model.

To test for the influence of interest groups, variables like the degree of unionization and the share of government employees in total employment are often used. The number of public employees has also been employed as a proxy for the influence of the bureaucracy.[8] It should, however, be pointed out that a growing number of civil servants as such may stimulate government investment due to a higher demand for government buildings. To take this possibility into account we include the growth rate of public employment in our model.

A factor that has been treated extensively in the literature on public sector growth is the possibility that governments of a socialist (or social-democratic) persuasion tend to increase public expenditures at a faster rate than do right-wing governments. Indeed, there are various studies that report evidence supporting this hypothesis (Cameron, 1978; Roubini and Sachs, 1989b; De Haan and Sturm, 1994). However, Henrekson (1988) has pointed out that there is a problem with linking public sector size to the 'colour' of the party in power. The attitudes of different parties towards public expenditures may depend on what kind of expenditure is at issue. Parties of the right may, for instance, be in favour of higher spending on defence and police, whereas parties of the left may favour spending of a social welfare character.[9] Van Dalen and Swank (1996) report evidence that spending on infrastructure in the Netherlands was higher under right-wing than under left-wing governments. In line with the approach of these authors we test whether governments dominated by left-wing parties are more willing to cut investment spending than are right-wing governments.[10]

It has also been argued by various authors that the kind of government (coalition, majority government or minority government) may influence both government debt accumulation and the level of government spending.[11] The reasoning behind this being that both broad coalition and minority governments may have more difficulty in reaching agreement to balance the budget. In that case, government investment spending will again be the more easy spending category to cut. However, Henrekson (1988) argues that a larger number of parties may increase the likelihood that an agreement between a party and an interest group is reached. In his model for Swedish government investment he therefore included a coalition dummy which turned out to be significantly negative, which is in line with the hypothesis of Roubini and Sachs (1989b).

The centralization of taxes is sometimes taken up to examine whether federalism is important. Various cross-section studies on the size of the public sector show that federalism is negatively related to the size of the government. In our model we have included the share of central government taxes in total tax revenues as an explanatory variable to test whether the degree of centralization of government affects government investment spending.[12]

To test for political business cycle considerations, electoral cycles are taken into account in some studies. Van Dalen and Swank (1996) found, for instance, that elections are important in explaining infrastructure spending in the Netherlands. We have therefore included an election variable in our model.

3.4   HYPOTHESES AND VARIABLES

3.4.1   Hypotheses

This section offers some hypotheses that may help explain the development of government capital spending. Very often it is maintained that in periods of fiscal consolidation government investment is an easy target. Roubini and Sachs (1989b, pp. 108–109) argue that "in periods of restrictive fiscal policies and fiscal consolidation capital expenditures are the first to be reduced (often drastically) given that they are the least rigid component of expenditures". Although this view is widely shared (see also the citation of Oxley and Martin (1991) in the introduction to this chapter), it has, to the best of our knowledge, only been tested for the Netherlands.[13] In Sturm and De Haan (1995b, 1998) and in the previous chapter, no significant effect of the rising public deficit or interest payments is found for the Netherlands. So our first hypothesis is that capital spending is reduced during periods of fiscal stringency, since this category of government spending is politically an easier target for cuts than other spending categories.

As pointed out in the previous section, the type of government may be relevant in explaining public sector investment. So our second hypothesis is that politically weak governments are more inclined to cut capital formation spending than are politically strong governments.

A third issue that we focus on is the political 'colour' of the government. As shown in the previous section, this variable was found to be important in explaining public sector size and may also be relevant in explaining public investment. We test whether left-wing governments give lower priority to public capital spending than do right-wing governments.

A fourth hypothesis that we will test is that myopic governments will cut investment spending more than governments which have a longer policy horizon. As the benefits of investment spending generally do not show up in the short-run, myopic policymakers will be inclined to cut capital spending. It is our contention that the government turnover may be a good proxy for the time-horizon of policymakers.[14]

As a fifth hypothesis we will examine whether private investment influences government investment spending, either because both types of investment are substitutes (as in public housing construction) or move in tandem. In Chapter 2 we found that both types of investment complement each other in the Netherlands. It is rather surprising, that in none of the studies summarized in table 3.1 has this issue been taken up.

Our final hypotheses are that the degree of centralization of government and elections may affect government investment spending. As pointed out in the previous section, these hypotheses were tested in various time-series models.

3.4.2 Variables

To test our first hypothesis, we have constructed three 'fiscal stringency' dummies. These dummies are 'one' if in a certain year the cyclically adjusted deficit is reduced by more than 0.5, 1.0 or 1.5 percentage points of GDP, respectively, and are 'zero' otherwise. To eliminate improvement of the financial position of government which is caused only by cyclical factors we have used the cyclically adjusted (or structural) deficit in constructing these dummies. Alternatively, we have employed the change in the structural deficit to test this hypothesis. The data are taken from the OECD Economic Outlook.

To capture possible effects of divided versus single party governments, and following Roubini and Sachs (1989b), we have constructed an index of power dispersion (POL) which measures the size of the governing coalition, ranging from 0 (smallest coalition) to 3 (minority government):[15]

0 = one-party majority parliamentary government;
1 = coalition parliamentary government with two or three coalition partners;
2 = coalition parliamentary government with four or more coalition partners;
3 = minority government.

The source of the data is Keesing's Archives.

Our third variable is the share of cabinet portfolios held by social democratic and other leftist parties (LEFT). This variable is constructed following the approach outlined by Cameron (1985). The total number of months that left-wing politicians held cabinet portfolios is divided by the total number of cabinet members, multiplied by twelve. For their sample of fourteen industrial countries Roubini and Sachs (1989b) concluded that this variable helps explain cross-country differences in government spending.[16]

Our variable CHANGE traces the frequency of government changes. It is our contention that this variable proxies for the time-horizon of policymakers. A government change occurs after each election and if a change takes place with respect to the parties participating in the governing coalition.[17] For example, when the social democrats left the three-party coalition in the Netherlands in 1982 and the remaining parties formed a minority government, we consider this a change of government. After the elections took place, a new centre-right government was formed, and this we consider as another change.[18]

To test our sixth hypothesis we have constructed a variable that measures the share of central government taxes in total tax revenues. This variable proxies the degree of centralization in a country. The data are taken from various issues of the OECD's Revenue Statistics of OECD Member Countries.

The variable ELECTION, which counts the number of elections in each year, is used to test our final hypothesis. The source of the data is Keesing's Archives.[19]

3.5 ESTIMATION RESULTS

Table 3.2 presents our estimation results for the model for government investment spending expressed as a fraction of GDP. Our testing approach is the following. We start with a basic model to which various variables are added, in order to test the hypotheses outlined in the previous section. The explanatory variables in the basic model are the lagged dependent variable, the difference between the deflator of government investment and the GDP deflator, the growth rate of real GDP and of the number of civil servants. These variables have been selected on the basis of the time-series models summarized in section 3.3 and on the basis of their robustness in the regression. As suggested by Blanchard (1992), we have estimated this model by Weighted Least Squares (WLS), correcting for the unbalanced dataset.[20] The model is estimated with both random and fixed effects. The results of a Hausman (1978) test taught that country dummies had to be included. Column (1) of table 3.2 shows the basic model. All explanatory variables have the theoretically expected sign and are highly significant.

Column (2) contains the results adding the fiscal stringency measure, which

Table 3.2 Explaining government investment as a share of GDP[a]

GOV.INV./GDP	(1)	(2)	(3)	(4)	(5)	(6)	(7)	(8)	(9)	(10)	(11)[b]
Lagged dependent variable	0.715 (21.62)	0.787 (23.98)	0.791 (25.92)	0.715 (21.46)	0.711 (21.22)	0.716 (21.57)	0.706 (21.53)	0.736 (19.42)	0.714 (21.56)	0.785 (23.97)	0.785 (24.69)
Gov.inv. inflation minus GDP infl.	0.027 (4.93)	0.020 (4.23)	0.016 (3.65)	0.027 (4.92)	0.027 (4.91)	0.027 (4.92)	0.024 (4.31)	0.027 (4.77)	0.027 (4.85)	0.017 (3.68)	0.016 (3.43)
Growth rate of real GDP	-0.022 (2.57)	-0.012 (1.58)	-0.012 (1.65)	-0.022 (2.57)	-0.022 (2.56)	-0.022 (2.56)	-0.027 (3.09)	-0.019 (2.05)	-0.022 (2.52)	-0.012 (1.65)	-0.011 (1.49)
Growth rate of civil servants	0.024 (2.34)	0.018 (2.01)	0.019 (2.23)	0.024 (2.34)	0.023 (2.29)	0.024 (2.28)	0.021 (2.09)	0.026 (2.50)	0.025 (2.42)	0.017 (1.87)	0.017 (1.93)
Fiscal stringency dummy		-0.0015 (4.10)								-0.0014 (3.90)	-0.0014 (4.00)
Structural deficit (Δ)			-0.0519 (6.98)								
Political cohesion variable, POL				-0.0001 (0.17)						-0.0003 (1.10)	-0.0002 (0.86)
Colour of government, LEFT					0.0005 (0.78)					0.0005 (0.80)	0.0005 (0.44)
Political stability, CHANGE						-0.0001 (0.17)				-0.0000 (0.12)	-0.0002 (0.84)
Private investment (percentage GDP)							0.0332 (2.76)			0.0354 (3.58)	0.0231 (2.86)
Centralization of taxes								-0.0121 (1.53)		-0.0142 (2.13)	-0.0077 (1.16)
Election year, ELECTION									-0.0003 (0.77)		
Observations	243	217[c]	217[c]	243	243	243	243	235	243	215[c]	214[c]
R^2 (adj.)	0.963	0.951	0.957	0.963	0.963	0.963	0.964	0.961	0.963	0.955	0.957

Sample: 22 OECD countries, 1980–92.
[a] Absolute values of t-statistics are shown in parentheses. Estimation is by WLS, correcting for unbalanced dataset. Country dummies are included.
[b] Outliers are removed from the sample.
[c] Iceland, New Zealand and Switzerland are not included.

is 'one' where the structural deficit is reduced by 1.0 percentage point or more, and which is 'zero' otherwise. Its coefficient is significantly different from zero, thereby providing support for our first hypothesis. Because data on the cyclically adjusted deficit are not available for Iceland, New Zealand and Switzerland, we had to exclude these countries from this regression. Similar results are found if other fiscal stringency dummies are employed (not shown). As shown in column (3) of table 3.2, the same conclusion is also reached if the change in the structural deficit series itself is included instead of the fiscal stringency dummy.

Column (4) of table 3.2 presents the outcomes if our variable POL is included as explanatory variable. It follows that its coefficient is not significantly different from zero, thereby refuting our second hypothesis. However, Edin and Ohlsson (1991) have pointed out that the construction of POL places a very restrictive form on its effects. Why should public capital spending under a minority government be three times as low as under a two-party majority coalition? Following Edin and Ohlsson (1991) we have therefore constructed a dummy variable for each 'political class'. None of these variables turned out to be significant (not shown).

In the fifth column of table 3.2 the variable LEFT is taken up as explanatory variable. Again, the coefficient is not significantly different from zero. This outcome does not support our third hypothesis. Also, the coefficient of our variable CHANGE is not significantly different from zero (column (6) of table 3.2), so that our fourth hypothesis is also refuted. However, one may express some doubts whether our variable CHANGE is a good proxy for the time horizon of policymakers if measured on an annual basis. Below we therefore present the estimation results using three year averages instead of annual observations.

Next, we have added private investment spending (excluding residential building) as explanatory variable. As follows from the seventh column of table 3.2, the coefficient of this variable is significantly positive, indicating that private and public capital spending are complementary.[21] In the previous chapter, we also found a complementary relationship using only Dutch data.[22]

Column (8) of table 3.2 shows the estimation outcomes if the centralization of taxes is added as an explanatory variable. Its coefficient is not significantly different from zero. This is also true for the election dummy (column (9) of table 3.2).

Finally, we have estimated the model including all variables (except, of course, the change of the structural deficit, which cannot be included together with the fiscal stringency dummy). As follows from column (10) of table 3.2 our basic conclusions do not change.

Because in most regressions a few outliers are present, we adjusted the sample accordingly and re-estimated all equations. Column (11) of table 3.2

Figure 3.3   Rolling regressions

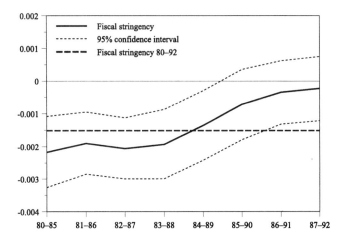

shows the results for the model including all variables. It follows that the results are robust; the model without outliers produces similar results, and our conclusions do not alter. To sum up so far we only find support for the views that during periods of fiscal stringency capital spending is a more easy target than other categories of public spending and that public and private investment spending are complements.

A final check on the robustness is carried out by performing so-called rolling regressions. In these regressions we set the number of years in our panel to six and let the sample period roll. Most coefficients stayed roughly the same over time. One possible exception is the coefficient of the fiscal stringency dummy which is used to test the first hypothesis, i.e. public capital spending is reduced during periods of fiscal stringency. Figure 3.3 shows how the estimated coefficient of the fiscal stringency variable evolves over time: there is a positive trend. Still, its coefficient is significantly negative in most of the regressions.

Table 3.3 presents our estimates of the model for public capital spending as a share of total government spending. The basic model is similar to the one used previously, except for the growth rate of GDP, which is not significantly different from zero and is therefore excluded in the basic model (column (1)). Testing results indicated again that country dummies had to be included.

The basic conclusions that follow from table 3.3 are the same as those drawn on the basis of table 3.2. The coefficients of POL, LEFT, CHANGE, centralization of taxes and ELECTION are not significantly different from zero. We find only supporting evidence for our first and fifth hypotheses. As shown in column (11) of table 3.3, removing outliers also does not affect our conclusions.[23]

As explained before, one may doubt whether our proxy for the time horizon of policymakers is appropriate if annual observations are used. One may doubt, for instance, whether the policy horizons of government in 1984–85 in Italy and Switzerland were the same, while CHANGE is zero in both countries. Therefore, we have re-estimated our models using three-year averages instead of annual observations. Columns (1) and (3) of table 3.4 present the basic model for government investment as a share of GDP and total government outlays, respectively. In columns (2) and (4) the variable CHANGE is added. It follows that now we find clear support for the hypothesis that the time horizon of policymakers is relevant. In both columns the coefficient of CHANGE has the predicted negative sign and is significantly different from zero. We have also re-estimated the models for the other political variables in similar vein, but this does not lead to different results. The coefficients of POL and LEFT remain insignificant (not shown).

3.6 CONCLUDING COMMENTS

In this chapter a model is estimated to examine whether various hypotheses put forward to explain downward trends in public capital spending are supported by the data. Using panel data for 22 OECD countries for the period 1980–92, the following hypotheses are tested:

(1) Capital spending is reduced during periods of fiscal stringency, since this category of government spending is politically an easier target for cuts than are other spending categories. Using 'fiscal stringency' dummies constructed on the basis of the cyclically adjusted deficit we find some evidence in support of this hypothesis.

(2) Politically weak governments are more inclined to cut capital formation spending than are politically strong governments. To capture possible effects of divided versus single party governments, we have constructed an index of power dispersion which measures the size of the governing coalition, ranging from 0 (smallest coalition) to 3 (minority government). This variable does not exert any significant influence on government investment spending. So, this hypothesis is not supported by our results.

(3) Governments which are dominated by left-wing parties are more willing to cut investment spending than are right-wing governments. This hypothesis

Table 3.3 Government investment as a share of total government outlays[a]

GOV.INV./GOV.OUTLAYS	(1)	(2)	(3)	(4)	(5)	(6)	(7)	(8)	(9)	(10)	(11)[b]
Lagged dependent variable	0.747 (21.94)	0.753 (22.26)	0.754 (22.43)	0.745 (21.78)	0.746 (21.58)	0.746 (21.94)	0.717 (21.03)	0.755 (22.69)	0.744 (21.79)	0.730 (21.71)	0.740 (26.61)
Gov.inv. inflation minus GDP infl.	0.040 (4.01)	0.038 (3.90)	0.037 (3.74)	0.039 (3.98)	0.040 (4.00)	0.039 (4.00)	0.031 (3.17)	0.038 (3.95)	0.039 (3.96)	0.030 (3.09)	0.032 (4.05)
Growth rate of civil servants	0.035 (1.80)	0.028 (1.43)	0.031 (1.60)	0.035 (1.82)	0.035 (1.78)	0.038 (1.94)	0.034 (1.80)	0.039 (2.08)	0.038 (1.92)	0.035 (1.85)	0.035 (2.25)
Fiscal stringency dummy		-0.0016 (2.18)								-0.0016 (2.18)	-0.0506 (2.85)
Structural deficit (Δ)			-0.0543 (2.68)								
Political cohesion variable, POL				-0.0003 (0.58)						-0.0004 (0.68)	-0.0004 (0.85)
Colour of government LEFT					0.0001 (0.11)					0.0002 (0.16)	0.0004 (0.43)
Political stability, CHANGE						-0.0006 (1.05)				-0.0007 (1.26)	-0.0005 (1.09)
Private investment (percentage GDP)							0.0762 (3.58)			0.0726 (3.47)	0.0749 (4.32)
Centralization of taxes								0.0002 (0.01)		-0.0052 (0.37)	0.0030 (0.25)
Election year, ELECTION									-0.0006 (0.91)		
Observations[c]	216	216	216	216	216	216	216	214	216	214	209
R^2 (adj.)	0.977	0.978	0.978	0.977	0.977	0.977	0.978	0.979	0.977	0.980	0.986

Sample: 19 OECD countries, 1980–92.
[a] Absolute values of t-statistics are shown in parentheses. Estimation is by WLS, correcting for unbalanced dataset. Country dummies are included.
[b] Outliers are removed from the sample.
[c] Iceland, New Zealand and Switzerland are not included.

Table 3.4   Government investment using 3-years averages[a]

	GOV.INV./GDP		GOV.INV./ GOV.OUTLAYS	
	(1)	(2)	(3)	(4)
Lagged dependent variable	0.193	0.079	0.173	0.052
	(1.69)	(0.69)	(1.14)	(0.35)
Gov.inv. inflation minus	0.075	0.076	0.091	0.119
GDP infl.	(2.12)	(2.36)	(1.35)	(1.87)
Growth rate of real GDP	−0.088	−0.076		
	(3.03)	(2.81)		
Growth rate of civil	0.128	0.105	0.297	0.240
servants	(2.67)	(2.35)	(2.84)	(2.41)
Political stability,		−0.0048		−0.0108
CHANGE		(2.57)		(2.36)
Observations	54	54	49[b]	49[b]
R^2 (adj.)	0.949	0.958	0.964	0.969

Sample: 22 OECD countries, 1980–92.
[a]Absolute values of *t*-statistics are shown in parentheses. Estimation is by WLS, correcting for unbalanced dataset. Country dummies are included.
[b]Iceland, New Zealand and Switzerland are not included.

is tested using a variable that measures the total number of months that left-wing politicians held cabinet portfolios, divided by the total number of cabinet members, multiplied by twelve. We do not report evidence in support of this hypothesis.

(4) Myopic governments will cut investment spending more than governments which have a longer policy horizon. Using the frequency of government changes as a proxy for the time-horizon of policymakers, we find supporting evidence for this hypothesis in the panel model where three year averages are used instead of annual observations.

(5) Private investment influences government investment spending, either because both types of investment are substitutes or move in tandem. Our findings indicate that private and public capital spending are complementary.

(6) Centralization of government may affect government investment spending as it is well known that in federal countries total government spending is generally lower than in non-federal countries. Using the share of central government taxes in total tax revenues as a proxy, we do not find support for this hypothesis.

(7) According to the political business cycle hypothesis government spending in election years will be higher than it is otherwise. This may also be true for investment spending. Using the number of elections in each year we do not

find support for this hypothesis.

Comparing these results with the outcomes of the previous chapter shows that public and private investment are positively related. Not only in the Netherlands, but apparently in most OECD countries, public and private investment are complements. However, compared to Chapter 2 in which public investment was the leading variable, the results presented here suggest that public investment follows private investments.

In Chapter 2, we did not find evidence that in the Netherlands public investment spending is reduced during periods of fiscal stringency. However, after refining our fiscal stringency measure and looking at the OECD level, the data do indeed reveal the relationship we hypothesized.

NOTES

1. Some studies, such as, e.g. Henrekson (1988) and Hackl *et al.* (1993), use time-series analysis to explain the growth of the public sector. These studies are discussed in greater detail in the third section of this chapter.
2. As we will discuss in Chapters 4 and 5, the findings of Aschauer (1989a) are—according to recent research—not very robust and can be criticized on various grounds.
3. Although we use the most consistent database available, it may be the case that some of these variations can partly be explained by differences in definition.
4. The data for figure 3.2 have been constructed using the data underlying figure 3.1 and total government outlays as a percentage of GDP as published in the OECD Economic Outlook (1995).
5. Wagner (1877, 1890) was the first to propose a coherent theory of the growth of government.
6. Baumol (1967) observed that productivity growth was much lower in the public than in the private sector, while wage increases were about the same. Hence, the nominal share of government in GDP will become larger even if the real rates of growth in the two sectors are the same.
7. For instance, Lybeck (1988) argues that "(t)he hypothesis in its original form depends on a true demand for society's services as a result of diminished home production. When one accepts a negative sign, the variable instead is transformed into a catch-all variable that captures all the economic, political and institutional elements of the service economy and their effects on the size of the public sector. This serves simply then to justify a certain variable in the explanatory equations, but it cannot be said to represent any particular theory, least of all Wagner's" (Lybeck, 1988, pp. 30–31).
8. As pointed out by Lybeck (1988) a significant relationship between government spending and the number of public employees does not imply any causal effort, as the SNA assumes away productivity changes.
9. Solano (1983) concludes that votes for leftist parties for seats in the central legislature does not account for differences in any type of spending that he discerns among high income democracies.
10. Kirchgässner and Pommerehne (1988) do not find much evidence that the strength of the social-democratic party in Germany has an impact on the share of investment outlays in total government spending.
11. See, e.g. Grilli *et al.* (1991) on the former and Roubini and Sachs (1989b) on the latter.
12. As in many countries part of the tax revenue is automatically redistributed, this yardstick is not perfect. However, data limitations force us to use this measure.
13. Not all authors agree with this hypothesis. Aubin *et al.* (1988) argue that since investment expenditure is usually more evident than consumption expenditure, an increase in taxes may

be more easily accepted by the electorate if it is followed by a rise in investment. Conversely, in periods of fiscal restraint, spending cuts have a less adverse political effect if consumption (and public wages) is curbed.

14. See also De Haan and Sturm (1994).
15. Note, however, that for several countries some differences exist between our index and the power dispersion index as presented by Roubini and Sachs (1989b). The Roubini and Sachs index for the Netherlands for the period 1983–85 (2) is, for instance, clearly wrong as the government coalition consisted of two parties during that period. See De Haan and Sturm (1994) for further details.
16. We refer to De Haan and Sturm (1994, 1997) for detailed information on this political variable.
17. This variable intends to measure the chance of being thrown out of office and therefore all elections are included even if the government is re-elected. See also De Haan and Sturm (1994).
18. We refer to De Haan and Sturm (1994) for detailed information on this variable.
19. The appendix of De Haan and Sturm (1994) also contains detailed information on this variable.
20. This unbalanced dataset is due to the fact that for some countries the sample period for which all data are available is shorter than 1980–92. Using standard ordinary least squares did not alter our conclusions.
21. Because of possible causality problems we also included lagged private investment instead. Using 1 or 2 lags did not change the outcome considerably.
22. However, in that chapter the causality ran in the opposite direction.
23. One might argue that the influence of political variables is different during periods of fiscal stringency than during other years. Therefore, we have re-estimated all models in which political variables are included, splitting all observations into two groups. In the first group only observations for which the fiscal stringency dummy is 'one' are included, while all other observations are included in the other group. The estimation outcomes for both groups of observations are very similar, indicating that there is no asymmetry (not shown).

PART TWO

Impact

4. Modelling Public Capital Spending and Growth[*]

4.1 INTRODUCTION

During the 1970s and 1980s many OECD countries have offset increases in debt interest payments and rising social security transfers by winding back public investment. As was illustrated in figure 1.1 of Chapter 1, public capital spending as a share of GDP declined in most countries between 1970 and 1992.

According to Oxley and Martin (1991, p. 161) the decline of government investment reflected "the political reality that it is easier to cut-back or postpone investment spending than it is to cut current expenditures." In Chapter 3 we have found evidence that during fiscal contractions capital spending is indeed reduced more than other categories of government spending. According to some authors this decline in public capital spending has an important negative impact on economic growth. For instance, Aschauer (1989a) has hypothesized that the decrease in productive government services in the United States (US) may be crucial in explaining the general decline in productivity growth in that country. Taking a production function approach and using annual data for the period 1949 to 1985, Aschauer (1989a) found a strong positive relationship between productivity and the ratio of the public to the private capital stock. Based on his results, a 1 per cent increase in the public capital stock might raise multifactor productivity by 0.39 per cent. The implications of these results for policymakers seem to be clear: public investment should go up to boost the economy. Because of these well-received policy implications—higher infrastructure spending formed a major part of President Clinton's economic plans—the findings of Aschauer (1989a) have sparked research into the impact of public sector capital spending on private sector output.

This chapter reviews empirical research on the impact of government capital spending on economic growth. Successively, the pros and cons of five different ways to model the relationship between public investment and economic growth are reviewed. We start with the production function approach (section

---

[*]This chapter is a revised version of Sturm et al. (1996).

4.2). Instead of adding the public capital stock as an additional input factor in a production function, a cost or profit function in which the public capital stock is included could also be estimated. This so-called behavioural approach is discussed in the third section. Section 4.4 reviews Vector Auto Regressions (VARs) which also have been employed to model the relationship between government investment and economic growth. By imposing as few economic restrictions as possible, this modelling technique tries to solve some of the problems related to the first two approaches. The previous lines of research are all based on time series (or panel data). An alternative way to model the growth effects of public capital spending is to include government investment spending in cross-section growth regressions (section 4.5). The sixth section reviews attempts to estimate the growth effects of public investment spending using structural econometric models. We review here only the impact of public capital on the supply side; demand raising effects of government investment spending in these models are not taken into account. The final section offers some concluding comments.

In the remainder of this book we will implement some of these approaches ourselves. Chapter 5 applies the production function approach to the Netherlands and the US. In Chapter 6 a cost function will be estimated to explore sectoral differences of the public capital impact in the Netherlands. Using Dutch historical data, the VAR approach will finally be implemented in Chapter 7.

4.2 PRODUCTION FUNCTION APPROACH

The stock of public capital (G_t) may enter the production function in two ways. First it may influence multifactor productivity (A). Second, it may enter the production function directly, as a third input:

$$Q_t = A(G_t) f(K_t, L_t, G_t),$$ (4.1)

where Q_t is real aggregate output of the private sector, L_t is (aggregate hours worked by) the labour force of the private sector and K_t is the aggregate non-residential stock of private fixed capital. It depends on the functional form of the production function whether both effects can be identified. At the end of this section we will elaborate on this problem.

In the first type of analysis generally an aggregated Cobb–Douglas production function is used in which the public capital stock is added as an additional input factor:

$$Q_t = A_t L_t^{\alpha} K_t^{\beta} G_t^{\gamma}.$$ (4.2)

Dividing both sides of equation (4.2) by K_t, taking the natural logarithm, and assuming constant returns to scale across all inputs, gives:

$$\ln \frac{Q_t}{K_t} = \ln A_t + \alpha \ln \frac{L_t}{K_t} + \gamma \ln \frac{G_t}{K_t}. \tag{4.3}$$

Aschauer (1989a) introduces a constant and a trend variable as a proxy for $\ln A_t$. The capacity utilization rate is added to control for the influence of the business cycle. Most authors have used this specification. Only a few studies have used a translog function, which is more general than the Cobb–Douglas function.[1] Another drawback of the estimated production functions is that labour and capital are exogenous; it is implicitly assumed that both factors are paid according to their marginal productivity. Tables 4.1 and 4.2 summarize all production function studies that we are aware of. Table 4.1 concentrates on US studies, whereas table 4.2 summarizes studies on other OECD countries. As can be seen from both tables the estimate of γ in the studies included there varies between -0.11 and 0.54, and it is often found to be insignificant.

Various authors have used regional or local data in their analysis. The use of such data may circumvent various implicit assumptions that are made when national data are employed, like: the marginal productivity is the same in all states; the rate of technological progress is uniform across states (Aaron, 1990). Unfortunately, many authors—e.g. Munnell and Cook (1990) and Garcia–Milà and McGuire (1992)—employ estimation techniques such as Ordinary Least Squares (OLS) that ignore state-specific effects—representing differences in underlying productivity stemming from location, climate, and endowments—thereby producing biased and inconsistent estimates.[2] Because more prosperous states are likely to spend more on public capital, there will be a positive correlation between the state-specific effects and public sector capital (Holtz–Eakin, 1992).

Studies using aggregated national data for the US apparently find higher production elasticities of public capital than those relying on more disaggregated data. Munnell (1992, pp. 193–194) ascribes this to possible spillover effects: "because of leakages, one cannot capture all of the payoff to an infrastructure investment by looking at a small geographic area." However, Holtz–Eakin (1992) and Holtz–Eakin and Schwartz (1994), who take the effects of aggregation explicitly into account, and Holtz–Eakin and Schwartz (1995), who explicitly estimate the spillover effects of motorway infrastructure in the US, find little evidence of spillovers.[3]

Hulten and Schwab (1991b, p. 125) also focus on externalities and use regional manufacturing data for the US because they "hope to isolate the externalities by concentrating on an important subsector of the economy in which the effects of public capital are likely to be confined to indirect effects, manufacturing." These authors find no systematic relationship between regional

Table 4.1   Studies using the production function approach for the US

STUDY	AGGREGATION LEVEL	SPECIFICATION	DATA	OUTPUT ELASTICITY OF PUBLIC CAPITAL
Ratner (1983)	National	Cobb–Douglas; log level	Time series, 1949–73	0.06
Aschauer (1989a)	National	Cobb–Douglas; log level	Time series, 1949–85	0.39
Ram & Ramsey (1989)	National	Cobb–Douglas; log level	Time series, 1949–85	0.24
Munnell (1990)	National	Cobb–Douglas; log level	Time series, 1949–87	0.31–0.39
Aaron (1990)	National	Cobb–Douglas; log level & delta log	Time series, 1952–85	not robust
Ford & Poret (1991)	National	Cobb–Douglas; delta log	Time series, 1957–89	0.39–0.54
Tatom (1991)	National	Cobb–Douglas; delta log	Time series, 1949–89	insignificant
Hulten & Schwab (1991a)	National	Cobb–Douglas; log level & delta log	Time series, 1949–85	not robust: 0.21 & insignificant, resp.
Finn (1993)	National	Cobb–Douglas; delta log	Time series, 1950–89	0.16
Eisner (1994)	National	Cobb–Douglas; log level	Time series, 1961–91	0.27
Sturm & De Haan (1995a)	National	Cobb–Douglas; log level & delta log	Time series, 1949–85	0.41 & insignificant, resp.
Ai & Cassou (1995)	National	Cobb–Douglas; delta log	Time series, 1947–89	0.15–0.20
Lau & Sin (1997)	National	Cobb–Douglas; log level	Time series, 1925–89	0.11
Costa *et al.* (1987)	48 states	Translog; level	Cross-section, 1972	0.19–0.26
Merriman (1990)	48 states	Translog; level	Cross-section, 1972	0.20
Munnell & Cook (1990)	48 states	Cobb–Douglas; log level	Pooled cross-section, 1970–86	0.15
Aschauer (1990)	50 states	Cobb–Douglas; log level	Cross-section, averaged 1965–83	0.055–0.11
Eisner (1991)	48 states	Cobb–Douglas & translog; log level	Pooled cross-section, 1970–86; Pooled time series, 1970–86	0.17; insignificant
Garcia–Milà & McGuire (1992)	48 states	Cobb–Douglas; log level	Panel data, 1969–82	0.04–0.05
Holtz–Eakin (1992)	48 states & 9 regions	Cobb–Douglas; log level	Panel data, 1969–86	insignificant
Munnell (1993)	48 states	Cobb–Douglas; log level	Pooled cross-section, 1970–86 (90)	0.14–0.17
Pinnoi (1994)	48 states	Translog; level	Panel data, 1970–86	−0.11–0.08
Evans & Karras (1994a)	48 states	Cobb–Douglas & translog; log level & delta log	Panel data, 1970–86	insignificant
Baltagi & Pinnoi (1995)	48 states	Cobb–Douglas; log level	Panel data, 1970–86	insignificant
Garcia–Milà, *et al.* (1996)	48 states	Cobb–Douglas; delta log	Panel data, 1970–83	insignificant
Eberts (1986)	38 metropolitan areas	Translog; level	Panel data, 1958–78	0.03–0.04

Table 4.2   Studies using the production function approach for other OECD countries

STUDY	COUNTRY	SPECIFICATION	DATA	OUTPUT ELASTICITY OF PUBLIC CAPITAL
Mera (1973)	9 Japanese regions	Cobb–Douglas; level	Panel data, 1954–63	0.12–0.50
Aschauer (1989c)	G-7	Cobb–Douglas; delta log	Panel data, 1966–85	0.34–0.73
Merriman (1990)	9 Japanese regions	Translog; level	Panel data, 1954–63	0.43–0.58
Ford & Poret (1991)	11 OECD countries	Cobb–Douglas; delta log	Time series, 1960–89	only significant in Belgium, Canada, Germany, Sweden
Berndt & Hansson (1991)	Sweden	Cobb–Douglas; log level	Time series, 1960–88	mixed & implausible results
Bajo–Rubio & Sosvilla-Rivero (1993)	Spain	Cobb–Douglas; log level	Time series, 1964–88	0.19, cointegrated
Mas et al. (1993)	17 Spanish regions (manufacturing)	Cobb–Douglas; log level	Panel data, 1980–89	0.21
Evans & Karras (1994b)	7 OECD countries	Cobb–Douglas; delta log	Panel data, 1963–88	estimates are fragile & generally insignificant
Mas et al. (1994a)	17 Spanish regions	Cobb–Douglas; log level	Panel data, 1980–89	0.24
Otto & Voss (1994)	Australia	Cobb–Douglas; log level	Time series, 1966–90	0.38–0.45 (poor results at sectoral level)
Toen–Gout & Jongeling (1994)	Netherlands	Cobb–Douglas; delta log	Time series, unknown	0.37
Sturm & De Haan (1995a)	Netherlands	Cobb–Douglas; log level & delta log	Time series, 1960–90	estimates are fragile, no cointegration
Dalamagas (1995)	Greece	Translog; level	Time series, 1950–92	0.53 (if budget deficit is included, otherwise negative)
Mas et al. (1996)	17 Spanish regions	Cobb–Douglas; log level	Panel data, 1980–89	0.08
Otto & Voss (1996)	Australia	Cobb–Douglas; log level	Time series, 1959:III–92:II	0.17, cointegrated
Wylie (1996)	Canada	Cobb–Douglas, translog; log level	Time series, 1946–91	0.11–0.52
Kavanagh (1997)	Ireland	Cobb–Douglas; log level	Time series, 1958–90	insignificant
Nazmi & Ramirez (1997)	Mexico	Cobb–Douglas; delta log	Time series, 1950–90	use investment series, find significant marginal productivity of public capital

growth rates of public capital and regional growth rates of productivity.

A conclusion initially drawn by various authors from the studies under review was that in the US public capital seems to have a significant positive effect on private sector productivity. Besides the already-mentioned problems concerning the *restrictive specification* of the production function and the *exogenous factor inputs*, several economists questioned the plausibility of the values of the estimated marginal productivity of public capital on the grounds that they are *implausibly high* (Aaron, 1990; Gramlich, 1994). Aschauer (1989a) points out, however, that a rate of return between 50 and 60 per cent, while substantial, is in line with estimates of the rate of return on Research and Development (R&D) capital. Still, expenditure on R&D is riskier and should yield higher rates of return. A related criticism is that the wide range of reported estimates of public capital's impact on output makes the empirical linkages *fragile* at best. Although Munnell (1993, p. 32) claims that "in almost all cases the impact of public capital on private sector output and productivity has been positive and statistically significant," table 4.1 shows that she is wrong; even for the case of the US, there are quite diverging outcomes.

The work of Aschauer (1989a)—and subsequent research by, e.g. Munnell (1990)—has also been criticized on other grounds.[4] A first issue is *causality*: does the levelling off of public capital reduce the growth of output, or does the reduced growth of output diminish the demand for public capital? (Eisner, 1991; Gramlich, 1994) To this criticism, Aschauer (1990, p. 35) has responded by stating that "this argument must confront the simple fact that public non-military investment expenditure . . . reached a peak in the period between 1965 and 1968, while the usual dating of the onset of the productivity decline is around 1973."[5,6]

Recently Finn (1993) and Ai and Cassou (1995) have captured the causality issue by applying a Generalized Method of Moments (GMM) estimator. This technique resembles an instrumental-variables procedure and therefore avoids the possible reverse-causation bias. Finn (1993) reports a significant elasticity of the stock of public motorways of 0.16. The elasticity estimates of Ai and Cassou (1995) for the stock of public capital range between 0.15 and 0.2.[7]

There is also another possible form of simultaneity bias (Gramlich, 1994). Even if the true aggregate supply effect of public capital were zero, a rise in public investment may raise aggregate demand and output in the short run, leading to an inappropriate inference of the productivity effects of public capital.

Second, various authors have taken issue with the *specification* of Aschauer's (1989a) *model*. For instance, Tatom (1991) argues that the reported large output elasticities are due to misspecification of the production function. He contends that the rising price of oil during the seventies made some private capital obsolete and therefore negatively affected productivity. Using another specification with energy prices included and capacity utilization entered multiplicatively to both the private and public capital stock, Tatom (1991) finds little evidence that public capital raises productivity. However, Duggal *et al.* (1995) criticize Tatom's (1991) approach arguing that the relative price of energy is a market cost factor that would be included in the firm's cost function and therefore also in the factor input demand functions. So, the relative price of energy should not be included directly in the production function, but the energy input instead.

Another specification issue is the inclusion of the degree of capacity utilization. As already pointed out, Aschauer (1989a) included this variable to account for business cycle fluctuations. Duggal *et al.* (1995) criticize studies in which this approach is followed—including Hulten and Schwab (1991a) and Sturm and De Haan (1995a)—since it is an additive factor in the estimated log equation, which implies that it is a multiplicative factor in the production function. A change in the capacity utilization causes an across-the-board change in the usage of all three factor inputs, such that the ratio of their marginal products remains the same. This is a very restrictive assumption. However, a specification in which the capacity utilization is not included at all is, of course, the other extreme. Chapter 5 and Sturm and De Haan (1995a) show that this issue is not crucial for the conclusions reached.

A final specification issue that we would like to address is the specification in the widely-cited paper by Ford and Poret (1991). These authors have estimated production functions in which the public capital stock is included as an input factor for eleven OECD countries. However, they combine private capital and labour into one private sector input variable, thereby imposing some restrictions which are not tested for. The same approach is followed by Toen–Gout and Jongeling (1994) for the Netherlands. Whereas Ford and Poret (1991) report very mixed outcomes for their sample of countries, Toen–Gout and Jongeling conclude that "infrastructure would ... appear to have a significant and positive influence on private output" (Toen–Gout and Jongeling, 1994, p. 13). This result contrasts sharply with the findings of Sturm and De Haan (1995a) who also use Dutch data but do not impose these restrictions.

A third reason to question the results of Aschauer (1989a) and others is the *non-stationarity* of the data which may render a spurious regression between the public capital stock and output growth (Aaron, 1990; Tatom, 1991). Sturm and De Haan (1995a) argue that if Aschauer's (1989a) model is estimated in first differences—which is necessary as the variables used are neither stationary nor cointegrated—the model produces only ambiguous results. However, first differencing also has its problems. As pointed out by Munnell (1992) it is assumed that output growth in one year is only correlated with input growth in that same year; it eliminates the ability to estimate the underlying long-term relationship between production and factor inputs.[8] Duggal *et al.* (1995, p. 6) argue: "(t)he fact that first-differenced equations generate *a priori* implausible labour and capital output elasticities is enough to question the capability of first-differenced equations to capture the long run relationships." Indeed, researchers should examine not simply the extent to which variables are non-stationary, but also whether they grow together over time and converge to their long-run relationship, i.e. whether they are cointegrated. Various authors have followed this approach, with rather mixed results. While Sturm and De Haan (1995a) conclude, for instance, that public capital and private sector output in the US and the Netherlands are not cointegrated, Bajo–Rubio and Sosvilla–Rivero (1993), Lau and Sin (1997) and Otto and Voss (1996) find that both variables are cointegrated in Spain, the US and in Australia, respectively.

In a recent paper Garcia–Milà *et al.* (1996) systematically test for various specification problems (including non-stationarity of the data) for the case of a state-level production function with public capital as an input. Although it is likely that this will be less of a problem with panel datasets, it is still possible that these kind of estimates are contaminated by non-stationarity of the variables. Indeed, in the preferred specification, which is in first differences with fixed states effects, Garcia–Milà *et al.* (1996) report no significant effects of public capital, thereby refuting earlier evidence, including their own.

A final problem according to Duggal *et al.* (1995) is that in all studies in the production function approach *public capital is treated as a factor input*, like private capital and labour. This violates standard marginal productivity theory in that it assumes a market determined per unit cost of infrastructure that is known to individual firms and can be used in calculating total costs. Aaron (1990) argues that the absence of a market price, coupled with government pricing inefficiencies makes it impossible to assume that infrastructure as a factor input will be remunerated in line with its marginal product.[9] The basic problem here is, however, that in a Cobb–Douglas function (estimated in log levels) it does not make any difference whether public capital is treated as a third production factor or as influencing output through the factor representing technology. Both ways of modelling the influence of public capital yield similar equations to be estimated. In other words, in these kinds of empirical models the direct and indirect impact of public capital cannot be disentangled.

A somewhat different approach, which also employs a production function and which is therefore finally taken up in this section, is 'growth accounting' or 'sources of growth analysis'. This method can be explained as follows. Assume a production function like equation (4.1) without the inclusion of public capital. If it is also assumed that each input is paid the value of its marginal product, then the output elasticities are equivalent to income shares. In that case, the well-known 'multifactor productivity' (MFP) can be estimated as a residual, since all other terms are directly observable. Apart from the rate of change of technical efficiency, all sorts of other items like errors in measurement and omitted variables are included in the MFP estimate. Public capital can affect MFP in two ways: indirectly, by enhancing productivity of all or some of the private inputs, or as a direct factor of production, as in Aschauer (1989a). Both factors lead to biased estimates of MFP. By comparing MFP-growth with public capital growth one might find indications for the importance of these biases. Hulten and Schwab (1991b) conclude that public capital is not a key determinant of multifactor productivity growth. Productivity grew slightly faster in the older, declining regions of the US during 1951–86 (North and

East), whereas in contrast, the public capital stock grew substantially faster in the Sun Belt (South and West). Nor do they find any significant link between MFP and public capital in their pooled regression for 16 regions over the period 1970–86. Similar results are reported in Hulten and Schwab (1993). However, Eberts (1990), who analyzed MFP-growth in 36 metropolitan areas between 1965 and 1977, reports somewhat different results. He finds that variation across these areas in public capital stock growth had a positive and statistically significant effect on MFP-growth over the period 1965–73; this relationship disappears during the second period 1973–77. Eberts (1990) also concludes that the public capital stock affects output, but only when private inputs are not included in the regression. When they are included, the size of the coefficient of public capital falls and becomes insignificant. According to this author, the primary channel through which public capital influences output growth is via private inputs.

4.3 BEHAVIOURAL APPROACH

Some of the drawbacks of the production function approach can be eliminated by describing optimizing behaviour of economic agents (i.e. firms) either by maximizing profits or minimizing costs. Given the cost function we can under certain regularity conditions derive a unique production function by applying duality theory (Diewert, 1974). For instance, one can specify a cost function for the private sector (C) in which firms are envisaged as attempting to produce a given level of output (Q_t) at minimum private cost. Because the input prices (p_t^i) are exogenously determined, the instruments of the firm are the quantities of private inputs (x_t^i). Alternatively, firms are assumed to maximize their profits (Π) given the output (p_t^Q) and input prices:

$$
\begin{aligned}
C\left(p_t^i, x_t^i, A_t, G_t\right) \quad &- \quad \min_{x_t^i} \sum_i p_t^i x_t^i \\
&\text{s.t. } Q_t = f\left(x_t^i, A_t, G_t\right), \\
\Pi\left(p_t^Q, p_t^i, x_t^i, A_t, G_t\right) \quad &= \quad \max_{Q_t, x_t^i} p_t^Q Q_t - \sum_i p_t^i x_t^i \\
&\text{s.t. } Q_t = f\left(x_t^i, A_t, G_t\right).
\end{aligned}
\tag{4.4}
$$

When private firms optimize, they take into account the environment in which they operate. One of these environmental variables is the state of technical knowledge (A_t).[10] Another environmental variable affecting production relationships to the firm is the amount of public infrastructure capital (G_t) available. The public capital stock enters the production function and thus also the cost or profit function as an unpaid fixed input.[11]

Table 4.3 Studies using the behavioural approach[a]

STUDY	FUNCTION	DATA	PUBLIC CAPITAL	OTHER INPUTS TO G	SUBST. TO G	COMPL. TO G	CONSTANT RETURNS	ELASTI-CITIES	CONCLUSIONS	COMMENTS
Berndt & Hansson (1991)	Cost: generalized Leontief	US, time series 1960–88 (private business)	Core	K, L			Rejected	MFP: (0.06;0.17)	Increase in G reduces costs; Excess G declined.	K is a quasi-fixed input; Government bond yield used as discount rate for G; Problems implementing a dynamic model. Only cost function estimated.
	Cost: generalized Leontief	US, time series 1960–88 (manufacturing)	Total	K, L, E, M			Rejected		Increase in G reduces costs; Excess G declined.	
Conrad & Seitz (1992)	Cost: translog	Germany, panel, 4 sectors, 1961–88	Core	K, L, M M	K, L		If homogeneity imposed then CRS accepted	Cost: (−0.07; −0.22)	Largest impact G in trade & transport sector; No productivity slowdown when taking account of G.	Estimating sector by sector leads to multicollinearity problems. Use mark-up to capture imperfect competition.
Conrad & Seitz (1994)	Cost: translog	Germany, panel, 3 sectors, 1961–88	Core	K, L, M L		K	If homogeneity imposed then CRS accepted		Increase in G reduces costs; Slowdown growth G partially responsible for productivity slowdown.	Use $CU \times G$ to measure flow of services and remove multicollinearity problems.
Dalamagas (1995)	Cost: translog	Greece, time series 1950–92 (manufacturing)	Total public investment	K, L, E K, L			imposed	Cost: −2.35	Government investment is important in determining the production cost in manufacturing.	All variables converted into indices. 3 models estimated: standard; using instrumental variables; augment system by reaction functions.
	Profit: translog	Greece, time series 1950–92 (manufacturing)	Infrastructure; Education; Health	K, L, Q Edu: K, L	Infra: K, L			Infra: Output: 1.06 Profit: 1.06	Spending on infrastructure leads to higher profits. Negative relationship between education and output.	All variables converted into indices.

(to be continued)

58

Table 4.3 *Studies using the behavioural approach (continued)*

STUDY	FUNCTION	DATA	PUBLIC CAPITAL	OTHER INPUTS TO G	SUBST. TO G	COMPL. TO G	CONSTANT RETURNS	ELASTI- CITIES	CONCLUSIONS	COMMENTS
Deno (1988)	Profit: translog	US, panel, 36 SMSA's, 1970–78 (manufacturing)	Motorways. Water; Sewers; Total	K, L, Q	K, L			Output: 0.69	G more effective in declining regions. G plays important role in output supply and input demand.	G multiplied by percentage of population employed in manufacturing in order to capture congestion. Only share equations estimated.
Keeler & Ying (1988)	Cost: translog	US, panel, 9 regions, 1950–73 (road freight transport sector)	Motorways	$K, L, E, M,$ Transport			Rejected, IRS		G improved productivity; Benefits for trucking sector cover at least 33 per cent of total capital costs of G.	All variables converted into indices.
Kitterer & Schlag (1995)	Cost: translog	Germany, time series, 1961–88 (private business)	Total; Core	K, L	L	K		Cost: −0.01	The effect G on costs is significant but decreases over time.	ECM used to capture non-stationarity of data.
Lynde (1992)	Profit: Cobb–Douglas	US, time series, 1958–88 (non-financial corporate sector)	Total; Federal; State & local	K, L			Accepted	Profit: 1.2	Significant share of profits attributable to G (especially State & local); Profit elasticity of K is higher.	Perfect competition imposed; Correction for heteroscedasticity and serial correlation carried out. Only profit function estimated.
Lynde & Richmond (1992)	Cost: translog	US, time series, 1958–89 (non-financial corporate sector)	Total; Federal; State & local	K, L	L	K	Accepted		G has a positive marginal product.	Perfect competition imposed; Statistical analysis indicates problems in the interpretation of the estimates. Only share equations estimated.
Lynde & Richmond (1993a)	Cost: translog	UK, time series, 1966:1–90:II (manufacturing)	Total excl. dwellings	K, L, M, Y			Rejected	Output: 0.20	Higher G in the 1980s could have increased labour productivity growth by 0.5 per cent per year.	ECM of Phillips & Hansen (1990) used to capture non-stationarity of data. Only share equations estimated.

(to be continued)

Table 4.3 Studies using the behavioural approach (continued)

STUDY	FUNCTION	DATA	PUBLIC CAPITAL	OTHER INPUTS	SUBST. TO G	COMPL. TO G	CONSTANT RETURNS	ELASTI-CITIES	CONCLUSIONS	COMMENTS
Lynde & Richmond (1993b)	Profit: translog	US, time series, 1958–89 (non-financial corporate sector)	Total excl. dwellings	K, L, M, Y			Rejected	Output: 0.20	40 per cent of productivity slowdown is explained by G/L.	Perfect competition imposed. ECM of Phillips & Hansen (1990) used to capture non-stationarity of data. Only share equations estimated.
Morrison & Schwartz (1992)	Cost: generalized Leontief	US, panel, 48 states, 1970–87 (manufacturing)	Motorways & water & sewers	K, Lprod, Ln-prod, E			Rejected	Cost: (0.07; –0.17)	G has been below social optimum; growth must more than keep up with output growth to have a positive productivity impact.	K is a quasi-fixed input; Problems concerning heteroscedasticity.
Morrison & Schwartz (1996)	Cost: generalized Leontief	New England states, 1970–78 (manufacturing)	Motorways & water & sewers	K, Lprod, Ln-prod, E	short run: K; Y-fixed: Lprod, Ln-prod	E; long run: K; profit-max: Lprod, Ln-prod			K is more valuable for society than G. Public investment is warranted if public policy is ineffective at increasing private investment.	K is a quasi-fixed input; Minor autocorrelation problems. Add short-run profit-maximization equation to the system. Calculate user cost of public capital similar to that of private capital.
Nadiri & Mamuneas (1994a)	Cost: generalized Cobb–Douglas	US, panel, 12 sectors, 1956–86 (manufacturing)	Total: R&D	K, L, M		K, L	Rejected, IRS	Cost: (–0.11; –0.21)	R&D and G are not major contributors to MFP; Contribution of G to MFP is twice as large as that of R&D.	Use $CU \times G$.
Nadiri & Mamuneas (1994b)	Cost: generalized Cobb–Douglas	US, panel, 12 sectors, 1956–86 (manufacturing)	Total: R&D	K, L, M M		K, L		Cost: (–0.10; –0.21)	R&D and K both have higher rates of return than G;	Results do not change if $CU \times G$ is used.
Seitz (1993)	Cost: generalized Leontief	Germany, panel, 31 sectors, 1970–89 (manufacturing)	Roads (monetary); Motorways (physical)	K, L	L	K			Shadow values of G are significant for 22 sectors. Complementary relationship between K and G is negligible.	Results using monetary measure for roads are comparable to the results using the physical measure for motorways.

(to be continued)

Table 4.3 Studies using the behavioural approach (continued)

STUDY	FUNCTION	DATA	PUBLIC CAPITAL	OTHER INPUTS TO G	SUBST. TO G	COMPL. TO G	CONSTANT RETURNS	ELASTICITIES	CONCLUSIONS	COMMENTS
Seitz (1994)	Cost: generalized Leontief	Germany, panel, 31 sectors, 1970–89 (manufacturing)	Total; Core	K, L	L	K	Rejected		G has a stabilizing but decreasing impact on private input demand, due to low G formation.	Use $CU \times G$ to get variation over industries.
Seitz & Licht (1995)	Cost: translog	Germany, panel, 11 states, 1971–88 (manufacturing)	Total	K^M, K^B, L	L	K^M, K^B	rejected	Cost: $(-0.10; -0.36)$	Distinction between K^B and K^M is crucial, former more affected by G than latter	
Shah (1992)	Cost: translog	Mexico, panel, 26 sectors, 1970–87 (manufacturing)	Core	$K, L, M\ M$	K, L		Rejected, IRS	Output: 0.05	K has larger impact than G; Under-investment in K and G.	K is a quasi-fixed input; G is like a private or highly congested public good.
Sturm & Kuper (1996)	Cost: translog	Netherlands, panel, 5 sectors, 1953–87 (manufacturing)	Total; Other; Buildings; Infrastructure	K, L, E	L, E			Output: (0.20;0.25) insign.	Multicollinearity and autocorrelation problems produce weird coefficients (not induced by public capital.).	All variables converted into indices. Autocorrelation problems exist with static version. Dynamic version results in violation of first order conditions.
Sturm (1997)	Cost: symm. gen. McFadden	Netherlands, exposed versus sheltered sector, 1953–93	Infrastructure	K, L			imposed	Cost: $(-0.2; -0.3)$	Increase in G mainly reduces costs of sheltered sector.	ECM used; relationship with private inputs unclear.

^{a} G: public capital stock; K: private capital stock; K^M private stock of machinery; K^B: private stock of buildings; L: private labour; E: energy; M: intermediate goods; Y: value added; Q: output; $Lprod$: production labour; $Ln\text{-}prod$: non-production labour; CU: capacity utilization rate.

The dual function that satisfies one of the optimization problems in equation (4.4) is normally tackled by a second-order Taylor approximation, like the transcendental logarithmic (translog) or the generalized Leontief function.[12] First-order conditions can be derived, which result into factor-share (translog) or factor-demand equations (generalized Leontief).[13] To increase efficiency, these first-order conditions and the cost or profit function are normally estimated simultaneously.[14] From these estimates, several elasticity measures can be revealed which fully describe the underlying production function. Besides estimating several elasticities, the behavioural approach also allows us to estimate the shadow value of public capital—as a proxy for the unknown market price—and therefore the long-run desired level of public capital, i.e. one can assess whether the amount of public capital is insufficient or excessive.[15]

Two differences are conspicuous when comparing the behavioural approach with the production function approach. First, the use of a flexible functional form hardly imposes any restrictions on the production structure. For example, *a priori* restrictions placed upon substitutability of production factors—as encountered in the production function approach—do not apply. Apart from the direct effect that is focused upon when production functions are estimated, public capital might also have indirect effects. Firms might adjust their demand for private inputs, if public capital is a substitute or a complement to these other production factors. It seems very plausible that, e.g. a larger stock of infrastructure raises the quantity of private capital used and therefore indirectly increases production. By using a flexible functional form, the influence of public capital via private inputs can be determined.

Second, as shown in the previous section, production function estimates may suffer from a simultaneous equations bias. Specifically, the right-hand variables in the various equations estimated by Aschauer (1989a) and Munnell (1990) include measures of labour input and utilization, and strong arguments have been made that such variables should be treated as endogenous. This problem does not arise in the behavioural approach, because costs or profits, and therefore input shares or demands, are directly represented. In the behavioural approach inputs are no longer exogenous to the level of output. However, input prices and—in case of the cost function approach, the level of output—are the exogenous variables. Therefore, the problem of possible endogeneity of variables remains, but does not concern the same variables as before.

Table 4.3 summarizes all studies we found in the literature which apply cost and/or profit functions. A flexible function not only consists of many parameters which need to be estimated, but also includes many second-order terms which are cross-products of the inputs.[16] These second-order variables create multicollinearity problems. Therefore, the dataset not only has to be relatively large, but must also contain a lot of variability so that problems of multicollinearity can be dealt with. Most studies therefore use panel data which combine a time dimension with either a regional or a sectoral dimension.

In most studies summarized in table 4.3 it is concluded that public capital reduces private sector costs or increases private sector profits. However, the estimated effects are generally significantly smaller than those reported by Aschauer (1989a). Only Deno (1988) and Lynde (1992) come up with a larger effect. The remaining studies roughly estimate less than half the impact reported by Aschauer (1989a). In a variable cost function framework, the cost saving effects of public capital only arise if the substitution effect of some private inputs outweigh the complementary effects of other private inputs. Several studies find that intermediate inputs (and sometimes also labour) are substitutes for public capital. On the other hand, private and public capital mostly bear a complementary relationship, which confirms the conclusion of Chapters 2 and 3 that public and private capital spending are complementary.

Most authors clearly reject the hypothesis of constant returns to scale to all inputs. Exceptions are Conrad and Seitz (1992, 1994), Lynde (1992) and Lynde and Richmond (1992). Conrad and Seitz (1992, 1994) even reject the hypothesis of price homogeneity of the cost function, which is assumed in most studies.[17] However, imposing price homogeneity results in accepting the hypothesis of constant returns to scale to all inputs.

It can easily be seen that the behavioural approach boils down to allocating economic profits to increasing returns to scale, imperfect competition, and public capital. Therefore, imposing constant returns to scale and perfect competition on the model implies that all profits are automatically allotted to the public capital stock. However, as already noted, Lynde and Richmond (1992, 1993a, 1993b) only estimate share equations, and because these share equations only contain some parameters of the cost function, the structure of the underlying production function cannot be resolved without imposing several restrictions, such as constant returns to scale and perfect competition. This makes clear that estimating all parameters of the dual function is crucial.

Many authors adjust the stock of public capital by an index, such as the capacity utilization rate, to reflect usage by the private sector (Conrad and Seitz, 1994; Deno, 1988; Nadiri and Mamuneas, 1994a; Seitz, 1994; Shah, 1992). The impression exists that this is mainly done to artificially increase the variability of the data in order to cope with multicollinearity problems. On a theoretical basis two reasons have been advocated for adjusting the stock of public capital. First, public capital is a collective input which a firm must share with the rest of the economy. However, since most types of public capital are subject to congestion, the amount of public capital that one firm may employ will be less than the total amount supplied. Moreover, the extent to which a capacity utilization index measures congestion is dubious. Second, firms might have some control on the usage of the public capital stock in existence. For instance, a firm may have no influence on the level of motorways provided by the government, but it can vary its usage of existing motorways by choosing routes. Therefore there are significant swings in the intensity with which public capital is used. Other authors explicitly "... refrain from all of these possible adjustment procedures because of their ad hoc character and because 'proper' adjustment makes virtually all results possible" (Seitz, 1993, p. 230).

Despite the fact that time-series properties are a main issue in the production function approach, they are hardly addressed in studies using the behavioural approach. Nevertheless, also in this line of research the results of many standard inference procedures are invalidated by non-stationary series. To make econometrically justifiable estimations one has to filter the time series to make them stationary or apply some kind of cointegration technique. The latter approach is followed by Lynde and Richmond (1993a, 1993b). They apply an error correction model (ECM) to capture the non-stationarity of the data.

Using an ECM approach also introduces dynamics in this framework. The standard behavioural approach assumes that all endogenous variables adjust to their equilibrium level within one period. Of course, it is hard to imagine that, e.g. the private capital stock fulfils this prerequisite. Not surprisingly, Sturm and Kuper (1996) report severe autocorrelation using the standard behavioural approach. Furthermore, they show that this problem can be overcome by adopting an ECM representation within a translog cost function. However, during the empirical implementation, they came up with other difficulties; several first-order conditions were no longer satisfied. Probably the increased flexibility was too much to be asked, for given the available data.

In estimating the optimal stock of public capital, the assumption regarding the public good character of infrastructure is crucial. In the case of pure public goods, one could define total marginal benefits of public capital as the sum of the shadow values over all private sector firms, plus the sum of corresponding marginal benefits over all final consumers, yielding what might be called the social or total marginal benefit of public capital. Alternatively, if there is no congestion in the consumption of public goods, the total marginal benefit could be the largest benefit accruing to any one or set of consumers and producers, rather than the addition over all consumers and producers. The simplest rule to determine the optimal provision of public capital is to calculate the amount of infrastructure for which social marginal benefits just equal marginal costs. The difficulty in the empirical implementation of this rule lies in approximating the marginal costs of public capital. Therefore, only a few studies have estimated the optimal amount of public capital to compare it with the actual stock. Berndt and Hansson (1991) report an excess in public capital in the US that has declined over time. In contrast, Shah (1992) concludes that there was under-investment in public capital in Mexico. These studies use some measure for the cost of borrowing, such as the government bond yield, to approximate the marginal costs of public capital. To get around the problem, Conrad and

Seitz (1994) interpret the case in which the social marginal benefit of public capital is greater than the price of private capital as indicative of a shortage of public capital, whereas the reverse indicates over-investment in public capital. They find that during 1961–79 the social marginal benefit of public capital in Germany exceeded the user cost of private capital, whereas in the 1980–88 period the opposite held true.

To summarize, the most appealing property of the behavioural approach induces also the biggest problem; the flexibility of the functional form requires a tremendous amount of information to be included in the database. Furthermore, several problems raised by the production function approach still remain. In most of the studies using the behavioural approach time-series properties are not taken into account.

4.4 VAR APPROACH

Another line of research to examine the effect of public capital spending on the economy, which we will label the VAR approach, is primarily data-oriented. By imposing as little economic theory as possible, this approach tries to solve some problems raised by the production and behavioural studies. In a VAR model a limited number of variables is distinguished that are explained by their own lags and lags of the other variables, meaning that all variables are treated as jointly determined. If necessary, deterministic variables, such as a constant or a trend, are included.[18] In this approach usually Granger-causality tests are carried out. As discussed in Chapter 2, some variable is said to 'Granger cause' another variable, if the time-series prediction of the latter from its own past improves when lags of the former are added to the equation. Therefore, Granger causality is a statistical concept of antecedence, or predictability. Granger-causality tests address the question of whether one variable helps to explain the subsequent time path of another. This interpretation of causality is, of course, intuitively attractive. It has therefore become widely accepted, although some of its implications are still under debate (Granger, 1980).

Besides conducting Granger-causality tests, a VAR model can be analyzed by observing the reactions over time of different shocks on the estimated system (impulse-response analysis). Rewriting the VAR into its Vector Moving Average (VMA) representation allows us to trace the time path of various shocks on the variables contained in the VAR system. However, there are many equivalent VMA representations for one VAR model. Because of this identification problem some economic structure has to be imposed, which reduces an important advantage of the VAR analysis. Furthermore, the model needs to be stable in order to make the conversion. A sufficient condition that makes the model stable is that the variables used are stationary or cointegrated. Problems

Table 4.4   VAR studies

STUDY	DATA	MODEL	VARIABLES[a]	CONCLUSIONS
Clarida (1993)	US, France, Germany, UK	VECM	MFP, G	MFP and public capital are cointegrated, but direction of causality is unclear
McMillin & Smyth (1994)	US, 1952–90	VAR, levels and first differences	H/K, P^E/P^Y, G/K, inflation	No significant effect of public capital
Sturm *et al.* (1995)	Netherlands, 1853–13	VAR	Y, K, G, L	Infrastructure Granger-causes output
Otto & Voss (1996)	Australia, 1959:III– 92:II	VAR	Y, K, G, H	No relationship between public capital and labour or output. Private capital affects public capital positively

[a]MFP: multifactor productivity; K: private capital stock; L: private labour; H: number of working hours; Y: private sector GDP; G: public capital stock; H/K: hours of work per unit of capital; P^E/P^Y: relative price of energy.

concerning non-stationarity and cointegration of the data may be solved within this framework by applying the Johansen (1988, 1991) cointegration technique (Gonzalo, 1994). This method consists of a VAR model in which an error correction mechanism is included.

The production function studies derive single-equation models from first principles, which are then estimated while conclusions are based on the estimated elasticities. The multi-equation regressions in the behavioural approach are also deduced from first principles. In order to derive these first principles, some economic structure has to be assumed. First of all, this implies that the causal relationships are determined by theory. However, causality is often an issue when discussing the results of the production function approach. An advantage of the VAR approach is that no *a priori* causality directions are imposed, or other identifying conditions derived from economic theory are needed. For instance, the causality might run from output to public capital, which is the opposite of what is usually assumed.

An additional advantage—compared to the production function approach— is that public capital might indirectly influence output by its effect on a third variable, e.g. private investment. Some authors, like Aschauer (1989b) and Erenburg (1993), report evidence for a complementary relationship between public and private capital, which suggests the existence of these indirect effects.

Because the VAR approach does not completely reveal the underlying production process, it is somewhat harder to get elasticity estimates. The only way to get specific elasticity estimates is via the impulse-response functions; they result in estimates of the long-run effects of various shocks.

Despite these advantages of the VAR approach, so far it has hardly been applied to the problem at hand. Besides the preliminary results presented in Chapter 2, we have traced only four studies in which some variant of the VAR approach is conducted to test the effects of public capital spending on the private sector: Clarida (1993); McMillin and Smyth (1994); Sturm *et al.* (1995); and Otto and Voss (1996). We will discuss these papers in chronological order. Table 4.4 provides a summary.

Clarida (1993) compares multifactor productivity (MFP) measures and public capital stocks for the US, France, Germany, and the United Kingdom. Clarida rejects stationarity in levels for both series in all four countries. The Johansen (1988, 1991) method leads to the conclusion that MFP and public capital cointegrate, i.e. there exists a long-run equilibrium relationship between these two variables. However, the causation is unclear. The Granger-causality tests produce evidence that public capital influences productivity as well as that productivity determines public capital.

McMillin and Smyth (1994) claim to stick to the production function framework as closely as possible in order to be able to compare their results with those reported in the production function literature. The variables that enter their VAR model are the private sector output per unit of private capital (Q/K), the hours of work per unit of private capital (H/K), government capital per unit of private capital (G/K), the relative price of energy (P^E/P^Q), and the inflation rate (π). However, not all of these variables can be described as typical for the single-equation estimates of the aggregate production function. For instance, inflation is included to incorporate another line of research, but how it can be seen as an additional production factor is unclear; including it is definitely not common for this line of literature. As already discussed in section 4.2, the inclusion of the relative price of energy is also debatable. Furthermore, both private and public capital are adjusted by the capacity utilization rate which may also be questioned (see section 4.3). The data relate to the US for the 1952–90 period. McMillin and Smyth (1994) do not test whether the variables are stationary or not. They decided to estimate the VAR model with both levels and first differences of the variables. As already mentioned, this may lead to inconsistent estimates or spurious regressions. To account for apparent non-stationarity, a trend term was added to each equation in the model estimated in levels. McMillin and Smyth (1994) analyze both VAR models by observing the reactions over time of different shocks on the estimated system (impulse-response analysis) and by computing the share of the forecast error variance for each variable that can be attributed to its own innovations and to shocks to the other variables in the system (variance decompositions).

McMillin and Smyth (1994) use impulse-response analysis and variance decompositions. In both models, i.e. in levels and first differences, they reach the same conclusion: public capital per unit of private capital has no significant role in explaining output per unit of private capital. However, McMillin and Smyth (1994) apply the Choleski decomposition of the covariance matrix in order to convert their VAR into a VMA representation. This approach implies an ordering of the variables from the most pervasive—a shock to this variable affects all the other variables in the current period—to least pervasive—a shock does not affect any other variables in the current period. Unfortunately, there are many ways to order the variables, and the choice of one particular ordering might not be innocuous. The ordering employed is P^E/P^Q, π, G/K, H/K, Q/K. Placing Q/K last is consistent with the production function studies, because these studies treat this variable as the endogenous variable. The importance of the ordering depends on the correlation between the residual terms. If the estimated correlations are almost zero, the ordering is immaterial. However, if a correlation coefficient is almost unity then a single shock in the system contemporarily affects two variables. McMillin and Smyth (1994) report large absolute correlations between several residual terms. To what extent the results change when other orderings are imposed is not discussed in their paper.

The third paper in which the VAR approach is employed and on which Chapter 7 is based, covers the Netherlands for the period 1853–1913. In contrast to the above-mentioned studies, Sturm *et al.* (1995) do not use capital stocks but utilize investment series in their analysis. Augmented Dickey–Fuller (ADF) tests show that the series for machinery investment, infrastructure investment, and output are trend stationary over the period considered. Therefore cointegration techniques like the Johansen (1988, 1991) method need not be applied. The multivariate VAR model that these authors estimate includes a trend in each equation. Granger-causality tests indicate large effects of infrastructure on output. No evidence is found for indirect effects of infrastructure via machinery investments. These findings are confirmed by impulse-response analysis and variance decompositions. These authors also apply an ordering of the variables that sticks to the production function approach. However, in contrast to McMillin and Smyth (1994), Sturm *et al.* (1995) check whether changing the ordering alters their conclusions. Because there is hardly any correlation between the residual terms in their VAR model, they are able to establish that the ordering does not influence the outcomes in a significant way.

Finally, Otto and Voss (1996) employ VAR techniques to Australian quarterly data covering the 1959:III–92:II period. Augmented Dickey–Fuller tests indicate that all four variables—output, private and public capital, working hours—are non-stationary. However, these authors decided to estimate a VAR model using levels of all variables. Impulse-response functions and variance decomposition are used to arrive at some conclusions about the short-run dynamics. They find that public capital is not affected by—and has hardly any effect on—both labour and output. The impulse-response functions show that a positive shock to public capital tends to have a positive lagged effect on private capital. Variance decompositions, however, indicate that private capital is largely exogenous, which argues against the conclusion that public investment can influence private investment. The other way around, public capital responds positively to private capital innovations. This is confirmed by the variance decompositions. As the correlations between the residuals are very close to zero, alternative orderings do not produce qualitatively different results.

To summarize these four papers, only the third paper of Sturm *et al.* (1995) finds clear evidence for the thesis that public capital spending influences output or productivity. Furthermore, not all four papers are on solid econometric ground or come up with unambiguous results. McMillin and Smyth (1994) and Otto and Voss (1996) do not take account of possible cointegrating relationships and present results that are possibly inconsistent or based on spurious regressions. Clarida (1993) reports that MFP and public capital influence each other mutually.

4.5 PUBLIC CAPITAL IN CROSS-SECTION MODELS

In the previous sections we discussed the impact of government capital on economic growth in models using mainly a time-series framework. Although it is generally accepted that public capital and economic growth are somehow related, the literature is not unambiguous with respect to the size of such effects. Here we review the empirical literature on the relationship between public capital and growth based primarily on the theory of (endogenous) economic growth.

Since the mid-1980s the study of economic growth and its policy implications vigorously re-entered the research agenda (Romer, 1986; Baumol, 1986). A diverse body of literature appeared trying to explain, both theoretically and empirically, why differences in income over time and across countries did not disappear as the neo-classical models of growth—developed by Solow (1956) and Swan (1956)—of the 1950s and 1960s predicted. The idea that emerged from this literature is that economic growth is endogenous. That is, economic growth is influenced by decisions made by economic agents, and is not merely the outcome of an exogenous process. Endogenous growth assigns a central role to capital formation, where capital is not just confined to physical capital, but includes human capital, infrastructure and knowledge.

The econometric work on growth is dominated by cross-country regressions (Barro, 1991; Mankiw *et al.* 1992). In these studies the model of growth collapses to a single growth equation by log-linearizing the model around the steady state. Empirically, growth of real per capita GDP is estimated by a catch-up variable, human capital, investment, and population factors like fertility. Public investment might be a relevant factor in these kind of models. Indeed, some studies employ government investment as an explanatory variable. Table

Table 4.5   Cross country growth regressions

STUDY	COUNTRIES	SAMPLE	GOVERNMENT CAPITAL CONCEPT	CONCLUSIONS
Barro (1989)	72 non-OPEC countries	1960–85	public investment	significant effect
Barro (1991)	76 countries	1960–85	public investment	no effect
Easterly & Rebelo (1993)	about 100 countries	1970–88	public investment or transport and communication spending	first variable not significant, second variable is significant

4.5 provides a summary of the equations estimated in various studies:[19]

$$\Delta \ln \left(\frac{Q}{L} \right)_{0,T} = c_0 + \beta \left(\frac{Q}{L} \right)_0 + \gamma \left(\frac{I^G}{Q} \right)_{0,T} + \delta \, (\text{conditional variables}), \quad (4.5)$$

where $(Q/L)_{0,T}$ is the average per capita GDP over a period $[0,T]$, $(Q/L)_0$ is the initial level of real per capita GDP, and $(I^G/Q)_{0,T}$ is the average rate of public investment (% GDP) over a period $[0,T]$. Obviously, the regression should include public capital and not public investment. In empirical work, however, public investment is used because data on public capital are difficult to come by or are not available at all. Furthermore, again due to (lack of) availability of data, the period over which investment rates are averaged may deviate from the period used to average the growth rates of per capita GDP. The set of conditional variables include averages of primary and/or secondary enrolment (as a proxy of human capital), measures of political instability (assassinations, revolts and coups, and war casualties), measures of economic freedom, and the ratio of government consumption to GDP. Parameter β in the equation above measures technological catch up (if negative).[20] Parameter γ measures the effect of public investment on growth and is therefore not the same as the marginal productivity of public capital. The data used are often based on the dataset compiled by Summers and Heston (1988, 1991) for a large sample of countries, and extended with investment data and information on other variables gathered by Barro and Wolf (1989) and Barro and Lee (1994).

The model of Barro (1989) builds on Romer (1989), Lucas (1988) and Rebelo (1991). Public services enter the production function: some infrastructure activities of government are inputs to private production and also raise the marginal product of private capital. Preliminary, but suggestive, findings are that public investment tends to be positively correlated with growth and private investment. In Barro (1991) growth is inversely related to the share of government consumption in GDP, but insignificantly related to the share of public investment. Once the total investment ratio is included in the model, there is no separate effect on growth from the breakdown of total investment between private and public components.

Easterly and Rebelo (1993) run pooled regressions (using decade averages for the 1960s, 1970s and 1980s) of per capita growth on (sectoral) public investment and conditioning variables (decade averages of primary and secondary enrolment, measures of political instability, and the ratio of government consumption to GDP). The share of public investment in transport and communication (infrastructure) is robustly correlated with growth in a Barro-type cross-section regression (including a set of conditioning variables like initial level of income, enrolment rates, measures of political instability and the ratio of government consumption to GDP). Using instrumental variables the size of the effect of investment in transport and communication on growth as reported by Easterly and Rebelo (1993) becomes disturbingly high. This issue requires more research.

Until now we have discussed cross-country models. In section 4.2 we have already referred to one study in which the growth approach has been applied using regional data (Holtz–Eakin, 1992). Table 4.6 summarizes these studies. In the remainder of this section the studies of Mas *et al.* (1994b, 1995a, 1995b) and Crihfield and Panggabean (1995) will be discussed, as they have not been addressed in previous sections.

Mas *et al.* (1994b, 1995a, 1995b) estimate growth equations directly. They conclude that for the Spanish regions the initial stock of public capital relative to gross value added affects output per capita positively. However, their result only applies to the period until 1967. Crihfield and Panggabean (1995) use quite a different approach to arrive at conclusions which are in line with those of other authors: public infrastructure surely plays a role, but its contribution may be less than that of other forms of investment. Crihfield and Panggabean (1995) adopt a two-stage estimation technique, since exogeneity of labour and capital, often implicitly assumed, is rejected in most of the cases they consider. In the first stage they estimate reduced-form equations for population growth and investment equations, including public capital data (state or local investment in various types of public capital like education, streets and motorways and sewerage and sanitation) as explanatory variables. The predicted values from these estimations enter the GDP per capita equation in the second stage. The implied elasticities of public capital are negative for both local and state public capital and ambiguous for most types of public capital, except for streets and motorways.

Various authors have pointed out problems associated with cross-country regressions. There are biases due to omitted variables, reverse causation (Levine and Renelt, 1992; Levine and Zervos, 1993) and sample selection (De Long, 1988). Furthermore, measurement may also be problematic (Baltagi and Pinnoi, 1995; Dowrick, 1992). The interpretation is often tempted by wishful thinking (Solow, 1994), perhaps because the interpretation becomes blurred due to the number of variables that are included in the regressions (Pack, 1994).

Table 4.6   Cross states growth regressions

STUDY	COUNTRIES	SAMPLE	PUBLIC CAPITAL CONCEPT	MARGINAL PRODUCTIVITY OF PUBLIC CAPITAL
Crihfield & Panggabean (1995)	282 US metropolitan areas	1960–77	local public capital, state public capital, types of public capital	negative, negative, ambiguous
Holtz–Eakin & Schwartz (1994)	48 US states	1971–86	public capital infrastructure	fragile, insignificant
Mas *et al.* (1994b)	17 Spanish regions	1955–91, 1955–67, 1967–79, 1979–91	public capital	0.005, 0.0097, insignificant, insignificant
Mas *et al.* (1995a)	17 Spanish regions	1955–91, 1955–61, 1961–67, 1967–73, 1973–79, 1979–85, 1985–91	public capital	0.005, 0.0061, 0.017, insignificant, insignificant, insignificant, insignificant
Mas *et al.* (1995b)	50 Spanish regions	1955–91, 1955–67, 1967–79, 1979–91	public capital	0.0043, 0.0094, 0.009, insignificant

Cross-section regressions, especially in a cross-section of heterogeneous countries, are often not very robust (Levine and Renelt, 1992). Finally, growth regressions are single-equation models. Economic theory may indicate, and economic data may not reject, that there is more than one endogenous variable in the system (Crihfield and Panggabean, 1995). This calls for a more structural approach which also reduces the problem of multicollinearity.

4.6 PUBLIC CAPITAL IN STRUCTURAL MODELS

The literature reviewed so far aimed at identifying and estimating the effect of (an increase in) government investment (public capital) on output (growth). Except for the VAR approach most models are single-equations models which are sensitive to problems of causation, multicollinearity and so on. In this section we will take a look at structural models for the Netherlands designed to illustrate the role of government investment. This means that we neglect macroeconometric models for the Netherlands, like the models of the CPB Netherlands Bureau for Economic Policy Analysis, the CCSO Centre for Economic Research and De Nederlandsche Bank.

Of the various papers within this approach, only Westerhout and Van Sinderen (1994) try to estimate the marginal productivity of public capital. The other papers *assume* a positive relationship between government investment and the performance of the economy simply by referring to Aschauer (1989a), thereby neglecting the criticism discussed in section 4.2. Indeed, the specification and the estimates of these studies are easily tainted by wishful thinking.

Using a small linearized macroeconomic model for the Netherlands, Westerhout and Van Sinderen (1994) assess the indirect effect of both government policies and external factors on economic growth through their effect on private investment. The model, which covers 1958–89, consists of four reduced-form equations. The rate of output growth depends on the private gross investment rate, whereas the private gross investment rate is assumed to be positively related to the rate of growth of public investment with the causality running from public to private investment. From the estimation results the long-run coefficient on the rate of growth of public investment in the equation for the private gross investment rate appears to be 0.23, while the coefficient for the gross private investment rate in the output growth equation is 0.48. This implies that in the long run the elasticity of output with respect to public investment equals 0.11 (0.23 × 0.48). In the short run it is only 0.02. If the ratio of public investment over output equals about 0.03, then the marginal product of public investment in the long run equals 3.7 which seems to be highly unrealistic. This might be caused by the fact that Westerhout and Van Sinderen (1994) use public investment data rather than data on public capital. Or perhaps the gross investment rate in the output growth equation picks up other influences as well.

In the other papers reviewed in this section public capital is included as an argument in the production function in a general equilibrium framework with optimizing agents. In all cases the production function is linearized and is written in terms of rates of growth. Most papers only report the output elasticity of public capital. The marginal product of capital can be derived as the ratio between the output elasticity of public capital and the average productivity of public capital. Only De Mooij *et al.* (1996) explicitly report the marginal productivity of public capital. Van de Klundert (1993) and De Mooij *et al.* (1996) assume constant returns to scale (CRS) to all private inputs and increasing returns to all inputs. Van Hagen *et al.* (1995) assumes CRS to all inputs, private and public. This has consequences for the way public inputs are financed. Except for Toen–Gout and Van Sinderen (1995) all the papers focus on long-run effects of public capital which seems the right thing to do since "... the benefits reaped from public investment are far ahead in the future..." (Van de Klundert, 1993, p. 273).

Toen–Gout and Van Sinderen (1995) concentrate on the effects of infrastructure investment in the Netherlands on economic growth and employment in the short and medium run using a general equilibrium model. They assume a positive relationship between government investment (especially infrastructure) and the performance of the economy and a negative impact due to financing these outlays. The production function includes public investment instead of public capital. Public investment is assumed to have the same elasticity as private investment (0.34). Public investment is supposed to have a direct (positive) effect on growth by raising private productivity. There is a negative effect between private and public capital due to substitution. They estimate the overall elasticity to be about 0.04. Even when the method of financing is taken into consideration these authors still find a positive effect between public capital and growth. Based on simulation exercises they favour a reduction of income transfers to pay for public investment.

Unlike Toen–Gout and Van Sinderen (1995), Van de Klundert (1993) focuses on long-run effects of crowding out of private and public capital accumulation. Van de Klundert (1993) uses a two-country general equilibrium model (with optimizing finitely lived agents) with imperfect commodity substitution and imperfect capital mobility. Consumers face an intertemporal optimization problem. Furthermore they have to decide between consumption of home and foreign goods. Firms produce under perfect foresight and maximize the net present value of the cash flow subject to the production function. Public capital is included in the production function with CRS to private factors. The output elasticity of public capital is set equal to 0.2.

Van Hagen *et al.* (1995) focus on long-run effects for the Dutch economy of an increase in public expenditures on education financed by either a cut in other public spending categories, or by taxes. They use a general equilibrium model including endogenous accumulation of human capital. They assume that government expenditures (be it infrastructure investment or investment in R&D and education) have a positive impact on productive capacity. Van Hagen *et al.* (1995) are inspired by Mankiw *et al.* (1992) by assuming CRS to all inputs, private and public. The output elasticity of infrastructure capital is set equal to 0.05. The parameters are fixed rather arbitrarily. In their model, labour is paid its marginal product so the model implies that the rents for public capital are paid for by private capital.

Van Hagen *et al.* (1995) conclude that the long-run effects on production and employment of a policy change aimed at a faster accumulation of skills are potentially large, especially when financed by reducing income transfers or by reducing the number of civil servants. The authors indicate that their results are sensitive to the degree of substitutability between high-skilled and low-skilled labour, the importance of human capital in production, and the effect of education on human capital.

Finally, De Mooij *et al.* (1996) focus on welfare effects of public expenditures using a general equilibrium model. The linearized production function implies that the marginal productivity of public capital amounts to 0.12. The output elasticity of public capital equals 0.04. This means that the rate of public capital to output is only 0.3 which does not seem to be very realistic. Here we have CRS to private inputs just as in the model by Van de Klundert (1993).

The production function includes labour-augmenting technical progress which is assumed to be negatively related to labour taxes.

De Mooij *et al.* (1996) conclude that cutting public investment may seriously harm economic performance. Furthermore, they show that investment in infrastructure has a positive effect on economic welfare and economic growth, especially when financed with lump sum taxes or labour taxes. Capital taxation results in negative effects. Again substitutability between private and public capital is important.

4.7 CONCLUSIONS

The final section of this chapter will first formulate our main conclusions with respect to the literature surveyed here. Next we add some general observations which are relevant for most studies surveyed.

The academic debate on public capital spending was stimulated by Aschauer (1989a, 1989b, 1989c, 1990). As Gramlich (1994, pp. 1176–1177) put it: "(h)e wrote a series of papers ... that put these movements (, i.e. the US productivity slowdown and the neglect of public capital,) together econometrically ... His work hit the magic button ... and Aschauer's papers were followed by an unusual amount of attention, from politicians and economists." This chapter takes stock of this literature. This implies that many of the issues dealt with are of an econometric nature. It also implies that some other research which has been used to assess whether there is a shortage of public capital (like engineering needs assessments, political voting outcomes and cost-benefit analyses) have not been discussed.[21]

We have reviewed the pros and cons of five different ways to model the relationship between public investment and economic growth. We started with the production function approach in which the public capital stock is added as an additional input factor in a production function, which is then estimated at a national or regional level. Initially, this approach yielded results "that were just too good to be true" (Aaron, 1990, p. 62). Indeed, the results of Aschauer (1989a) and Munnell (1990) have been criticized on various grounds. The most serious objections are related to (1) the assumed causality between public capital and output, (2) the specification and restrictiveness of the estimated model, and (3) the time-series characteristics of the data. With respect to this last issue, the proper way to proceed is to analyze whether the data are stationary or cointegrated. As we will see in the next chapter and as has been shown by Sturm and De Haan (1995a), applying this procedure in the case of the Netherlands reveals that public capital and private sector inputs are only cointegrated if the variables are in first differences. This specification eliminates the ability to estimate the underlying long-term relationship between production and factor inputs. As to the second issue, a serious shortcoming of much of this literature is that most authors employ a Cobb–Douglas production function, thereby simply following the lead of Aschauer (1989a). This implies, however, that various restrictions are introduced.

An alternative for the production function approach is to estimate a cost or profit function in which the public capital stock is included. Some of the drawbacks of the production function approach can be eliminated by using this so-called behavioural approach. However, the flexibility of the functional form requires the database used to contain a tremendous amount of information. Furthermore, most problems raised in production function estimates still remain. In most of the studies using the behavioural approach time-series properties are not taken into account. The issue of causality is also problematic. Most studies following the behavioural approach conclude that public capital reduces private sector costs or increases private sector profits. However, the estimated effects are generally significantly smaller than those reported by Aschauer (1989a).

A third way to examine the relationship between government investment and economic growth is the so-called VAR approach. By imposing as few economic restrictions as possible, this way of modelling tries to solve some of the problems raised by the production and behavioural approach. An advantage of VAR models is that no *a priori* causality directions are imposed or other identifying conditions derived from economic theory are needed. Indirect effects of public capital are also taken into account. As the VAR approach does not completely reveal the underlying production process, only impulse-response functions yield estimates of the long-run effects of different shocks. So far, there are only a few studies in which VARs have been used to analyze the problem at hand; therefore it is too early to reach definite conclusions. Still, it seems a promising approach.

The first three approaches are all based on time series (or panel data). A fourth way to model the growth effects of public capital spending is to include government investment spending in cross-section growth regressions. Problems associated with these cross-section regressions include biases due to omitted variables and reverse causation. The two-step approach adopted by Crihfield and Panggabean (1995) seems a promising way to deal with problems related to the single-equation nature of most cross-section regression models. Conclusions based on such regressions, especially in a cross-section of heterogeneous countries, are often not very robust and this also holds true for the outcomes with respect to the growth-raising effects of public investment.

Finally some attempts to estimate the growth effects of public investment spending using structural econometric models have been discussed. The conclusions from this approach to model the impact of public capital on economic growth are twofold. First, in most cases it is simply assumed that there exists a causal and positive relationship between public capital on the one hand, and economic growth on the other. However, this assumption may not be warranted as the previous sections have shown. Second, even if we assume that such a positive relationship exists, the conclusions of studies in this approach should be interpreted with great care. Not only the size of the effect of public capital on output varies considerably among the various studies, but some authors also point at the importance of the degree of substitutability in the system in order to assess the importance of public capital for the performance of the economy. Here, we enter another discussion—which actually takes us back to the Cambridge-Cambridge controversy in the 1960s—since economists do not agree on the degree of substitution in an economy.

Finally, we have some general observations relating to all approaches discussed. One issue that is not always dealt with carefully is that the concept of the stock of public capital includes rather diverse items, like motorways and streets, gas, water and electricity facilities, water supply, bridges and water transportation systems. Indeed, the evidence of Sturm *et al.* (1995) and Chapter 7 suggests that different types of infrastructure can have different effects. Most authors employ data in their analyses which are generally chosen on the ground of their availability, without analyzing whether their conclusions are sensitive not only to the concept of the public capital stock (narrow versus broad definitions), but also to the way the capital stock has been constructed. For instance, most data on the capital stock are constructed using the perpetual inventory method, in which assumptions about the expected life of the assets are crucial. Few authors experiment with different definitions of the stock of public capital, which indeed, sometimes lead to diverging outcomes (Sturm and De Haan, 1995a; Garcia–Milà *et al.* 1996). Although some authors, including Aschauer (1989a), differentiate between the total stock of non-military public capital and the stock of infrastructure, one may wonder whether this suffices. It is likely, that regions and industries react differently to various types of public capital. Indeed, Pinnoi (1994) finds strong evidence in support of this view.

Another issue to which hardly any attention has been paid is the fact that what really matters from a theoretical perspective is the amount of services yielded by the public capital stock. In all empirical research it is implicitly assumed that these can be proxied by the stock of public capital or the level of government investment spending, which may not be true. For instance, the amount of services provided is also determined by the efficiency with which they are provided from the stock of public capital. Indeed, according to Munnell (1993) and Boarnet (1997) there is substantial room for improving the efficiency.

A further general observation that we would like to make concerns the implicit assumptions about the time it takes for public capital to affect output growth. There may well be a substantial lag before the building of say a new road leads to new businesses being set up. A simple Cobb–Douglas production function, as often applied in the literature, will probably not reflect this effect. Similarly, it does not allow for network effects, whereby the quality of the connections facilitated by infrastructure investments may be more important than the level of the public capital stock itself (Garcia–Milà *et al.*, 1996). It may also make quite a difference whether the investment concerns infrastructure which previously did not exist at all, or simply adds to existing public capital (compare: a new two-lane road versus a two-lane road turned into a four-lane road).

To summarize, we come up with only very modest conclusions. First, public capital probably enhances economic growth, a conclusion that most economists intuitively would ascribe to. Second, we are less certain about the magnitude of this effect which is a disappointing outcome, given the enormous amount of research that has been done in this field.

NOTES

1. For instance, the Cobb–Douglas production function restricts—by definition—the substitution elasticities of the production factors to be equal to one.
2. Hulten and Schwab (1993) estimate the level of multifactor productivity (MFP) in each region in four versions of their model: constrained (assuming the same level and growth of MFP across regions), including only regional intercepts, including only regional time effects and including both regional intercepts and time effects. The results of their various specifications are quite different.
3. Holtz–Eakin (1992) and Holtz–Eakin and Schwartz (1994) incorporate infrastructure (streets and motorways, sanitation and sewage, and electric, gas, and water utilities) as a component of aggregate production. Holtz–Eakin (1992) estimates the model without fixed effects and including both state and time effects. The estimated values for γ imply that the macroeconomic impact of public sector capital on private productivity has been small. Holtz–Eakin and Schwartz (1994) first estimate the model without fixed effects to find negative values for γ. Controlling for state-specific differences in productivity changes parameters dramatically, but the effects are still not very significant. Both Holtz–Eakin (1992) and Holtz–Eakin and Schwartz (1994) conclude that there is little support for claims of a dramatic productivity decline due to decreased infrastructure spending. Holtz–Eakin and Schwartz (1995) examine the degree to which motorways provide productivity benefits beyond the confines of each state's border. They find no evidence of quantitatively important productivity spillovers.
4. Earlier, Ratner (1983) had already reached similar conclusions. Costa *et al.* (1987) also found a significant impact of the public capital stock on output.
5. Aschauer (1989a, 1990) also employed instrumental variables to estimate his production functions. This did not affect his basic conclusions.
6. As figure 1.2 of Chapter 1 demonstrates, in the Netherlands the fall in public investment also preceded the productivity slowdown.
7. Formally, as several Euler equations have to be specified, the GMM procedure implies that a more behavioural approach is used. However, as essentially a production function is estimated, we opted to include these two papers in this section.
8. The GMM procedure adopted by Finn (1993) and Ai and Cassou (1995) also follows the first-differencing suggestion. However, these authors suggest that, because the GMM procedure tightly identifies the parameters, their estimates are not sensitive to the differencing. Holtz–Eakin and Schwartz (1995) on the other hand use so-called long differences; the data for each year is entered as differences from the initial year. In this way cumulative growth rates

are used. All three studies report labour and capital elasticities which are in accordance with theoretical predictions.

9. Duggal *et al.* (1995) develop an alternative approach in which infrastructure is incorporated as part of the technological constraint, rather than as a factor input. Infrastructure reduces production costs, thereby raising the productivity of factor inputs, and it expands markets, thereby lowering production costs through economies of scale and also allowing the implementation of technological innovations that do not become cost effective until an output threshold is reached. However, estimating their theoretical model for the US over the period 1960–89 these authors find estimates of the marginal product of infrastructure which exceed even those of Aschauer (1989a) and Munnell (1990). In the authors' view these results are not implausible when one stops thinking of infrastructure as a factor input that siphons off its factor share of income.

10. Most studies approximate the state of technical knowledge by a time trend. Nadiri and Mamuneas (1994a, 1994b) are exceptions in which public R&D capital is also taken into account.

11. There is, of course, a price to be paid for the services of public capital through the tax system. However, by assuming that firms do not have direct control over how much capital the government supplies to them, all studies treat these services as 'unpaid' factors of production.

12. Exceptions are Lynde (1992) who employs a standard Cobb–Douglas function and thereby eliminates most advantages of the behavioural approach, and Nadiri and Mamuneas (1994a, 1994b) who use a generalized Cobb–Douglas function which can also be seen as a restricted translog function.

13. Diewert and Wales (1987) have shown that the translog and the generalized Leontief functions frequently fail to satisfy the appropriate curvature conditions. This is confirmed by Sturm and Kuper (1996) who have used a translog specification. Chapter 6 and Sturm (1997) report results using a modified symmetric generalized McFadden (SGM) function on which the appropriate curvature conditions can easily be imposed without destroying the flexibility properties. Using Dutch data, their results suggest that this modified SGM specification outperforms the translog specification.

14. Exceptions are Berndt and Hansson (1991) and Lynde (1992), who only estimate the dual function, and Lynde and Richmond (1992, 1993a, 1993b), who only estimate share equations, thereby reducing estimation efficiency. As no additional information is added by incorporating the symmetric generalized McFadden cost function, only the factor-demand equations are estimated in Chapter 6 and in Sturm (1997).

15. The shadow value of public capital measures the impact on the private firm's costs of there being an exogenous increase in the amount of available public capital.

16. If there are n production factors in the cost functions, then $2n + n(n - 1)/2$ coefficients need to be estimated besides the constant and possible dummy-variables.

17. Price homogeneity of the cost functions means that doubling the input prices implies a doubling of the cost.

18. In case n variables are included with each p lags, $n^2 \times p$ coefficients need to be estimated, besides the deterministic variables.

19. Since we are interested in government investment, we restrict ourselves to models including some measure of government investment. Consequently we do not include studies that include total investment (Dowrick, 1992), nor do we review articles on government consumption expenditures. Furthermore, as we concentrate on the OECD countries, studies of, e.g. Devarajan *et al.* (1996), Hulten (1996), Kelly (1997), Khan and Kumar (1997), Khan and Reinhart (1990) and Ram (1996)—which focus solely on developing countries—are not included in table 4.5.

20. Note that this β is not the same as in equation (4.2).

21. See Gramlich (1994) for a discussion of these other methods.

5. Productivity Effects of Public Capital[*]

5.1 INTRODUCTION

Initially, the post-war decades brought unprecedented levels of productivity growth to most Western industrialized countries. Near the end of the 1960s productivity growth plummeted almost everywhere, notably in the United States (US). As discussed in Chapter 4, Aschauer (1989a) has hypothesized that the decrease in productive government services in the US may be crucial in explaining the decline. Taking a production function approach and using annual data for the period 1949–1985, Aschauer (1989a) found that a one per cent increase in the public capital stock might raise multifactor productivity by 0.39 per cent. As the previous chapter has shown, this seminal work inspired a lot of research into the impact of public sector capital spending on private sector output. Much follow-up research has been conducted specially for the US.

This chapter presents some new estimates for the US and the Netherlands. The aim is to examine whether Aschauer's (1989a) approach is—from an econometric point of view—justifiable. We conclude that the conjecture of a positive relationship between public capital and productivity is not well founded. It will be argued that Aschauer's (1989a) results for the US are suspect from an econometric perspective. If his model is estimated in first differences—which is necessary as the variables used are neither stationary nor cointegrated—the model produces only ambiguous results.[1]

Similar results are found in the case of the Netherlands. As in the American case, we must use first-differenced series in order to produce econometrically sound results. Consequently, the values of the estimated coefficients do not lie in a theoretically justifiable interval. Our conclusion is that an economically sensible interpretation of the outcomes rooted in the production function approach is not possible.

This chapter will mainly focus on the remarkable results found when using first-differenced data. Other problems concerning this approach—such as, e.g. the possible endogeneity of public capital—have already been discussed in Chapter 4.

---

[*]This chapter is a revised version of Sturm and De Haan (1995a).

The remainder of the chapter is organized as follows. The next section will outline the procedure followed by Aschauer (1989a). Section 5.3 presents our estimation results for the US, while section 5.4 contains outcomes for the Netherlands. Section 5.5 summarizes the paper.

5.2   THEORETICAL FRAMEWORK

The analysis uses an aggregate Cobb–Douglas production function:

$$Q_t = A_t L_t^\alpha K_t^\beta G_t^\gamma, \tag{5.1}$$

where Q_t is real aggregate output of the private sector, A_t is multifactor productivity, L_t is aggregate hours worked by the labour force of the private sector, K_t is aggregate non-residential stock of private capital, and G_t is aggregate non-military stock of public capital.

Using the standard production function, without the public capital stock, various authors have been unable to explain the productivity slowdown experienced in the US since the 1970s. Several hypotheses have been put forward, including a reduction in research and development expenditures, a decline in the quality of labour, the energy price rise, and a decline in capital stock services. However, none of these variables has explained the slowdown satisfactorily.

By introducing the public capital stock as another input to the national production function, Aschauer (1989a) tried to find an alternative explanation for the productivity slowdown. Dividing both sides of equation (5.1) by K_t, taking the natural logarithm, and *assuming* constant returns to scale across all inputs, gives:

$$\ln\left(\frac{Q_t}{K_t}\right) = \ln(A_t) + \alpha \ln\left(\frac{L_t}{K_t}\right) + \gamma \ln\left(\frac{G_t}{K_t}\right). \tag{5.2}$$

Aschauer (1989a) introduces a constant and a trend variable as a proxy for $\ln(A_t)$. The capacity utilization rate is added to control for the influence of the business cycle. The equation to be estimated is then given by:

$$\ln\left(\frac{Q_t}{K_t}\right) = c + \tau t + \alpha \ln\left(\frac{L_t}{K_t}\right) + \gamma \ln\left(\frac{G_t}{K_t}\right) + \delta \ln(CU_t), \tag{5.3}$$

where t is a deterministic trend, and CU_t is the capacity utilization rate of the private sector. Since the assumption of constant returns to scale may not be

Figure 5.1   US data[a]

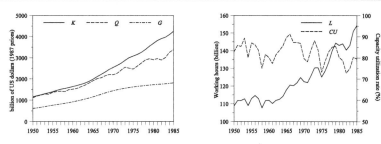

[a]K_t: private non-residential capital stock, Q_t: real aggregate output of the private sector, G_t: public non-military capital stock, L_t: private labour hours input, CU_t: capacity utilization rate of the private sector.
Source: Federal Reserve Bank of St Louis.

valid, we also use the following equation, to test for this restriction:

$$\ln\left(\frac{Q_t}{K_t}\right) = c + \tau t + \alpha \ln\left(\frac{L_t}{K_t}\right) + \gamma \ln\left(\frac{G_t}{K_t}\right)$$
$$+ (\alpha + \beta + \gamma - 1)\ln(K_t) + \delta \ln(CU_t), \quad\quad (5.4)$$

If the assumption of constant returns to scale holds (i.e. $\alpha + \beta + \gamma = 1$) equation (5.4) reduces to (5.3).

5.3   NEW EMPIRICAL EVIDENCE FOR THE UNITED STATES

As we saw in the previous chapter, most studies for the US economy use equations like (5.3) to estimate the production elasticity of public capital. Under the assumptions made in section 5.2 the coefficient γ equals this elasticity measure. As can be seen from table 4.1 of Chapter 4 the estimate of γ in the studies for the US varies between -0.11 and 0.54, and is often found to be significant.

The studies which report an insignificant production elasticity of public capital, have used disaggregated or first-differenced data. Munnell (1992, pp. 193–194) points out that "because of leakages, one cannot capture all of the payoff to an infrastructure investment by looking at a small geographic area." This might explain the lower and sometimes even insignificant elasticity estimates found by studies using more regional data. The aspect of using first-differenced series will be discussed in greater detail in this and subsequent sections.

All data we use for the US have been kindly provided by the Federal Reserve Bank of St Louis. Figure 5.1 displays the series used. The series Q_t, K_t, G_t and

Table 5.1   Estimation results using levels for the US[a]

$\ln(Q_t/K_t)$	ASCHAUER (1989A)	OWN RESULTS	
c	−2.42	−0.30	0.38
	(21.58)	(0.84)	(0.99)
Trend	0.008	0.010	0.013
	(4.62)	(3.63)	(4.49)
$\ln(L_t/K_t)$	0.35	0.47	0.58
	(4.85)	(5.61)	(6.41)
$\ln(G_t/K_t)$	0.39	0.41	0.45
	(16.23)	(8.09)	(8.39)
$\ln(CU_t)$	0.43	0.36	0.27
	(12.28)	(8.98)	(6.31)
ρ			0.28
			(1.85)
R^2 (adj.)	0.976	0.985	0.990
D–W	1.79	1.34	1.75

Sample: US, 1949–85.
[a]See figure 5.1 for variable definitions. Absolute values of t-statistic are shown in parentheses.

L_t steadily rise over time. L_t is relatively high (low) when CU_t is high (low). As expected the number of hours worked reflects the economic climate.

Using these data we have estimated equation (5.3) for the same sample period as Aschauer (1989a), namely 1949–1985. Table 5.1 shows both our results and those of Aschauer (1989a). It follows that, except for the constant term, the estimated coefficients are comparable. Differences must be the consequence of using another data source. The low Durbin–Watson statistic suggests that the residuals may be serially correlated. That is the reason why the last column of table 5.1 shows the results when equation (5.3) is corrected for first-order autocorrelation.[2] This hardly affects the coefficients. In all cases the production elasticity of public capital (γ) is significantly different from zero, ranging between 0.39 and 0.45. These outcomes seem to support the hypothesis that public capital belongs in the production function and that its reduction may explain a (large) part of the productivity slowdown.

The capital elasticity in the production function (β) can be calculated from these outcomes. Aschauer's (1989a) results imply a private capital elasticity of 0.26; we estimate an elasticity of 0.12, and, when corrected for first-order autocorrelation, of −0.03.[3] Such low values lead to suspicion about the validity of the specification.

A common econometric problem with time-series modelling is the existence of a unit root in the variables used. In standard inference procedures it is assumed that the variables concerned are stationary, i.e. they do not have a

Table 5.2 Stationarity testing for the US^a

Series	AUGMENTED DICKEY–FULLER TEST				LEYBOURNE & MCCABE TEST^d	
	Trend		Constant		Trend	Constant
	Lags	$\tau_\tau{}^b$	Lags	$\tau_\mu{}^c$	$\hat{s}$-trend^e	$\hat{s}^f$
$\ln(Q_t/K_t)$	1	−3.39	2	−0.49	0.343**	2.943**
$\ln(L_t/K_t)$	2	−0.63	2	−1.88	0.584**	3.299**
$\ln(G_t/K_t)$	2	−2.27	3	−0.83	0.716**	1.471**
$\ln(K_t)$	3	−2.10	2	−0.54	0.374**	3.227**
$\ln(CU_t)$	1	−3.42	1	−3.25*	0.191*	0.587*
$\Delta\ln(Q_t/K_t)$	1	−4.77**	1	−4.83**	0.020	0.106
$\Delta\ln(L_t/K_t)$	1	−5.03**	1	−4.49**	0.055	0.768**
$\Delta\ln(G_t/K_t)$	1	−4.34**	2	−0.91	0.109	2.789**
$\Delta\ln(K_t)$	1	−3.14	1	−3.16*	0.319**	0.446
$\Delta\ln(CU_t)$	1	−5.12**	1	−5.22**	0.024	0.061

Sample: US, 1949–85.
^{a} See figure 5.1 for variable definitions.
^{b} At a five (one) per cent significance level the MacKinnon (1991) critical values are −3.58 (−4.32) when a trend and a constant are included (τ_τ).
^{c} At a five (one) per cent significance level the MacKinnon (1991) critical values are −2.97 (−3.69) when only a constant is included (τ_μ).
^{d} The number of autoregressive lags is set at three for series in levels and two for first-differenced series.
^{e} The asymptotic critical values for the significance levels of five and one per cent are respectively 0.146 and 0.216.
^{f} The asymptotic critical values for the significance levels of five and one per cent are respectively 0.463 and 0.739.
* Significant at a five per cent level.
**Significant at a one per cent level.

unit root. Non-stationary series invalidate many standard results.[4]

To determine whether the series are stationary, we use three different testing procedures: the augmented Dickey–Fuller (ADF) test, a test developed by Harris (1992), which we will call the bootstrapped unit root (BUR) test, and a newly developed test by Leybourne and McCabe (1994), which has stationarity as its null hypothesis. Appendix A briefly discusses the ideas behind these tests.

The left-hand side of Table 5.2 reports the outcomes of the ADF tests for the US. The series tested are displayed in the first column. The second column reports the number of recorded lags where a trend and a constant are included. In the third column the corresponding ADF *t*-statistic (τ_τ) is reported. The next two columns (Constant) show the optimal number of lags and the corresponding ADF *t*-statistic when only a constant is included (τ_μ).

Table 5.3   Augmented Engle–Granger test for the US[a]

$$\ln\left(Q_t/K_t\right) = c + \tau \times Trend + \alpha \ln\left(L_t/K_t\right) + \gamma \ln\left(G_t/K_t\right) + \delta \ln\left(CU_t\right)$$

Lags of first-differenced residuals		0
t-statistic		−3.8742
MacKinnon (1991) critical values	1%	−5.7218
	5%	−4.9016
	10%	−4.5060

Sample: US, 1949–85.
[a]See figure 5.1 for variable definitions. Absolute values of *t*-statistic are shown in parentheses.

From this table, it is clear that with the possible exception of $\ln\left(CU_t\right)$ none of the series are stationary in levels. Their first differences are clearly (trend) stationary. So, from the ADF test we conclude that all series used are I(1).[5]

The outcomes of the BUR test are generally very similar to those of the ADF test, and are, therefore, not shown. The outcomes of the test developed by Leybourne and McCabe (1994) are also shown in table 5.2. None of the series is stationary in levels. As the null-hypothesis of (trend) stationarity is never rejected when using first-differenced data, we again conclude that all series must be first differenced to achieve stationarity.

Therefore, only when the series concerned are cointegrated, i.e. they move together in time, thereby assuring existence of a long-run relationship, one may estimate equation (5.3) in levels. Several of the studies summarized in table 4.1 of Chapter 4 do not test for this.

We have used the augmented Engle–Granger test to examine cointegration.[6] This test consists of a unit root test on the residuals of the cointegration equation. The hypothesis of a unit root is rejected if the *t*-statistic lies to the left of the relevant critical values, which were computed by MacKinnon (1991) for any sample size and up to six variables. As can be seen from table 5.3 the hypothesis that the level of the series concerned are cointegrated must be rejected. Consequently, the estimated coefficients of table 5.1 cannot be interpreted in the usual way.

To make econometrically justifiable estimations we have to first difference the time series to turn them into stationary ones. Consequently, re-estimating equation (5.3) is necessary. Writing equation (5.3) in first differences yields:

$$\Delta\ln\left(\frac{Q_t}{K_t}\right) = \tau + \alpha\Delta\ln\left(\frac{L_t}{K_t}\right) + \gamma\Delta\ln\left(\frac{G_t}{K_t}\right) + \delta\Delta\ln\left(CU_t\right). \qquad (5.5)$$

This equation still assumes constant returns to scale. We therefore also estimate equation (5.6), which is a first-differenced version of equation (5.4), to test for

Table 5.4   Estimation results using first differences for the US[a]

$\Delta \ln(Q_t\,K_t)$	(1)	(2)	(3)	(4)
$\Delta Trend$	0.008	0.022	0.031	0.025
	(1.62)	(3.21)	(7.08)	(2.31)
$\Delta \ln(L_t/K_t)$	0.36	0.13	1.13	1.13
	(2.39)	(0.83)	(10.37)	(10.29)
$\Delta \ln(G_t/K_t)$	0.43	0.26	0.67	0.71
	(3.03)	(1.78)	(3.55)	(3.58)
$\Delta \ln(K_t)$		−0.58		0.19
		(2.71)		(0.67)
$\Delta \ln(CU_t)$	0.33	0.42		
	(5.82)	(6.84)		
R^2 (adj.)	0.871	0.892	0.747	0.743
D–W	1.95	2.17	1.59	1.63

Sample: US, 1949–85.
[a]See figure 5.1 for variable definitions. Absolute values of t-statistic are shown in parentheses.

this restriction:

$$\Delta \ln\left(\frac{Q_t}{K_t}\right) = \tau + \alpha \Delta \ln\left(\frac{L_t}{K_t}\right) + \gamma \Delta \ln\left(\frac{G_t}{K_t}\right)$$
$$+ (\alpha + \beta + \gamma - 1)\Delta \ln(K_t) + \delta \Delta \ln(CU_t). \qquad (5.6)$$

As noted in section 5.2, if $\alpha + \beta + \gamma - 1$ is insignificant, we cannot reject the assumption of constant returns to scale.

Table 5.4 reports the outcomes.[7] We will first discuss column (2) (our estimate of equation (5.6)). The hypothesis of constant returns to scale is not valid; the term $\alpha + \beta + \gamma - 1$ is significantly different from zero. Another striking result is that the coefficient of public capital is only significant at the 10 per cent level. So, if Aschauer's (1989a) model is estimated in first differences—which is necessary as the variables used are neither stationary nor cointegrated—the results are, at best, ambiguous.

As column (1) of table 5.4 shows, the estimated labour elasticity is 0.36, and the estimated (private) capital elasticity 0.21 when constant return to scale is imposed. Given the high public capital elasticity of 0.43, we expected a labour elasticity of $(2/3 \times (1 - 0.43) =)$ 0.38, and likewise 0.19 for (private) capital elasticity. So, these estimates are as anticipated. However, when the restriction of constant returns to scale over all inputs is dropped and if we let the data decide whether the restriction prevails (column (2) of table 5.4), we find an insignificant labour elasticity of 0.13 and a capital elasticity of 0.03, lying both

Table 5.5   Correlations using first differences for the US[a]

	$\Delta\ln(L_t/K_t)$	$\Delta\ln(G_t/K_t)$	$\Delta\ln(K_t)$	$\Delta\ln(CU_t)$
$\Delta\ln(L_t/K_t)$	1	−0.26	−0.05	0.85
$\Delta\ln(G_t/K_t)$	−0.26	1	−0.24	−0.07
$\Delta\ln(K_t)$	−0.05	−0.24	1	0.18
$\Delta\ln(CU_t)$	0.85	−0.07	0.18	1

Sample: US, 1949–85.
[a]See figure 5.1 for variable definitions. Absolute values of t-statistic are shown in parentheses.

far below their expected values. If constant returns to scale prevailed, we would have anticipated elasticities of $(2/3 \times (1-0.26)=) 0.49$ and 0.25, respectively. If only the two private inputs exhibit constant returns to scale and public capital causes increasing returns over all inputs, we would have expected them to be even 0.67 and 0.33, respectively. Because of the significance of $\ln(K_t)$, the data clearly suggest that decreasing returns to scale is relevant.[8]

Finally, we have examined whether our results have been influenced by multicollinearity problems. As can be seen from table 5.5, the highest correlation between $\ln(K_t)$ and any other variable is only −0.24. However, the correlation between $\ln(L_t/K_t)$ and $\ln(CU_t)$ is quite high. Therefore, we omitted $\ln(CU_t)$ from equations (5.5) and (5.6); the outcomes are reported in the last two columns of table 5.4. The results are striking. Not only is the hypothesis of constant returns accepted, but the coefficient of public capital remains highly significant. However, the estimated coefficients suggest a labour elasticity of approximately 1.13, and a private capital elasticity of −0.80 when constant returns to scale is imposed, and −0.64 otherwise. The estimated public capital elasticity of 0.7 is incredibly high.

All these results are clearly at odds with Aschauer's (1989a) conclusions. If stationarity of the variables is carefully tested for, it is quite clear that the model needs to be estimated in first differences, in which case the restriction of constant returns to scale has to be rejected. Multicollinearity is also a problem in Aschauer's (1989a) model. We conclude that the conjecture of a positive relationship between public capital and productivity in the US is not well founded, as far as it is based on the production function approach as suggested by Aschauer (1989a) and followed by many other authors.

As mentioned in Chapter 4, seven other studies have used first-differenced time series to estimate (variants of) equation (5.5) for the US (see table 4.1). Five of them (Aaron, 1990; Evans and Karras, 1994a; Garcia–Milà et al. 1996; Hulten and Schwab, 1991a; Tatom, 1991) also found no significant relationship between public capital and productivity. Only Finn (1993) and Ford and Poret (1991) report a significant positive relation for the US. However,

Finn (1993) used a Generalized Method of Moments (GMM) estimator which incorporated several Euler equations describing the economic behaviour of the private sector. Ford and Poret (1991) estimated an equation to explain the multifactor productivity in which private capital and labour are replaced by one variable in which both are weighted by their sample averaged factor share. Multifactor productivity was also computed using this compounded variable. This implies that Ford and Poret (1991) incorporated a number of additional restrictions into equation (5.5) which are unlikely to hold true and which they do not test for.

As mentioned in Chapter 4, it is difficult to interpret the regression outcomes when using first-differenced data. First differencing eliminates the ability to estimate the underlying long-term relationship between production and factor inputs, because in this case it is assumed that output growth in one year is only correlated with input growth in that same year.

In the following section we will examine whether our conclusion for the US also holds for the Netherlands.

5.4   EMPIRICAL RESULTS FOR THE NETHERLANDS

To test whether outcomes reported in the previous section are specific for the US, we will apply the same procedure for the case of the Netherlands. For the Netherlands, Aschauer's (1989a) model has hardly been estimated before.[9]

The output and labour measures for the Netherlands are from the data bank kept by the CCSO Centre for Economic Research of the University of Groningen and Twente. Gross value added of the private sector is used as the output measure Q_t; total employment in the private sector we call L_t. Series describing the capacity utilization rate (CU_t) were kindly provided by the CPB Netherlands Bureau for Economic Policy Analysis. All data are on an annual basis.

The upper-left panel of figure 5.2 displays the capacity utilization rate and the number of workers in the private sector.

Because no official estimates are available for the public capital stock in the Netherlands, we had to construct these estimates ourselves, using investment data extracted from the National Accounts of Statistics Netherlands. The capital stock are constructed using the 'dead loss' method, which is a special form of the well known perpetual inventory method. The dead loss method assumes that all assets are scrapped when their expected life expires. Maddison (1992, p. 3) argues: "it is the concept which is most appropriate for measuring factor productivity and assessing production potential, because most assets in use are repaired and maintained in such a way that their productive capacity remains near to their original level throughout their life." Following Maddison (1993) we presumed that the asset lives are 39 years for buildings, 14 years for other

Figure 5.2   Dutch data[a]

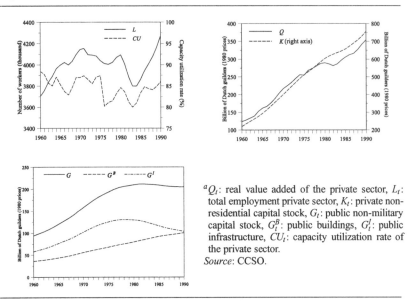

[a]Q_t: real value added of the private sector, L_t: total employment private sector, K_t: private non-residential capital stock, G_t: public non-military capital stock, G_t^B: public buildings, G_t^I: public infrastructure, CU_t: capacity utilization rate of the private sector.
Source: CCSO.

investments (mainly machinery and equipment), and corrected the capital stock estimates for war damage by assuming a 10 per cent loss.[10]

Applying the described method, we constructed four capital stocks for the Netherlands. One for the private sector, containing all assets, and three for the public sector. For the public sector we split total investment into investment in buildings and a remainder, which we call investment in infrastructure, because the largest part exists of civil engineering works. In this way we were in able to estimate three different public capital stocks, namely one including only buildings (G_t^B), one including only, what we call, infrastructure (G_t^I), and one combining the two into the aggregate capital stock (G_t).

Together with our output measure, the private capital stock is pictured in the upper-right panel of figure 5.2. The lower-left panel of figure 5.2 displays all three public capital stocks. Apparently, the public infrastructure stock deteriorates in the course of time, which yields a similar pattern for the total public capital stock.

As we will soon see, the series for the Netherlands do not all have the same order of integration. The left-hand side of table 5.6 shows the ADF results. With the possible exception of $\ln(L_t/K_t)$, it is very clear that none of the series are stationary in levels.

A look at their first differences demonstrates that at least $\ln(CU_t)$ and probably $\ln(Q_t/K_t)$ are I(1). Changing the number of lags does not make much dif-

Table 5.6   Stationarity testing for the Netherlands[a]

Series	AUGMENTED DICKEY–FULLER TEST				LEYBOURNE & MCCABE TEST[d]	
	Trend		Constant		Trend	Constant
	Lags	$\tau_\tau{}^b$	Lags	$\tau_\mu{}^c$	$\hat{s}$-trend[e]	$\hat{s}^f$
$\ln(Q_t/K_t)$	1	−1.75	1	−1.14	0.264**	2.612**
$\ln(L_t/K_t)$	2	0.21	2	−3.56*	0.549**	2.640**
$\ln(G_t/K_t)$	4	1.19	4	3.39	0.323**	2.518**
$\ln(G_t^B/K_t)$	3	−2.56	4	−2.28	0.209**	1.421*
$\ln(G_t^I/K_t)$	3	−1.84	3	−0.29	0.247**	2.261**
$\ln(K_t)$	3	−2.62	4	−0.85	0.255**	2.900**
$\ln(CU_t)$	1	−2.46	1	−2.40	0.072	0.090
$\Delta\ln(Q_t/K_t)$	0	−3.61	0	−3.63*	0.090	0.206
$\Delta\ln(L_t/K_t)$	1	−4.61**	2	−0.76	0.240**	2.130**
$\Delta\ln(G_t/K_t)$	3	−3.32	4	0.92	0.390**	2.113**
$\Delta\ln(G_t^B/K_t)$	3	−1.64	3	−1.94	0.350**	1.419*
$\Delta\ln(G_t^I/K_t)$	3	−3.27	4	0.38	0.440**	2.678**
$\Delta\ln(K_t)$	2	0.75	3	−1.96	0.328**	1.470**
$\Delta\ln(CU_t)$	0	−4.09*	0	−4.18**	0.053	0.091
$\Delta^2\ln(L_t/K_t)$	1	−4.34*	1	−4.45**	0.059	0.111
$\Delta^2\ln(G_t/K_t)$	3	−4.24*	3	−3.82**	0.040	0.215
$\Delta^2\ln(G_t^B/K_t)$	3	−3.46	3	−3.06^g**	0.091	0.467*
$\Delta^2\ln(G_t^I/K_t)$	3	−3.45	3	−3.40*	0.061	0.200
$\Delta^2\ln(K_t)$	1	−3.35	1	−2.49^g*	0.282**	0.394

Sample: the Netherlands, 1960–90.
[a] See figure 5.2 for variable definitions.
[b] At a five (one) per cent significance level the MacKinnon (1991) critical values are −3.63 (−4.44) when a trend and a constant are included (τ_τ).
[c] At a five (one) per cent significance level the MacKinnon (1991) critical values are −3.00 (−3.77) when only a constant is included (τ_μ).
[d] The number of autoregressive lags is set at three for series in levels, two for first-differenced, one for second-differenced and zero for third-differenced series.
[e] The asymptotic critical values for the significance levels of five and one per cent are respectively 0.146 and 0.216.
[f] The asymptotic critical values for the significance levels of five and one per cent are respectively 0.463 and 0.739.
[g] No constant included. At a five (one) per cent significance level the Dickey–Fuller critical values are −1.96 (−2.68) when no constant is included.
* Significant at a five per cent level.
**Significant at a one per cent level.

ference. Table 5.6 suggests that $\ln(L_t/K_t)$ is I(1) as well. However, this is only the case when one lag is included. All other lag-structures make us conclude

Table 5.7 Estimation results using first differences for the Netherlands[a]

$\Delta\ln(Q_t/K_t)$	TOTAL PUBLIC CAPITAL		BUILDINGS AND INFRASTRUCTURE		BUILDINGS		INFRASTRUCTURE	
$\Delta Trend$	0.038 (2.55)	0.032 (2.07)	0.047 (2.80)	0.031 (0.84)	0.004 (0.56)	−0.018 (1.49)	0.046 (2.83)	0.048 (2.06)
$\Delta\ln(L_t/K_t)$	0.69 (2.90)	0.99 (3.28)	0.93 (3.15)	1.00 (3.03)	0.29 (1.39)	0.94 (2.82)	0.93 (3.22)	0.93 (3.06)
$\Delta\ln(G_t/K_t)$	1.16 (2.57)	1.15 (2.60)						
$\Delta\ln(G_t^B/K_t)$			0.09 (0.35)	0.40 (0.60)	−0.10 (0.33)	0.98 (1.87)		
$\Delta\ln(G_t^I/K_t)$			0.80 (2.79)	0.63 (1.39)			0.78 (2.84)	0.80 (2.31)
$\Delta\ln(K_t)$		0.41 (1.54)		0.42 (0.50)		1.31 (2.39)		−0.04 (0.11)
$\Delta\ln(CU_t)$	0.20 (1.41)		0.12 (0.82)	0.10 (0.64)	0.15 (0.91)	0.06 (0.42)	0.10 (0.76)	0.11 (0.73)
R^2 (adj.)	0.223	0.261	0.230	0.207	0.037	0.179	0.255	0.227
D–W	2.13	2.19	2.12	2.13	2.00	2.11	2.10	2.10
E–G cointegration[b]	−4.88**	−4.91**	−5.42**	−5.10**	−1.81	−4.59*	−5.30**	−5.02**

Sample: the Netherlands, 1960–90.
[a] See figure 5.2 for variable definitions. Absolute values of t-statistic are shown in parentheses.
[b] Tests whether the variables which were not stationary after first-differencing are cointegrated. At a five (one) per cent significance level the MacKinnon (1991) critical values are −4.55 (−5.40) in case of four non-stationary variables, −4.08 (−4.90) in case of three non-stationary variables, and −3.58 (−4.35) in case of two non-stationary variables.
* Significant at a five per cent level.
** Significant at a one per cent level.

that $\ln(L_t/K_t)$ is neither I(0) nor I(1).[11] $\ln(G_t/K_t)$, $\ln\left(G_t^B/K_t\right)$, $\ln\left(G_t^I/K_t\right)$ and $\ln(K_t)$ are definitely not I(1).

So, we have to go one step further, and difference these five series once more. Now, $\Delta^2\ln(L_t/K_t)$, $\Delta^2\ln(G_t/K_t)$, $\Delta^2\ln\left(G_t^B/K_t\right)$, and $\Delta^2\ln\left(G_t^I/K_t\right)$ are clearly stationary, as can be seen from table 5.6. $\Delta^2\ln(K_t)$ seems to be stationary too, when the constant is omitted from the ADF test.

From the ADF test we must therefore conclude, that $\ln(Q_t/K_t)$ and $\ln(CU_t)$ are I(1), $\ln(L_t/K_t)$, $\ln(G_t/K_t)$, $\ln\left(G_t^B/K_t\right)$, $\ln\left(G_t^I/K_t\right)$ and $\ln(K_t)$ are I(2).

The BUR test clearly rejects the null hypothesis of a unit root in case of $\Delta^2\ln(K_t)$ (not shown). From the BUR test we therefore conclude that this series is definitely I(2). All other conclusions do not change.

Finally, we have applied the new test of Leybourne and McCabe (1994). The right-hand side of table 5.6 shows the results. They suggest that the capacity utilization rate might even be stationary in levels. Furthermore, the outcomes confirm our belief that $\Delta\ln(Q_t/K_t)$ is I(1) and the remaining series are I(2).

Taking all evidence together, we conclude that $\ln(Q_t/K_t)$ is I(1), $\ln(CU_t)$ is either I(0) or I(1) and all the remaining series, i.e. $\ln(L_t/K_t)$, $\ln(G_t/K_t)$, $\ln\left(G_t^B/K_t\right)$, $\ln\left(G_t^I/K_t\right)$, and $\ln(K_t)$, are I(2).

Because the series are non-stationary in levels equations (5.5) and (5.6) have been estimated.[12] This is justified, since the variables which were not stationary in first differences are cointegrated, as is shown in the last row of table 5.7, which presents the augmented Engle–Granger statistics for this test. As pointed out by Banerjee *et al.* (1993, pp. 167–168) it is necessary that the regressors have—either jointly or individually—the same order of integration as the regressand in order to interpret the results in the normal way. Because the regressand (the first difference of $\ln(Q_t/K_t)$) is now stationary and some regressors are still not stationary individually, we test whether these regressors are stationary jointly, i.e. whether they cointegrate. As follows from the last row of table 5.7, this is the case in all but one equation, meaning that only one cannot be interpreted in the usual way.

The first observation to be made is that, in contrast to the case of the US, we now find low values for the adjusted R^2. Furthermore, government buildings do not play a significant role in the explanation of the capital-productivity of the private sector.[13] Infrastructure clearly does. However, the estimated elasticities of both the public infrastructure stock and labour are very high. γ_{G^I} ranges from 0.63 and 0.80, and α lies in the interval between 0.93 and 1.00 in the equations which include public infrastructure. This implies that the private capital elasticity must be negative and lying somewhere between -0.61 and -0.82, which is highly improbable.

Another result that catches the eye, is that in three out of four cases the hypothesis of constant returns to scale cannot be rejected. Only when government buildings are included, do increasing returns to scale prevail. However,

Figure 5.3   Different private capital and public infrastructure stocks for the Netherlands[a]

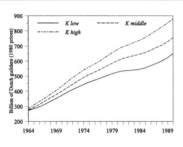 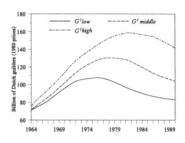

[a]See figure 5.2 for variable definitions.

since the coefficient for the stock of government buildings is insignificant, this suggests that increasing returns to scale prevail over labour and private capital, which contradicts the other findings.[14]

Again we checked whether there is a problem concerning multicollinearity. This is definitely not the case. As an example, the correlation between $\Delta \ln(L_t/K_t)$ and $\Delta \ln(CU_t)$ is only 0.25. We also performed the same regressions without the capacity utilization rate. As might be expected, the results did not change significantly.

Since it is possible that incorrect construction of the capital stock variable produces the strange coefficient in table 5.7, we also made two alternative estimates of this variable, by changing the assumption about the length of asset lives. For all capital stocks we constructed a low, middle and high estimator. In the lower ones we assumed that the asset lives are 34 years for buildings and nine years for other investments. The higher ones assume 44 and 19 years, respectively. Figure 5.3 shows the estimates for the public infrastructure and the private capital stock for the interval 1964–90. The two series G^I middle and K middle are the same as displayed in figure 5.2. As these figures show, the levels of all capital stocks definitely depend upon the assumptions made.

Table 5.8 reports results for the most interesting case, i.e. including the public infrastructure capital stock. Estimated labour and public infrastructure elasticities do not differ much across the table. The restriction of constant returns to scale is never rejected, and private capital elasticities (which can be calculated out of these results) are again negative in all three cases. However, it must be noted that using the 'low' capital stocks the non-stationary variables do not cointegrate, indicating that the construction of the two capital stocks is essential to finding a long-run relationship. So, we must conclude that the data suggest a role for public infrastructure capital, but the estimated coefficients are so large that the normal interpretation of the results seems not to be justified.

Table 5.8 *Estimation results using different capital stocks for the Netherlands*[a]

$\Delta\ln(Q_t/K_t)$	LOW		MIDDLE		HIGH	
$\Delta Trend$	0.050	0.048	0.058	0.051	0.033	0.020
	(4.44)	(3.30)	(3.46)	(2.12)	(1.58)	(0.94)
$\Delta\ln(L_t/K_t)$	0.87	0.90	1.13	1.16	0.78	1.04
	(3.77)	(3.46)	(3.84)	(3.78)	(2.28)	(2.81)
$\Delta\ln(G_t^I/K_t)$	0.88	0.86	0.94	0.86	0.59	0.47
	(4.52)	(3.85)	(3.34)	(2.40)	(1.57)	(1.25)
$\Delta\ln(K_t)$		0.08		0.15		0.47
		(0.26)		(0.42)		(1.60)
$\Delta\ln(CU_t)$	−0.03	−0.05	−0.05	−0.08	−0.03	−0.14
	(0.25)	(0.34)	(0.35)	(0.48)	(0.21)	(0.86)
R^2 (adj.)	0.421	0.396	0.330	0.305	0.122	0.178
D–W	2.13	2.12	1.87	1.86	1.58	1.67
E–G cointegration[b]	−1.84	−2.55	−4.53**	−4.38*	−4.16*	−4.73*

Sample: the Netherlands, 1964–90.
[a] See figure 5.2 for variable definitions. Absolute values of t-statistic are shown in parentheses.
[b] Tests whether the variables which were not stationary after first-differencing are cointegrated. At a five (one) per cent significance level the MacKinnon (1991) critical values are −4.15 (−5.02) in case of three non-stationary variables, and −3.63 (−4.44) in case of two non-stationary variables.
* Significant at a five per cent level.
**Significant at a one per cent level.

5.5 CONCLUSIONS

The productivity slowdown in most western industrialized countries has recently been linked to lower levels of public capital spending. However, as data series used in most papers about the economic effects of public capital are neither stationary nor cointegrated, the conclusion that public capital has a positive significant influence on private sector productivity is not well founded. We agree with Jorgenson (1991) that empirical results based on the production function approach are built on 'fragile statistical foundations' and should be viewed with extreme scepticism. Indeed, when Aschauer's (1989a) model for the US is estimated in first differences it produces very peculiar results. The estimated coefficients are so weird that economic justifiable interpretation is not possible. In several cases we found a negative private capital elasticity and a labour elasticity above one; both outcomes definitely do not correspond to economic theory. This conclusion also holds using Dutch data.

Our main conclusion is that an alternative approach has to be taken to test whether public capital has a significant influence on the private sector. Therefore, the so-called behavioural approach will be eplored in the next chapter.

NOTES

1. As discussed in the previous chapter, the argument that the variables used may not be stationary nor cointegrated has been addressed previously by other authors (Aaron, 1990; Tatom, 1991). In this chapter we apply various testing procedures to examine this issue more carefully.
2. The method used to correct for first-order autocorrelation is Cochrane–Orcutt.
3. The private capital elasticity can be calculated as $1 - \alpha - \gamma$.
4. See Engle and Granger (1987) for details.
5. Changing the number of lags in the ADF test does not alter the conclusions.
6. This test is also referred to as the (cointegration regression) ADF test. To make a clear distinction between this test and the ADF test on stationarity we follow Davidson and MacKinnon (1993) and name this test the augmented Engle–Granger cointegration test. The difference between both tests is the critical values which have to be used. We prefer the use of the augmented Engle–Granger test, instead of the Durbin–Watson test on cointegration. As argued by Banerjee *et al.* (1993, p. 207): "The use of (the Durbin–Watson) statistic is problematic in the present setting. First, the test statistic for co-integration depends upon the number of regressors in the co-integrating equation and, more generally, on the data-generation process and hence on the precise data matrix. Second, the bounds diverge as the number of regressors is increased, and eventually cease to have any practical value for the purpose of inference. Finally, the statistic assumes the null where (the residual vector) is a random walk, and the alternative where (the residual vector) is a stationary first-order autoregressive process... However, the tabulated bounds are not correct if there is higher-order residual autocorrelation, as will commonly occur."
7. To be on the safe side, we performed the augmented Engle–Granger cointegration test on each of the estimated equations in table 5.4. The hypothesis of no cointegration can clearly be rejected in all cases.
8. Similar results are reported by Hulten and Schwab (1991a). They estimated a labour, private capital, and public capital elasticity for the United States of respectively 0.11, 0.19 and 0.03. All three estimates do not differ significantly from zero.
9. An exception is Toen–Gout and Jongeling (1994) who estimate a specification comparable to the specification of Ford and Poret (1991) in which private capital and labour are combined into one private input variable. This implies a number of restrictions which the authors do not test for. Nevertheless, Toen–Gout and Jongeling conclude that "infrastructure would ... appear to have a significant and positive influence on private output" (Toen–Gout and Jongeling, 1994, p. 13). Using our own dataset and the specification of Toen–Gout and Jongeling (1994), we produced similar regression results. However, testing the imposed restrictions reveals that these are strongly rejected by the data.
10. As pointed out by Van Zanden and Griffiths (1989), war damage in the Netherlands was not as severe as often suggested in earlier work.
11. Taking one lag more or less reduces the τ_τ to respectively -3.40 and -2.28. Omitting the trend leads to $\tau_\mu = -0.76$ (with two lags). Also omitting the constant gives us $\tau = -1.22$ (with two lags), which is definitely insignificant.
12. Naturally, we have also tested whether the series are cointegrated in levels. This is definitely not the case. The augmented Engle–Granger test statistic for equation (5.3) is -2.45, which is highly insignificant (the MacKinnon (1991) five per cent critical value is -5.02).
13. The variables $\Delta \ln(L_t/K_t)$ and $\Delta \ln\left(G_t^B/K_t\right)$ do not even cointegrate, suggesting there does not exist a long-run relationship between these variables.
14. This is also the only case where the capital elasticity adopts a positive value; it becomes 0.37.

6. Sectoral Cost Elasticities of Public Infrastructure[*]

6.1 INTRODUCTION

As figure 1.1 of Chapter 1 illustrates, public capital outlays have decreased dramatically in most OECD countries since the early 1970s. At approximately the same time productivity growth plummeted almost everywhere, including the Netherlands (see figure 1.2). As discussed in Chapter 4, Aschauer (1989a) has hypothesized that the decrease in productive government services may be crucial in explaining the general decline in productivity growth.

The purpose of this chapter is to analyze possible effects of public capital on the performance of the exposed and sheltered sectors of the Dutch economy during the post-World War II period. The exposed sector is relatively capital intensive and consists of agriculture, manufacturing and transport, whereas trade, banking and other private services form the sheltered sector. Most previous studies concentrate on the US. With the exceptions of Sturm and De Haan (1995a) and Toen–Gout and Jongeling (1994), so far hardly any studies have been conducted for the Netherlands. Despite the development of public investment and productivity as shown in figure 1.2, the previous chapter did not produce solid econometric results. This is probably due to the over-simplifying character inherent to the production function approach.

As discussed in Chapter 4, studies in the early literature were largely based on the analysis of a production function, often assumed to be of the Cobb–Douglas form, which allows the signs and magnitudes of marginal products to be estimated, but requires restrictive assumptions about firm behaviour. Furthermore, questions as to the endogeneity of the variables and therefore the extent to which the production function estimates suffer from a simultaneous equations bias, have been raised.

These considerations led us to base our analysis on what we call the behavioural approach.[1] One can describe the behaviour of agents (firms) by assuming that they minimize costs. From this cost function we can, under certain

---

[*]This chapter is a slightly revised version of Sturm (1997).

regularity conditions, derive a unique production function by applying duality theory (Diewert, 1974). Furthermore, input shares or factor-demand equations, both directly derived from the cost function, can be incorporated in the regression analysis, thereby avoiding the exogeneity assumption on the private production factors as employed in the production function approach. Besides explicitly modelling economic behaviour, a major advantage of the behavioural approach is that we can use flexible functional forms which hardly enforce any restrictions on the production structure. For example, *a priori* restrictions placed upon substitutability of production factors—as often encountered in the production function approach—do not apply anymore.

We have opted for the symmetric generalized McFadden (SGM) cost function, and augmented it with public capital. So far, the only second-order Taylor approximations which have been used in this line of research are the transcendental logarithmic (translog) and the generalized Leontief function.[2] As shown by Diewert and Wales (1987) both functions frequently fail to satisfy the appropriate theoretical curvature conditions, as is confirmed by Sturm and Kuper (1996). Using the (modified) SGM cost function, it turns out that imposing the appropriate curvature conditions at one datapoint imposes the curvature conditions globally without destroying the flexibility property. Imposing curvature conditions on other flexible functional forms, such as the translog, often results in biased estimates and the loss of its flexibility (Diewert and Wales, 1987).

The modified SGM specification enables us to estimate several elasticities which uncover the productivity effects of public capital. Besides using this framework for the total private economy, we will estimate the specification for the exposed and the sheltered sector. We expect both to react differently to a change in public capital because of their distinct characters. Production costs of the total private economy are shown to be significantly reduced by public infrastructure. However, by differentiating between the two it appears that the relatively capital intensive exposed sector does not benefit as much from the provision of infrastructure as the sheltered sector of the Dutch economy.

As discussed in Chapter 4, most previous studies conclude that public and private capital are complements. This outcome supports the hypothesis that public capital might enhance the productivity of private capital. The relationship between labour and public capital is less clear.[3] Furthermore, most studies clearly reject the hypothesis of constant returns to scale in all inputs, including public capital.[4] All studies conclude that public capital reduces private sector costs. However, their estimated effects are mostly significantly smaller than those reported by Aschauer (1989a). Only Deno (1988) and Lynde (1992) come up with a larger impact of public capital on the private sector. The remaining studies roughly estimate less than half the impact that Aschauer (1989a) reported, i.e. a public capital elasticity of approximately 0.15.

This chapter is organized as follows. The theoretical framework is set forth in section 6.2, whereas section 6.3 describes the database. In section 6.4 the estimation results will be discussed. Finally, section 6.5 offers some concluding remarks and suggestions for further research.

6.2 THEORETICAL FRAMEWORK[5]

This section develops our theoretical framework which aims to incorporate public capital into the cost function and therefore into the underlying production function. For expositional purposes the section is subdivided into four subsections. The first subsection will discuss the general cost function framework. The second subsection derives some elasticities which reveal all relevant characteristics. In the third subsection the symmetric generalized McFadden cost function will be discussed and modified by incorporating public capital. Finally, the long-run relationship between production costs and public capital will be incorporated into an error correction model.

6.2.1 Cost function

Starting-point in constructing our theoretical framework is a variable cost function (C^*) which results from minimizing private variable production costs subject to the production function, $Q = f^*(x,t,G)$, where $x \equiv (x_1, \ldots, x_N)^T$ is the vector of private inputs utilized, t denotes technology, and G the services rendered by the public capital stock. The latter two variables form the environmental variables in our model. They are exogenous and enter the production function and thus also the cost function as unpaid fixed inputs.[6] Furthermore, we allow the environment to influence the productivity of specific inputs differently. Given a positive vector of input prices, $p \equiv (p_1, p_2, \ldots, p_N)^T \gg 0_N^T$, the cost function C^* dual to the production function f^* may be defined as follows:

$$C^*(p,Q,t,G) \equiv \min_x \{p^T x : f^*(x,t,G) \geq Q, x \geq 0_N\}, \qquad (6.1)$$

where 0_N is a vector of zeros with dimension N.

All relevant characteristics of the underlying production function can be summarized with this cost function if six conditions are satisfied. These conditions are:

$$
\begin{aligned}
C^*(\lambda p, Q, t, G) &= \lambda C^*(p, Q, t, G), \forall \lambda \geq 0, & (6.2) \\
C^*(p, Q, t, G) &> 0, \forall p > 0_N, \forall Q > 0, & (6.3) \\
\nabla_p C^*(p, Q, t, G) &\geq 0_N, & (6.4) \\
\nabla_{pp}^2 C^*(p, Q, t, G) &= \text{negative semidefinite}, & (6.5)
\end{aligned}
$$

$$\nabla_G C^* (p,Q,t,G) \leq 0, \tag{6.6}$$
$$\nabla_{GG}^2 C^* (p,Q,t,G) \geq 0, \tag{6.7}$$

where ∇_i is the column vector of the first order partial derivatives with respect to the components of i, and ∇_{ij}^2 denotes the matrix of second-order partial derivatives with respect to the components of i and j.

The first condition of linear homogeneity in prices is a restatement of the familiar principle that only relative prices matter to optimizing agents. Or, as long as input prices only vary proportionally, the cost-minimizing choice of inputs will not change. The non-negativity condition (6.3) simply says that producing a positive output at zero cost is impossible, whereas equation (6.4) indicates that increasing any input price cannot decrease cost. The concavity condition (6.5) assures that we are minimizing—instead of maximizing—cost. The final two conditions assure that public capital cannot increase the costs of the private sector (equation (6.6)) and that the marginal benefits of each additional unit of public capital do not increase (equation (6.7)). The free disposal assumption (6.6) means that production cost cannot rise as a consequence of an increase in public capital, because otherwise firms simply would not use the additional public capital in their production process.

6.2.2 Elasticities

Using a flexible cost function it is possible to reveal all relevant characteristics of the underlying production function.[7] Several interesting elasticities can be derived from a flexible cost function. For instance, the cost elasticities of all inputs—including public capital—can be calculated as:

$$\varepsilon_{Cj} = \frac{\partial \ln C^*}{\partial \ln j} = \frac{\partial C^*}{\partial j} \frac{j}{C^*}, \quad j = p_1, \ldots, p_N, Q, G,$$
$$\varepsilon_{Ct} = \frac{\partial \ln C^*}{\partial t}. \tag{6.8}$$

As we will use a second-order flexible cost function, we can even go a step further and calculate several price and demand elasticities. For that purpose we first have to apply Shephard's Lemma to the cost function, $C(p,Q,t,G)$, which yields the cost minimizing conditional factor-demand equations for the private inputs:

$$\nabla_p C(p,Q,t,G) = x^* = x(p,Q,t,G). \tag{6.9}$$

The price and demand elasticities can now be calculated by:

$$\varepsilon_{ij} = \frac{\partial \ln x_i^*}{\partial \ln j} = \frac{\partial x_i^*}{\partial j} \frac{j}{x_i^*} = \frac{\partial^2 C}{\partial p_i \partial j} \frac{j}{x_i^*}, \quad j = p_1, \ldots, p_N, Q, G,$$

$$\varepsilon_{it} = \frac{\partial \ln x_i^*}{\partial t}, \qquad\qquad\qquad i = 1, \ldots, N. \tag{6.10}$$

If the sign of such an elasticity for $j = Q, G$ is positive, factor j and the ith private input are complements. For $j = p_1, \ldots, p_N$ a positive sign indicates that the two inputs are substitutes.

Differentiating the cost function with respect to G yields the shadow price, p_G^s, associated with public capital:

$$p_G^s = -\frac{\partial C(p, Q, t, G)}{\partial G}, \tag{6.11}$$

which denotes the change in private production cost caused by one additional unit of public capital, G. Differentiating equation (6.11) with respect to the variable t yields insight into the impact of public capital on multifactor productivity. If $\partial p_G^s / \partial t$ is greater than, equal to, or less than zero, public capital respectively supports, does not affect, or discourages technological progress.

Using the conditional factor-demand equations (6.9), we can rewrite production costs as:

$$C = p^T x^*. \tag{6.12}$$

Applying Shephard's Lemma to equation (6.12) yields:

$$p_G^s = -p^T \nabla_G x^*, \tag{6.13}$$

which decomposes the cost changes associated with an increase in G into adjustment effects on the private inputs. $\partial x_i^* / \partial G$ denotes the response of the demand for private input x_i, $i = 1, \ldots, N$, to an increase in public capital, G. Equation (6.13) reveals that an increase in public capital is always cost saving if all private inputs are substitutes with respect to public capital, i.e. $\partial x_i^* / \partial G < 0$, $\forall i = 1, \ldots, N$. However, if one of the private inputs is complementary to the public input, cost savings arise only if the substitution effects outweigh the complementary effect.

The final step is to establish a link between the 'production function approach' and our 'behavioural approach'. For this we have to go back to the cost minimization problem and solve the Lagrangian:

$$\pounds(p, Q, t, G) = p^T x + \lambda [Q - f(x, t, G)]. \tag{6.14}$$

Note that in the optimum λ equals marginal cost, $\partial C^*/\partial Q$. Differentiating with respect to public capital yields:

$$-p_G^s = \frac{\partial \pounds}{\partial G} = -\lambda \frac{\partial f}{\partial G} = -\frac{\partial C^*}{\partial Q}\frac{\partial f}{\partial G}, \tag{6.15}$$

in the optimum, which is at minimum cost. Therefore the following property holds:

$$\frac{\partial f(x,t,G)}{\partial G}\frac{G}{Q} = \frac{p_G^s}{\partial C^*/\partial Q}\frac{G}{Q}. \tag{6.16}$$

The relation in equation (6.16) provides a link between the 'production function approach' and the 'behavioural approach' and can be used to compare results derived from both approaches. Note that if the cost function is linearly homogeneous in output, equation (6.16) states that the absolute value of the cost elasticity of public capital equals the absolute value of the output elasticity of public capital.

6.2.3 Modified SGM specification

Now we will define the modified symmetric generalized McFadden (SGM) cost function C.[8] The term 'modified' stems from the fact that we allow for a fixed input, i.e. public capital G.[9] Consider the following functional form for the cost function:

$$\begin{aligned}
C(p,Q,t,G) \equiv g(p)Q \quad &+b_{ii}^T pQ+b_i^T p+b_{it}^T ptQ+b_{iG}^T pGQ\\
&+b_{QQ}\beta^T pQ^2+b_t\alpha^T pt+b_{tt}\gamma^T pt^2Q\\
&+b_G\delta^T pG+b_{GG}\eta^T pG^2Q\\
&+b_{tG}\tau^T ptGQ,
\end{aligned} \tag{6.17}$$

where the function $g(p)$ is defined by

$$g(p) \equiv \tfrac{1}{2}\frac{p^T Sp}{\theta^T p}, \tag{6.18}$$

where $\theta \equiv (\theta_1,\ldots,\theta_N)^T \geq 0_N^T$, $b_{ii} \equiv (b_{11},\ldots,b_{NN})^T$, $b_i \equiv (b_1,\ldots,b_N)^T$, $b_{it} \equiv (b_{1t},\ldots,b_{Nt})^T$, $b_{iG} \equiv (b_{1G},\ldots,b_{NG})^T$, $b_{QQ}, b_t, b_{tt}, b_G, b_{GG}, b_{tG}, \alpha \equiv (\alpha_1,\ldots,$ $\alpha_N)^T$, $\beta \equiv (\beta_1,\ldots,\beta_N)^T$, $\gamma \equiv (\gamma_1,\ldots,\gamma_N)^T$, $\delta \equiv (\delta_1,\ldots,\delta_N)^T$, $\eta \equiv (\eta_1,\ldots,$ $\eta_N)^T$, and $\tau \equiv (\tau_1,\ldots,\tau_N)^T$ are the parameters of our model. To generate elasticities which are invariant to scale changes in the units of measurement, the econometrician has to set $\theta_i = \bar{x}_i$ for $i = 1,\ldots,N$.[10] The $7N$ number of parameters, α, β, γ, δ, η, τ, and θ are arbitrarily selected by the econometrician.

Since these values may be selected arbitrarily, it means that we are considering a whole family of flexible functional forms rather than just one form. If we choose $\alpha_i = \beta_i = \gamma_i = \delta_i = \eta_i = \tau_i = \theta_i = \bar{x}_i$ for $i = 1,\ldots,N$, where $\bar{x}_i$ is the average amount of input i used over the sample period, then again the elasticities generated by our estimated cost function will be invariant to scale changes. Alternatively, if there are ample degrees of freedom, the econometrician may set $b_{QQ} = b_t = b_{tt} = b_G = b_{GG} = b_{tG} = 1$ and estimate α, β, γ, δ, η, and τ. In this case the cost function becomes third-order flexible in Q, t and G, and therefore the factor-demand equations are second-order flexible in Q, t and G. Finally, S is an $N \times N$ symmetric negative semidefinite matrix that satisfies the N extra restrictions $Sp = 0$ for some $p \gg 0_N$.

Note that C is linearly homogeneous in p and that its factor-demand functions are linear in the unknown parameters. By differentiating equation (6.17) with respect to input prices, and then employing Shephard's Lemma, it can be shown that the factor-demand equations are:[11]

$$x^* = \frac{Sp}{\theta^T p} - \tfrac{1}{2}\theta\frac{p^T Sp}{(\theta^T p)^2} \quad \begin{aligned}&+b_{ii}Q + b_i + b_{it}tQ + b_{iG}GQ \\ &+b_{QQ}\beta Q^2 + b_t\alpha t + b_{tt}\gamma t^2 Q \\ &+b_G\delta G + b_{GG}\eta G^2 Q + b_{tG}\tau t GQ,\end{aligned} \qquad (6.19)$$

where $x^* \equiv (x_1^*,\ldots,x_N^*)^T$.

It can easily be verified that the concavity restrictions (6.5) for all $p \gg 0_N$, $Q > 0, t > 0, G > 0$ are satisfied if and only if the S matrix is negative semidefinite. Thus if our estimated S matrix turns out to be negative semidefinite, C will be globally concave. If furthermore $\nabla_{GG}C(p,Q,t,G) = 2b_{GG}\eta^T pQ \geq 0$ for all $p \gg 0_N, Q > 0, t > 0, G > 0$ we may call C globally curvature correct.

Using this functional form Diewert and Wales (1987) show that it is possible to impose the concavity in factor prices. Following a technique due to Wiley et al. (1973, p. 318), they reparameterize the S matrix by replacing it by minus the product of a lower triangular matrix of dimension $N \times N$, A say, times its transpose, A^T, i.e.

$$S = -AA^T, \qquad (6.20)$$

where $A = [a_{ij}]$ and $a_{ij} = 0$ for $i < j, i, j = 1,\ldots,N$. It must be emphasised that using this technique to impose negative semidefiniteness on S does not destroy the flexibility of the modified SGM function.

It should be noted that it is relatively easy to impose several restrictions on the modified SGM defined by (6.17) and (6.18). For instance, in order to make C linearly homogeneous in output Q (so that the dual production function exhibits constant returns to scale in the private inputs), we only need impose the following $N+3$ additional linear restrictions on the b parameters:

$$b_t = b_{QQ} = b_G = 0, \quad b_i = 0_N, \quad j = 1,\ldots,N. \tag{6.21}$$

6.2.4 Error correction specification

Equation (6.19) represents the long-run relation. It is unlikely that factor demand equals the long-run equilibrium in every time period because of habits
persistence, adjustment costs, incorrect expectations and misinterpreted real
price changes. Therefore, we introduce a first-order error correction model:

$$\Delta x = \Psi \Delta x^* + \Phi [x^* - x]_{-1}, \tag{6.22}$$

where x^* stand for the long-run factor-demand equations as given by equation (6.19), whereas Ψ and Φ represent parameter matrices. The first matrix
estimates the impact effects of short-run changes, whereas the second is the
error correction term, which determines the dynamic behaviour.[12] We chose
this simple model, because our main interest lies in estimating the long-run
relationship.

6.3   DUTCH DATA

In the empirical analysis we will distinguish two, and sometimes three, production factors controlled by the private sector ($N = 2$, or $N = 3$): Labour
(L)—which we will divide later on into low-skilled labour (L^l) and high-skilled
labour (L^h)—and capital (K). Technology and the services that stem from the
stock of public capital are two variables that might influence the cost minimization problem which firms face; these variables will be approximated by time
(t) and the stock of public capital (G), respectively.[13]

   Accordingly, factor demand is a function of factor prices, output, time,
public capital and the parameters of the cost function. Therefore, we need
data on prices and quantities of all factor inputs, and quantities of the public
capital stock and output. Because our analysis will concentrate on the sheltered
and the exposed sectors of the Dutch economy, we need all data—except of
course public capital—at the sectoral level.[14] Unless mentioned otherwise, the
data are extracted from the databases kept by the CPB Netherlands Bureau for
Economic Policy Analysis, which are based on the Dutch National Accounts of
Statistics Netherlands. Furthermore, price indices equal one in the year 1973.

   Low-skilled labour is defined as labour with primary and extended education. High-skilled labour involves labour with secondary, higher vocational

and university education. Statistics Netherlands (1996) provides data on employment and wages by education for the period 1969–93. As this is a short
period, we will start off by using total labour input. Data on total labour cover
the 1952–93 period. All labour variables are adjusted for the number of hours
worked. In a final stage we will make the division in labour in order to say
something more about the relationship between labour and public capital.

To get a more accurate estimate of the total private capital stock and its price,
we build up both measures from stocks and user costs of structures (buildings)
and equipment (machinery and equipment). Both the stock of private structures
and the stock of private equipment (K^j) are constructed through the perpetual
inventory method, i.e. through the accumulation of investments (I^j), assuming
a depreciation rate which is constant over time but varies with type and sector
(δ^j):

$$K_t^j = \left(1 - \delta^j\right) K_{t-1}^j + I_{t-1}^j, \qquad (6.23)$$

where j stands for structures or equipment. Both capital stocks are available
from 1952 until 1993. Initial capital stocks and depreciation rates are taken
from unpublished data on quantities and depreciations of the private capital
stock which were kindly provided by Statistics Netherlands.[15]

Following Jorgenson (1986), we express the user cost of both parts of the
private capital stock, i.e. structures and equipment, as a function of the interest
rate, tax parameters and the investment price index:

$$p_k^j = \frac{\left(1 - wir^j - u * ia^j\right)}{(1-u)} \left[(1-u)r + \delta^j + risk^j - \hat{\pi}^j\right] p_{inv}^j, \qquad (6.24)$$

where the corporate tax rate is given by u, and wir^j and ia^j stand for certain tax
reductions. The long-term interest rate on central government debt is given by
r, δ^j is the depreciation rate, and $risk^j$ is a mark-up for risk.[16] The price index
of investment is given by p_{inv}^j and $\hat{\pi}^j$ is the expected inflation of investment
goods.[17]

Once these rental prices and capital service flows have been separately
measured, we aggregate them to get the total stock of private capital and the
aggregate rental price of private capital by employing the familiar Tornqvist
discrete approximation to the continuous Divisia index.[18]

We also use the Tornqvist approximation of the Divisia index to aggregate
our data over both sectors. In this way we get estimates of prices and quantities
of all private input factors and private output for almost the entire private
sector. Only the construction sector and the Dutch gas industry are not taken
into account.[19] As we will see, using these aggregated data makes it easier to
interpret the results on a sectoral level.

The public capital stock is also constructed using the perpetual inventory method. In the empirical analysis we will concentrate on the stock of civil engineering works, which we will label infrastructure.[20] Following the definition of Statistics Netherlands, public firms like the Dutch railway company (NS) are not part of the public sector, their capital outlays are considered as private investment.[21] Initial capital stocks and depreciation rates are taken from unpublished data on quantities and depreciation rates of the public capital stock which were kindly provided by Statistics Netherlands.[22] Both infrastructure and the total public capital stock cover the 1949–93 period.

Many authors adjust the stock of public capital by an index, such as the capacity utilization rate, to reflect their private sector usage.[23] As discussed in Chapter 4, two main arguments are advanced to adjust the stock of public capital. The first argument is that public capital is a collective input which a firm must share with the rest of the economy. Since most types of public capital are subject to congestion, the amount of public capital that one firm may employ will be less than the total amount supplied. The second reason for adjustment is that firms might have some control over the usage of existing public capital. Other authors explicitly "... refrain from all of these possible adjustment procedures because of their ad hoc character and because 'proper' adjustment makes virtually all results possible." (Seitz 1993, p. 230) For the same reason, we will also refrain from adjusting the stock of public capital by some utilization index.

On average, approximately 20 per cent of the total capital stock in the Netherlands consists of public capital. However, according to unpublished data of Statistics Netherlands, almost 80 per cent of all infrastructure capital belongs to the public sector. This share has steadily declined from almost 90 per cent in the early 1950s to 72 per cent in 1990. The private stock of infrastructure is mainly possessed by firms in the exposed sector.[24]

As we know from Chapter 2, there are large fluctuations in the capital outlays of the public sector. Until the early 1970s public investment (in constant prices) increased substantially over the years. After 1971 the reverse happened; in 1987 public investment was almost 40 per cent below the 1971 level. Capital spending on infrastructure has the largest share in total public investment. However, the importance of this category has substantially decreased over time. In the 1958–80 period almost 70 per cent of all public investment was in infrastructure, whereas in the 1980–90 period this reduced to 58 per cent. Investment in machinery and transport equipment compensated for this. The share of investment in buildings remained constant over time, covering approximately 25 per cent of total public capital spending.

6.4 EMPIRICAL ANALYSIS

6.4.1 Estimation procedure

In the empirical application of the theoretical framework outlined in section 6.2, only the N factor-demand equations defined in equation (6.19) which are inserted in the error correction model (6.22) need to be estimated, so as to obtain estimates for all parameters of the cost function. The cost function itself does not have to be estimated, since it contains no additional information. To keep the error correction model as simple as possible, we assume both Ψ and Φ to be diagonal.[25]

We estimate the model for the aggregate, the exposed and the sheltered sectors of the Dutch economy for the 1952–93 period. Where labour is divided into low-skilled and high-skilled labour, data availability forces us to restrict our attention to the 1969–93 period. Initially, concavity in factor prices (6.5) is not imposed. However, where our estimated cost function was not concave at all datapoints, we re-estimated the model and imposed the concavity restrictions (6.20). For all our regressions we have used the software-package *Time Series Processor* Version 4.2, and applied a Seemingly Unrelated Regression (SUR) procedure which accommodates cross-equation restrictions and correlations among the disturbances by estimating the model as a system of equations.

The multivariate least squares method used is a generalized least squares method: the disturbances of the model are assumed to be independent across observations, but to have a free covariance across equations. We write the objective function as $Q(b) = e(b)^T (V^{-1} \otimes I_T) e(b)$, where $e(b)$ is the vector of residuals, V is an estimated covariance matrix of the disturbances, I_T is the identity matrix of order of the number of observations, and $\otimes$ is the Kronecker operator. V is recomputed from $b(i)$ at each iteration, so assuming the disturbances are multivariate normal, the estimator converges to the maximum likelihood estimator (implying that the standard errors are maximum likelihood estimates). The numerical method used is a generalized Gauss–Newton method, in which 'generalized' refers to the fact that the objective function contains a fixed weighting matrix (rather than being a simple sum of squares). The presented standard errors are heteroscedastic-consistent.[26]

We have estimated several models. Because our main interest lies in the effect of infrastructure, we choose to concentrate on models ensuring second-order flexibility of the factor-demand equations in Q, t, and G, i.e. to estimate the α, β, γ, δ, η and τ vectors of parameters instead of the b_{QQ}, b_t, b_{tt}, b_G, b_{GG} and b_{tG} parameters (see section 6.2). Especially attractive is the fact that in this case the effect of public infrastructure on private input factors is modelled somewhat more flexibly. The estimated parameters of these models will not be presented because little direct interpretation of these values is possible, given

Table 6.1   Elasticity estimates in the midpoint of the sample, 1973[a]

	Total	Sheltered	Exposed
ELASTICITIES OF PUBLIC INFRASTRUCTURE			
ε_{CG}	−0.676	−1.708	−0.073
	(0.248)	(0.340)	(0.243)
ε_{LG}	−0.565	−1.848	0.494
	(0.360)	(0.438)	(0.433)
ε_{KG}	−0.929	−1.212	−1.041
	(0.128)	(0.220)	(0.183)
$\partial p_G^s/\partial t$	0.092	0.040	0.081
	(0.079)	(0.028)	(0.075)
OTHER INTERESTING ELASTICITIES			
ε_{Ct}	−0.017	0.022	−0.041
	(0.006)	(0.010)	(0.006)
$\varepsilon_{C_{PL}}$	0.697	0.779	0.631
	(0.010)	(0.007)	(0.017)
$\varepsilon_{C_{PK}}$	0.303	0.221	0.369
	(0.010)	(0.007)	(0.017)
ε_{Lt}	−0.031	0.021	−0.071
	(0.009)	(0.012)	(0.010)
$\varepsilon_{L_{PL}}$	−0.054	−0.042	−0.097
	(0.009)	(0.010)	(0.022)
$\varepsilon_{L_{PK}}$	0.054	0.042	0.097
	(0.009)	(0.010)	(0.022)
ε_{Kt}	0.015	0.029	0.011
	(0.003)	(0.004)	(0.004)
$\varepsilon_{K_{PL}}$	0.125	0.147	0.165
	(0.019)	(0.034)	(0.032)
$\varepsilon_{K_{PK}}$	−0.125	−0.147	−0.165
	(0.019)	(0.034)	(0.032)

[a]The cost function is assumed to be homogeneous in output. The elasticities are evaluated in the midpoint of the sample, 1973. The standard errors in parentheses are heteroscedastic-consistent and are computed assuming that—apart from the parameter estimates—all variables are constants equal to their values in the midpoint of the sample.

the generality of the functional form. Several elasticity estimates summarize all relevant information and are therefore used to present the results. First, the elasticities are evaluated in the midpoint of the sample, i.e. 1973, and their t-statistics are computed assuming that all variables entering the elasticities formulas—except the parameter estimates—are constants. After that, we will analyze how the elasticities have developed over time.

6.4.2   Estimation results

We start off by estimating the model without any prior restrictions. Irrespective of the sector, several problems arise. For instance, concavity in factor prices is rejected by the data. To be more precise, one parameter from the S-matrix is estimated to be positive, whereas concavity implies that this parameter should be negative. By imposing the concavity restrictions defined in equation (6.20) we try to solve this problem. However, introducing these nonlinear restrictions into the model makes it impossible to get meaningful parameter estimates, because now the parameter does not converge. We therefore assume that the cost function is homogeneous in output, i.e. we impose the restrictions defined in equation (6.21) in the remainder of this chapter. This implies that the underlying production function is still allowed to exhibit increasing returns to scale to all inputs, but that we enforce constant returns to scale to the private input factors (CRS). This does not conflict with earlier empirical results in which constant returns to scale over all inputs is usually rejected (see section 4.3). As already noted in section 6.2, this implies that the output elasticity of infrastructure equals minus one times the cost elasticity of infrastructure (see equation 6.16).

Table 6.1 displays the first outcomes with this restricted cost function in the midpoint of the sample, 1973. First of all, note that the cost elasticity of public infrastructure (ε_{CG}) has the expected negative sign in 1973 for both sectors as well as for the total private sector. However, especially for the total and the sheltered sector, this point estimate is large when compared with previous research (see section 4.3). A ten per cent rise in public infrastructure will—according to the point estimate—decrease the costs of the private sector by almost seven per cent. The cost elasticity of infrastructure for the exposed sector of -0.07 is more in line with previous research. However, this elasticity is insignificant. So, these first results suggest that most benefits accrue to the sheltered sector.

The dependence of the sheltered sector on national infrastructure is not very surprising. Our infrastructure stock includes besides motorways, mainly local infrastructure such as roads, parking places and sewer systems which are all important environmental variables for sectors like the retail trade and the services sector, which are both part of the sheltered economy. For the exposed sector local infrastructure is not that crucial. By definition, the exposed sector depends more on international trade and therefore on only a subset of the national infrastructure stock, namely on those components that enhance international trade, such as motorways and (main) ports. Furthermore, international spillover effects from, e.g. foreign motorway infrastructure, might be important for the exposed sector. These spillovers are not captured by our infrastructure variable. Last, but certainly not least, the main part of the private infrastructure stock is owned by the exposed sector. Therefore, the exposed sector probably does not depend as much on the publicly provided part of the total infrastructure stock as does the sheltered sector, which hardly invests in infrastructure.

As table 6.1 shows, the labour elasticity of infrastructure (ε_{LG}) is negative for the total economy as well as for the sheltered sector.[27] In the exposed sector

Table 6.2   Dynamic parameters and equation statistics[a]

	Total private sector		Sheltered sector		Exposed sector	
	ΔL	ΔK	ΔL	ΔK	ΔL	ΔK
DYNAMIC PARAMETERS						
ψ_{ii}	0.38	−0.01	0.34	0.01	0.35	−0.03
	(0.04)	(0.02)	(0.06)	(0.03)	(0.04)	(0.02)
ϕ_{ii}	0.24	0.21	0.25	0.26	0.23	0.13
	(0.08)	(0.02)	(0.06)	(0.02)	(0.09)	(0.03)
EQUATION STATISTICS						
R^2	0.75	0.95	0.71	0.98	0.73	0.86
D–W	1.77	1.76	1.74	1.59	2.17	1.89

Sample: the Netherlands, 1952–93.
[a]The cost function is assumed to be homogeneous in output. The standard errors in parentheses are heteroscedastic-consistent.

a complementary relationship between labour and infrastructure seems to exist. Note, however, that only the point estimate for the sheltered sector differs significantly from zero. The relationship between private capital and public infrastructure—as denoted by ε_{KG})—is less ambiguous and approximately the same for all three sectors; there is a significant substitutive relationship between both variables in the midpoint of our sample. As explained in section 6.2 after equation 6.13, at least one of the two private inputs must bear a substitutive relationship and outweigh the possible complementary relationship in order to let infrastructure be cost saving and output augmenting. As the low point estimate of the cost elasticity of public infrastructure in the exposed sector indicates, the substitutive relationship of private capital and public infrastructure barely outweighs the (insignificant) complementary relationship between labour and public infrastructure in that sector. As indicated by the insignificant estimate of $\partial p_G^s / \partial t$, no correlation exists between infrastructure and technological progress.

Most of the other elasticity estimates stay roughly the same for different models. For example, we also estimated some models in which infrastructure was omitted. Although likelihood ratio tests indicated that infrastructure should be included, the estimated elasticities for the other elasticities hardly changed.

Table 6.2 shows the estimates of the dynamic parameters as well as some usual statistics. All dynamic parameters are pretty robust over the sectors. For both equations the error-correction coefficients lie somewhere around the 0.2 and they are highly significant. Therefore an actual factor-demand below its long-run level leads to an increase in factor-demand in the next period. As we restricted the off-diagonal elements of the Ψ-matrix to zero, these parameters are also the eigenvalues of that matrix, which implies that the dynamic system is definitely stable. Whereas significant short-run effects arise in the

Table 6.3   *Average elasticity estimates over time*

	Total	Sheltered	Exposed
ELASTICITIES OF PUBLIC INFRASTRUCTURE			
ε_{CG}	0.068	−1.261	1.076
	(0.786)	(0.913)	(1.774)
ε_{LG}	0.260	−1.598	2.054
	(1.171)	(0.807)	(3.007)
ε_{KG}	−0.433	−0.290	−0.662
	(0.517)	(1.189)	(0.474)
$\partial p_G^s / \partial t$	0.136	0.062	0.121
	(0.135)	(0.062)	(0.120)
OTHER INTERESTING ELASTICITIES			
ε_{Ct}	−0.019	0.010	−0.039
	(0.002)	(0.014)	(0.009)
ε_{Cp_L}	0.689	0.758	0.634
	(0.044)	(0.047)	(0.041)
ε_{Cp_K}	0.311	0.242	0.366
	(0.044)	(0.047)	(0.041)
ε_{Lt}	−0.027	0.016	−0.062
	(0.004)	(0.006)	(0.016)
ε_{Lp_L}	−0.052	−0.053	−0.086
	(0.014)	(0.026)	(0.025)
ε_{Lp_K}	0.052	0.053	0.086
	(0.014)	(0.026)	(0.025)
ε_{Kt}	0.001	0.003	0.001
	(0.013)	(0.040)	(0.009)
ε_{Kp_L}	0.112	0.156	0.146
	(0.013)	(0.051)	(0.024)
ε_{Kp_K}	−0.112	−0.156	−0.146
	(0.013)	(0.051)	(0.024)

[a]The cost function is assumed to be homogeneous in output. The elasticities estimates are averages over the 1953–93 period. The standard errors in parentheses are computed assuming that the parameter estimates are constants.

labour-demand equations, short-run changes do not have a significant effect on investment decisions of private firms. Apparently, investment decisions are based more on long-term considerations in stead of short-run fluctuations. The reported adjusted R^2's indicate that the model fits the data very well. The Durbin–Watson statistics are—especially for the sheltered sector—somewhat low but do not provide evidence of misspecification.

So far, we have analyzed the model by looking at elasticity estimates in the midpoint of the sample. However, these elasticities may vary over time. And so table 6.3 summarizes the variability of the elasticities by reporting the averages and their corresponding standard deviations over our time-interval. As the lower panel of the table shows, the standard deviations of the elasticities concerning the private inputs and technological progress are generally very low, and their averages correspond to their midpoint estimates reported in table

Table 6.4   Elasticity estimates using a prior[a]

	1973[b]			1953–93[c]		
	Total	Sheltered	Exposed	Total	Sheltered	Exposed
ELASTICITIES OF PUBLIC INFRASTRUCTURE						
ε_{CG}	−0.525	−0.528	−0.364	−0.308	−0.283	−0.201
	(0.120)	(0.098)	(0.126)	(0.114)	(0.143)	(0.086)
ε_{LG}	−0.358	−0.368	0.018	−0.243	−0.363	0.187
	(0.165)	(0.133)	(0.201)	(0.236)	(0.288)	(0.353)
ε_{KG}	−0.930	−1.103	−1.074	−0.526	−0.265	−0.852
	(0.100)	(0.210)	(0.138)	(0.519)	(1.070)	(0.544)
$\partial p_G^s / \partial t$	−0.008	−0.007	0.008	−0.032	−0.020	0.005
	(0.012)	(0.004)	(0.010)	(0.043)	(0.027)	(0.008)
OTHER INTERESTING ELASTICITIES						
ε_{Ct}	−0.025	−0.008	−0.040	−0.017	−0.009	−0.026
	(0.004)	(0.004)	(0.005)	(0.011)	(0.007)	(0.018)
ε_{Cp_L}	0.707	0.783	0.650	0.687	0.761	0.624
	(0.311)	(0.003)	(0.005)	(0.044)	(0.050)	(0.040)
ε_{Cp_K}	0.293	0.217	0.350	0.313	0.239	0.376
	(0.003)	(0.003)	(0.005)	(0.044)	(0.050)	(0.040)
ε_{Lt}	−0.042	−0.018	−0.069	−0.025	−0.009	−0.044
	(0.006)	(0.004)	(0.008)	(0.016)	(0.008)	(0.028)
ε_{Lp_L}	−0.051	−0.035	−0.086	−0.052	−0.045	−0.087
	(0.007)	(0.009)	(0.015)	(0.014)	(0.022)	(0.025)
ε_{Lp_K}	0.051	0.035	0.086	0.052	0.045	0.087
	(0.007)	(0.009)	(0.015)	(0.014)	(0.022)	(0.025)
ε_{Kt}	0.015	0.027	0.012	0.004	−0.001	0.006
	(0.003)	(0.004)	(0.003)	(0.013)	(0.035)	(0.008)
ε_{Kp_L}	0.122	0.126	0.160	0.110	0.133	0.141
	(0.016)	(0.032)	(0.027)	(0.012)	(0.043)	(0.022)
ε_{Kp_K}	−0.122	−0.126	−0.160	−0.110	−0.133	−0.141
	(0.016)	(0.032)	(0.027)	(0.012)	(0.043)	(0.022)

[a]The cost function is assumed to be homogeneous in output. The cost elasticity of public infra-structure is assumed to lie within a certain bandwidth.

[b]The elasticities are evaluated in the midpoint of the sample, 1973. The standard errors in parentheses are heteroscedastic-consistent and are computed assuming that—apart from the parameter estimates—all variables are constants equal to their values in the midpoint of the sample.

[c]The elasticities estimates are averages over the 1953–93 period. The standard errors in parentheses are computed assuming that the parameter estimates are constants.

6.1. We hoped that the same would be true for the elasticities concerning public infrastructure. Unfortunately, and as the upper panel of the table shows, this is clearly not the case. Not only do both factor-demand elasticities with respect to public infrastructure alter sign during our sample period, the cost elasticity of public infrastructure even becomes significantly positive over time which is theoretically unjustifiable (not shown). This leaves little room for interpreting the dynamic behaviour of these elasticities.

In our opinion, it is hard to imagine why the cost elasticity of public capital in particular has changed so dramatically over time. We therefore stipulate that the

Figure 6.1   *Cost elasticities of public infrastructure* $(\varepsilon_{CG})^a$

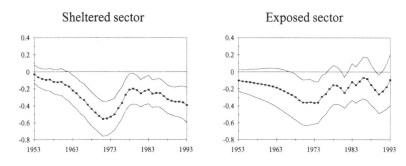

Sheltered sector   Exposed sector

[a]Including their 95 per cent confidence intervals.

95 per cent confidence interval around this elasticity has a maximum bandwidth of approximately 1, i.e. the standard deviation of the cost elasticity of public capital over time is bounded by $\frac{1}{4}$. We implemented this prior by adding the following equation to our system:[28]

$$u_t = \bar{\varepsilon}_{CG} + \frac{\partial C^*}{\partial G}\frac{G}{C^*}, \qquad (6.25)$$

where $u_t \sim iid\left(0, \frac{1}{16}\right)$ and which is uncorrelated with the residuals of the factor-demand equations. Furthermore, $\bar{\varepsilon}_{CG}$ represents a new parameter which equals the average cost elasticity of public infrastructure over time. Note that we do not impose restrictions on the level of this new parameter $\bar{\varepsilon}_{CG}$; only its standard deviation over time is bounded.

Together with the factor-demand equations in error correction form, as defined by equations (6.19) and (6.22), we then re-estimated the system. The results are presented in table 6.4. As the right-hand panel of that table shows, the standard deviation of the cost elasticity of public infrastructure over time is relatively low if compared to our previous results. Of course this is not surprising, because we have enforced this elasticity to stay within a certain bandwidth. However, we did not impose restrictions on the size of this elasticity and its standard deviation at each separate datapoint. For both sectors and their aggregate, table 6.4 shows that this cost elasticity is indeed negative and highly significant in the midpoint of our sample. Therefore, public infrastructure plays a significant role in the production process of private firms. As both tables show, again public infrastructure affects the sheltered sector of the economy more than it does the exposed sector. On average the cost elasticities of infrastructure for the aggregated, the sheltered and the exposed sectors are respectively -0.31, -0.28 and -0.20, which is somewhat high, but not out of line with previous research. The dynamic parameters hardly change and are therefore not reported.

Figure 6.1 shows the development of the cost elasticity of public infrastructure and its 95 per cent confidence interval over time. Clearly, the point estimates of the exposed sector are often insignificant whereas this is seldom the case for the sheltered sector. Furthermore, although both panels in figure 6.1 show that the cost elasticities of public infrastructure develop similarly in both sectors, the elasticity for the sheltered sector shows larger oscillations, indicating that this sector is more vulnerable to changes in the stock of public infrastructure than is the exposed sector.

The pattern is clear in both pictures. The build-up of infrastructural works after World War II increased the effect of infrastructure on the private sector. Its influence peaks in the early seventies, just a couple of years after government investment has reached its highest level (see figure 1.2 of Chapter 1). After a lag of approximately two or three years, the cut-backs in public infrastructure expenditure start to affect the private sector; the influence of infrastructure diminishes. After the eighties the curves of the sheltered and the exposed sector show different patterns. Whereas the effect of infrastructure on the latter is becoming more volatile and often insignificant, its influence on the sheltered sector steadily increases. Because public investment did not substantially rise in the early nineties, this suggests that infrastructural projects in that period were aimed at solving domestically-oriented problems, and/or that the sheltered sector found a way to use the available infrastructure more efficiently.

Another positive aspect of introducing the prior-equation (6.25) is that we now find a substitutive relationship between labour and technological progress in the sheltered sector. Despite the use of our prior, all other elasticities roughly stay the same. This also holds for both factor-demand elasticities with respect to infrastructure: still no clear picture emerges from the relationships between private inputs and infrastructure. As before, in the midpoint private capital and infrastructure behave as substitutes in all sectors. The relationship between labour and public infrastructure is ambiguous. For the exposed sector we again find an insignificant complementary relationship, whereas a significant substitutive relationship prevails in the sheltered sector. However, over time and for all sectors, both elasticities alter sign. For instance, in the first half and in the last two years of our sample private capital of the sheltered sector behaves as a complement to infrastructure, whereas an opposite relationship prevails between 1972 and 1991. The pattern between labour and public infrastructure roughly mirrors the pattern between the two capital stocks. Therefore, despite the fact that most empirical research report a complementary relationship between public and private capital, we come up with very mixed results. As indicated by the insignificant estimate of $\partial p_G^s / \partial t$, still no clear relationship

Table 6.5   *Elasticity estimates using a two-year lag on infrastructure[a]*

	1973[b]			1953–93[c]		
	Total	Sheltered	Exposed	Total	Sheltered	Exposed
ELASTICITIES OF PUBLIC INFRASTRUCTURE						
ε_{CG}	−0.196	−0.748	−0.102	−0.078	−0.447	−0.052
	(0.075)	(0.084)	(0.096)	(0.056)	(0.141)	(0.066)
ε_{LG}	0.053	−0.733	0.576	0.111	−0.513	0.687
	(0.099)	(0.107)	(0.150)	(0.210)	(0.281)	(0.494)
ε_{KG}	−0.760	−0.800	−1.168	−0.548	−0.438	−1.117
	(0.110)	(0.141)	(0.231)	(0.557)	(0.884)	(0.639)
$\partial p_G^s / \partial t$	0.033	−0.007	0.040	0.028	−0.024	0.057
	(0.009)	(0.004)	(0.009)	(0.037)	(0.033)	(0.055)
OTHER INTERESTING ELASTICITIES						
ε_{Ct}	−0.036	0.001	−0.047	−0.024	−0.001	−0.029
	(0.003)	(0.003)	(0.003)	(0.016)	(0.004)	(0.021)
ε_{CpL}	0.694	0.774	0.611	0.673	0.750	0.589
	(0.003)	(0.002)	(0.006)	(0.044)	(0.051)	(0.041)
ε_{CpK}	0.306	0.226	0.389	0.327	0.250	0.411
	(0.003)	(0.002)	(0.006)	(0.044)	(0.051)	(0.041)
ε_{Lt}	−0.057	−0.007	−0.088	−0.038	−0.003	−0.059
	(0.004)	(0.004)	(0.006)	(0.024)	(0.008)	(0.033)
ε_{LpL}	−0.064	−0.042	−0.126	−0.067	−0.055	−0.128
	(0.007)	(0.009)	(0.017)	(0.017)	(0.027)	(0.037)
ε_{LpK}	0.064	0.042	0.126	0.067	0.055	0.128
	(0.007)	(0.009)	(0.017)	(0.017)	(0.027)	(0.037)
ε_{Kt}	0.013	0.026	0.018	0.005	0.010	0.015
	(0.003)	(0.003)	(0.007)	(0.014)	(0.026)	(0.008)
ε_{KpL}	0.145	0.143	0.198	0.134	0.152	0.180
	(0.015)	(0.031)	(0.025)	(0.015)	(0.047)	(0.029)
ε_{KpK}	−0.145	−0.143	−0.198	−0.134	−0.152	−0.180
	(0.015)	(0.031)	(0.025)	(0.015)	(0.047)	(0.029)

[a]The cost function is assumed to be homogeneous in output. A two-year lag is placed on the public infrastructure variable. The cost elasticity of public infrastructure is assumed to lie within a certain bandwidth.
[b]The elasticities are evaluated in the midpoint of the sample, 1973. The standard errors in parentheses are heteroscedastic-consistent and are computed assuming that—apart from the parameter estimates—all variables are constants equal to their values in the midpoint of the sample.
[c]The elasticities estimates are averages over the 1953–93 period. The standard errors in parentheses are computed assuming that the parameter estimates are constants.

between infrastructure and technological progress is found.

To test the robustness of the model and remove some potential autocorrelation problems, we opt for putting a lag on our infrastructure variable. Furthermore, the lumpy character of infrastructure investment implies that the private sector needs some time to adapt to new infrastructure. Noting the pattern of the public investment share and labour productivity growth, as depicted in figure 1.2 of Chapter 1, and the reaction lag observed when discussing figure 6.1, we choose a two-year lag on our infrastructure variable. An additional advan-

Figure 6.2   Cost elasticities of public infrastructure (ε_{CG}) using a two-year lag on infrastructure[a]

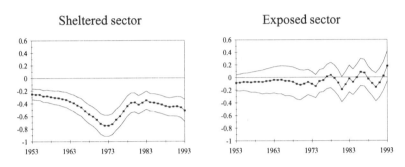

[a]Including their 95 per cent confidence intervals.

tage of introducing this two-year lag on infrastructure is that it might remove fears concerning the causality between infrastructure and our private variables. The theoretical model underlying our regressions assumes that infrastructure influences the private sector. No room is left for the private sector to influence the decision-making process that underlies the investments in infrastructure. If under these modifications similar conclusions are reached as before, this can be seen as indirect proof that our causality assumptions are correct.

Table 6.5 evaluates the elasticity estimates in the midpoint of our sample and over time. A comparison of these results with the previous ones reveals that the differences between the two sectors are being amplified. As figure 6.2 shows, the cost elasticity of infrastructure is getting larger in the sheltered sector, whereas for the exposed sector the estimated effect of infrastructure on costs is becoming insignificant at every datapoint. For the aggregate sector the absolute value of the cost elasticity of infrastructure is in general somewhat larger than it is for the exposed sector, but—and this is in contrast with our earlier results—it is often also estimated to be insignificant. The magnitude of the cost elasticity for both the aggregate as well as the exposed sector—respectively -0.07 and -0.05—are in line with previous research. However, the average cost elasticity of infrastructure for the sheltered sector has become more negative (-0.45). As before, the relationship between public infrastructure and factor-demand is unclear. Therefore, these results do not contradict our previous outcomes. On the contrary, they strengthen our conclusion that the sheltered sector depends especially on the stock of infrastructure.

To increase the degrees of freedom and to further check whether the effect of infrastructure on both the exposed and the sheltered sector is statistically

Table 6.6　Elasticity estimates using the 1969–93 sample[a]

	1973[b]			1969–93[c]		
	Total	Sheltered	Exposed	Total	Sheltered	Exposed
ELASTICITIES OF PUBLIC INFRASTRUCTURE						
ε_{CG}	−1.094	−1.333	−0.994	−1.034	−1.265	−0.943
	(0.160)	(0.210)	(0.170)	(0.059)	(0.069)	(0.046)
ε_{LG}	−1.375	−1.582	−1.240	−1.490	−1.679	−1.253
	(0.207)	(0.263)	(0.198)	(0.395)	(0.391)	(0.240)
ε_{KG}	−0.381	−0.399	−0.479	−0.013	0.044	−0.392
	(0.462)	(0.755)	(0.307)	(0.645)	(1.019)	(0.245)
$\partial p_G^s / \partial t$	−0.032	−0.012	−0.018	−0.141	−0.062	−0.065
	(0.016)	(0.006)	(0.009)	(0.076)	(0.034)	(0.034)
OTHER INTERESTING ELASTICITIES						
ε_{Ct}	−0.001	0.011	−0.006	−0.005	0.008	−0.012
	(0.005)	(0.007)	(0.005)	(0.002)	(0.002)	(0.004)
ε_{CpL}	0.717	0.789	0.676	0.721	0.793	0.669
	(0.003)	(0.005)	(0.003)	(0.051)	(0.046)	(0.059)
ε_{CpK}	0.283	0.211	0.324	0.279	0.207	0.331
	(0.003)	(0.005)	(0.003)	(0.051)	(0.046)	(0.059)
ε_{Lt}	−0.003	0.013	−0.013	−0.005	0.009	−0.018
	(0.007)	(0.008)	(0.006)	(0.006)	(0.006)	(0.005)
ε_{LpL}	−0.033	−0.033	−0.035	−0.031	−0.028	−0.036
	(0.005)	(0.008)	(0.008)	(0.011)	(0.012)	(0.013)
ε_{LpK}	0.033	0.033	0.035	0.031	0.028	0.036
	(0.005)	(0.008)	(0.008)	(0.011)	(0.012)	(0.013)
ε_{Kt}	0.003	0.002	0.008	−0.001	0.008	0.001
	(0.017)	(0.027)	(0.011)	(0.010)	(0.016)	(0.008)
ε_{KpL}	0.084	0.125	0.073	0.076	0.101	0.069
	(0.012)	(0.029)	(0.017)	(0.009)	(0.021)	(0.007)
ε_{KpK}	−0.084	−0.125	−0.073	−0.076	−0.101	−0.069
	(0.012)	(0.029)	(0.017)	(0.009)	(0.021)	(0.007)

[a]The cost function is assumed to be homogeneous in output. The cost elasticity of public infrastructure is assumed to lie within a certain bandwidth.

[b]The elasticities are evaluated in 1973. The standard errors in parentheses are heteroscedastic-consistent and are computed assuming that—apart from the parameter estimates—all variables are constants equal to their values in the midpoint of the sample.

[c]The elasticities estimates are averages over the 1969–93 period. The standard errors in parentheses are computed assuming that the parameter estimates are constants.

the same, we constructed a panel dataset covering both sectors. In our first panel regression all parameters are modelled to be sector-specific. As expected, the outcomes resemble our previous results (not shown). In the next step we assume the effect of infrastructure to be the same over both sectors. A likelihood ratio test indicates that this assumption is strongly rejected by the data (not shown). Apparently, the exposed and the sheltered sector are quite dissimilar and should therefore be modelled separately.

Other ways in which we checked the robustness of the outcomes is by changing the initial private capital stocks and their depreciation rates. The

Table 6.7　Elasticity estimates using low-skilled and high-skilled labour[a]

	1973[b]			1969–93[c]		
	Total	Sheltered	Exposed	Total	Sheltered	Exposed
ELASTICITIES OF PUBLIC INFRASTRUCTURE						
ε_{CG}	−1.021	−1.644	−0.906	−0.899	−1.513	−0.829
	(0.244)	(0.359)	(0.220)	(0.072)	(0.131)	(0.078)
ε_{L^lG}	−4.007	−4.628	−2.794	−10.244	−9.416	−7.014
	(1.073)	(3.047)	(0.528)	(5.701)	(3.606)	(4.461)
ε_{L^hG}	3.508	1.648	2.367	5.869	2.300	5.094
	(1.905)	(3.988)	(1.335)	(1.808)	(2.330)	(2.402)
ε_{KG}	−1.400	−1.359	−1.086	−1.305	−0.520	−1.225
	(0.456)	(0.933)	(0.318)	(0.956)	(1.691)	(0.262)
$\partial p^s_G/\partial t$	0.062	−0.018	0.036	0.098	−0.033	0.055
	(0.049)	(0.037)	(0.022)	(0.096)	(0.052)	(0.019)
OTHER INTERESTING ELASTICITIES						
ε_{Ct}	0.000	0.027	−0.006	−0.003	0.019	−0.011
	(0.008)	(0.013)	(0.007)	(0.002)	(0.004)	(0.003)
$\varepsilon_{Cp_{L^l}}$	0.416	0.424	0.422	0.331	0.308	0.351
	(0.003)	(0.005)	(0.002)	(0.082)	(0.091)	(0.076)
$\varepsilon_{Cp_{L^h}}$	0.298	0.366	0.261	0.387	0.485	0.321
	(0.004)	(0.008)	(0.002)	(0.063)	(0.078)	(0.045)
ε_{Cp_K}	0.286	0.209	0.317	0.283	0.207	0.327
	(0.002)	(0.003)	(0.002)	(0.056)	(0.052)	(0.061)
ε_{L^lt}	0.060	0.068	0.020	0.085	0.097	0.030
	(0.041)	(0.117)	(0.020)	(0.022)	(0.048)	(0.021)
$\varepsilon_{L^lp_{L^l}}$	−0.401	−0.770	−0.085	−0.768	−1.404	−0.182
	(0.151)	(0.449)	(0.092)	(0.272)	(0.460)	(0.067)
$\varepsilon_{L^lp_{L^h}}$	0.496	0.918	0.143	0.896	1.603	0.270
	(0.155)	(0.466)	(0.087)	(0.302)	(0.509)	(0.093)
$\varepsilon_{L^lp_K}$	−0.095	−0.149	−0.058	−0.128	−0.199	−0.089
	(0.020)	(0.033)	(0.015)	(0.033)	(0.058)	(0.028)
ε_{L^ht}	−0.112	−0.017	−0.090	−0.092	−0.028	−0.081
	(0.073)	(0.157)	(0.051)	(0.019)	(0.041)	(0.012)
$\varepsilon_{L^hp_{L^l}}$	0.692	1.064	0.231	0.708	0.938	0.274
	(0.217)	(0.550)	(0.141)	(0.081)	(0.121)	(0.047)
$\varepsilon_{L^hp_{L^h}}$	−0.928	−1.321	−0.439	−0.884	−1.112	−0.451
	(0.224)	(0.576)	(0.134)	(0.071)	(0.140)	(0.023)
$\varepsilon_{L^hp_K}$	0.236	0.257	0.207	0.176	0.174	0.177
	(0.029)	(0.050)	(0.025)	(0.042)	(0.056)	(0.026)
ε_{Kt}	0.030	0.020	0.027	0.024	0.026	0.017
	(0.016)	(0.031)	(0.012)	(0.018)	(0.026)	(0.011)
$\varepsilon_{Kp^l_L}$	−0.138	−0.301	−0.077	−0.148	−0.289	−0.093
	(0.029)	(0.067)	(0.020)	(0.038)	(0.072)	(0.024)
$\varepsilon_{Kp^h_L}$	0.246	0.451	0.171	0.239	0.403	0.174
	(0.031)	(0.087)	(0.021)	(0.036)	(0.074)	(0.020)
ε_{Kp_K}	−0.108	−0.149	−0.094	−0.091	−0.114	−0.081
	(0.013)	(0.038)	(0.012)	(0.011)	(0.024)	(0.008)

[a]The cost function is assumed to be homogeneous in output. The cost elasticity of public infrastructure is assumed to lie within a certain bandwidth.

[b]The elasticities are evaluated in 1973. The standard errors in parentheses are heteroscedastic-consistent and are computed assuming that—apart from the parameter estimates—all variables are constants equal to their values in the midpoint of the sample.

[c]The elasticities estimates are averages over the 1969–93 period. The standard errors in parentheses are computed assuming that the parameter estimates are constants.

conclusions do not alter (not shown). These results strengthen our impression that the findings are very robust.

As already noted, despite the fact that estimates of the price elasticities are highly significant, they are extremely low. Using a similar specification without infrastructure, for the Dutch economy covering the 1972–93 period, Draper and Manders (1996b) report price elasticities for aggregate labour ranging from -0.02 in the exposed to -0.05 in the sheltered sector, in line with our own findings. However, after dividing labour into low-skilled and high-skilled types their price elasticities rise considerably, but still well below unity. To check whether the same prevails in our model using infrastructure, and to see whether infrastructure has a different effect on low-skilled versus high-skilled labour, we will now concentrate on the 1969–93 period for which disaggregated labour data is available. Note that by using this shorter time interval, degrees of freedom are severely reduced. This might result in less precise elasticity estimates.

Before estimating the model using the two labour inputs, we first estimated the same model as before for the 1969–93 period. As shown in table 6.6, the standard elasticity estimates, i.e. those without infrastructure, are again pretty robust; the sign of none of the significant elasticities alters and their magnitudes are still very low and quite comparable with our previous results. However, the absolute size of all elasticities of infrastructure definitely increases. For instance, the overall effect of infrastructure on private cost rises considerably. By using the shorter time interval our point estimates of the cost elasticity of infrastructure in the sheltered sector even surpass our previous results which already were high as compared to other research; now the point estimates suggest that a one per cent rise in infrastructure decreases cost by approximately one per cent. In line with our previous results is the finding that the sheltered sector has benefited more from infrastructure than the exposed sector of the Dutch economy. However, this time we find a significant substitutive relationship between aggregate labour and infrastructure which does not alter sign during our (short) time interval. The relationship between private capital and infrastructure is still unclear.

Keeping these results in mind, we now divide labour into high-skilled and low-skilled labour, and re-estimate the expanded model. The results are presented in table 6.7 and confirm the outcomes of Draper and Manders (1996b, 1996a): the price elasticities of both labour inputs are much higher than the price elasticity of our aggregated labour input. The main difference with the outcomes of Draper and Manders (1996b, 1996a) is that we come up with a complementary relationship between low-skilled labour and private capital, whereas they found a substitutive relationship. High-skilled labour and private capital are substitutes. The overall effect of infrastructure on private cost is approximately the same as when we use the aggregated labour variable over the short time interval; the cost elasticity of public infrastructure is incredibly large. Infrastructure seems to have the opposite effect on low-skilled labour as compared with its effect on high-skilled labour. Whereas a clear substitutive relationship between low-skilled labour and infrastructure prevails, the point estimates of ε_{L^hG} suggest that high-skilled labour and infrastructure are complements. Note, however, that the magnitudes of these factor-demand elasticities with respect to infrastructure are incredibly large. This might indicate a structural break between 1953–93. However, likelihood ratio tests indicate that including dummy-variables in the models covering the entire sample period does not significantly increase their likelihood functions. Apparently, it is the reduction in degrees of freedom that has big consequences for the precision of the coefficients concerning infrastructure. This is not very surprising, as using a shorter time interval reduces the variability of—and therefore the information contained in—especially our infrastructure stock. Infrastructure then starts to resemble the trend variable and consequently causes multicollinearity problems. This might explain the opposite effect infrastructure has on low-skilled versus high-skilled labour; the amount of high-skilled labour has increased continuously over the 1969–93 period, whereas the opposite is the case for the low-skilled.

6.5   CONCLUDING REMARKS

After incorporating a public capital variable in a symmetric generalized Mc-Fadden cost function, our empirical analysis yields some very interesting results. For the post-World War II period in the Netherlands we find a significant influence of infrastructure on output and production costs of the private sector. A ten per cent rise in the stock of public infrastructure has reduced the cost of the private economy on average by three per cent.[29] This is perhaps somewhat high, but in line with previous research. However, neither labour nor private capital has a very distinct relationship with infrastructure: sometimes private inputs behave as substitutes for public infrastructure, at other times there seems to exist a complementary relationship between them.

Looking at a sectoral level reveals large differences between the exposed and the sheltered sectors of the Dutch economy. As a more substitutive relationship between both private inputs and infrastructure exists in the sheltered sector, it seems to have benefited significantly from increases in infrastructure. In the exposed sector, the quantitatively smaller substitutive and larger complementary effects of infrastructure on both private inputs almost level off, resulting in a statistically insignificant cost elasticity of infrastructure. No significant relationship between public infrastructure and technological progress is found in either sector.[30]

The insignificant effect of infrastructure on output and production cost of the exposed sector can be explained by referring to the fact that only a small part of our infrastructure variable is relevant for that sector. The exposed sector—by definition internationally oriented—is dependent upon those components of the infrastructure stock that enhance international trade. However, motorways and other 'internationally-oriented' infrastructure only play a minor role in our infrastructure variable. The sheltered sector benefits mainly from 'locally-oriented' infrastructure, which forms the major part of our infrastructure stock. Furthermore, foreign infrastructure might be expected to be equally important to the exposed sector and is not included as an additional variable. Finally, the exposed sector is probably not that dependent on the publicly provided part of infrastructure as is the sheltered sector, because the exposed sector itself invests in infrastructural works. Nowadays, more than 80 per cent of all private infrastructure investment is done by the exposed sector, which means that it accounts for approximately 25 per cent of all infrastructure investments in the Netherlands. Therefore, it does probably not depend upon the publicly provided part of the total infrastructure stock as much as the sheltered sector.

Disaggregating the labour-input variable into low-skilled and high-skilled reveals that the former especially has a substitutive relationship with infrastructure, whereas the latter often shows a complementary relationship with infrastructure. However, the point estimates are very imprecise, possibly because of the loss in degrees of freedom as the number of variables increases and the sample size decreases.

NOTES

1. See Chapter 4 for a survey of the pros and cons of the different empirical approaches used in researching the impact of public capital.
2. See table 4.3 of Chapter 4.
3. Whereas Conrad and Seitz (1994), Lynde and Richmond (1992) and Seitz (1993, 1994) find a substitutive relationship, Conrad and Seitz (1992), Deno (1988), Nadiri and Mamuneas (1994b) and Shah (1992) report that labour and public capital are complements.
4. Exceptions are Conrad and Seitz (1992, 1994), Lynde (1992) and Lynde and Richmond (1992). Conrad and Seitz (1992, 1994) even reject the hypothesis of price homogeneity of the production function. However, when these authors impose homogeneity they cannot reject the hypothesis of constant returns to scale in all inputs.
5. This section draws upon Diewert and Wales (1987, 1995) and Seitz (1994).
6. There is, of course, a price paid for the services of the public capital stock through the tax system, but it is assumed that firms do not have direct control over how much capital the government supplies to them, so that we can treat these services as 'unpaid' factors of production.
7. A functional form is flexible if it can provide a second-order approximation to a function which is twice continuously differentiable and which satisfies the regularity conditions defined in equations (6.2) to (6.7). It can be shown that our candidate cost function must contain at least $N(N+7)/2+6$ free parameters in order to be flexible. See Allen (1997) for an excellent survey of flexible functional forms applied to production analysis.

8. The functional form is a (modest) generalization of a functional form due to McFadden (1978, p. 279), in which $g(p)$ is defined to be symmetric. See Diewert and Wales (1987, p. 51–54) for details. Recent applications of this specification can be found in Rask (1995), Coelli (1996) and Terrell (1996).

9. Rask (1995) also modifies the original SGM proposed by Diewert and Wales (1987) to allow for fixed factors of production. However, the function which he defines is not second-order flexible in the fixed inputs.

10. See Diewert and Wales (1987).

11. See, e.g. Diewert (1974).

12. Using this specification we assume that impact effects of price and production changes are equal.

13. In this line of research most studies approximate the state of technical knowledge by a time trend. Nadiri and Mamuneas (1994b, 1994a) are the only ones who also take public Research and Development (R&D) capital into account.

14. As noted in the introduction, the exposed sector includes agriculture, manufacturing and transport, whereas trade, banking and other private market services form the sheltered sector.

15. The depreciation rate of structures equals 2 per cent for both sectors, whereas the depreciation rate of equipment is set to 5 per cent in the exposed and 8 per cent in the sheltered sector. In prices of 1990 the initial stock of structures for the exposed sector is set at 250 billion guilders, whereas for the sheltered sector this stock equals almost 100 billion guilders. The initial stocks of equipment equal approximately 70 billion and 14 billion guilders for the exposed and sheltered sectors of the economy respectively.

16. We have set the mark-up for risk at 2 percentage points, as a lower risk premium sometimes leads to negative capital rental prices.

17. Following Broer and Jansen (1989), we calculate the expected inflation of investment goods by using $\hat{\pi}_t^j = \alpha \hat{\pi}_{t-1}^j + (1-\alpha) \pi_{t-1}^j$, where we picked $\alpha = 0.1$, and where π_{t-1}^j is the realized inflation of investment good j in period $t-1$.

18. The Tornqvist approximation of the Divisia index has attractive properties. Diewert (1976) has shown that it can be viewed as an exact index corresponding to a second-order approximation in logarithms of an arbitrary production or cost function (Caves *et al.* 1982). In particular, this index places no prior restrictions on the substitution elasticities among the goods being aggregated. With the Tornqvist approximation, the change in aggregate private capital service flow is a weighted sum of the changes in both asset-specific private capital stocks, where the weights are relative cost shares.

19. Unlike Draper and Manders (1996b, 1996a), the construction sector is left out of the analysis in order to minimize the influence of possible backward linkages, i.e. direct impulses on the economy through the demand for labour, raw materials and other capital goods in the construction of the infrastructural work.

20. We have also used the total public capital stock, which is the sum of five types of public capital: buildings; civil engineering works; machinery; road transport equipment; and other transport equipment. The qualitative conclusions do not change when we use the total public capital stock.

21. Consequently, privatization of these public firms does not influence our data.

22. The initial infrastructure stock in 1949 was set at approximately 60 billion guilders in 1990 prices. The depreciation rate of infrastructure is taken to be two per cent.

23. See, e.g. Conrad and Seitz (1994), Deno (1988), Nadiri and Mamuneas (1994a), Seitz (1994), Shah (1992).

24. In 1990 over 80 per cent of all private infrastructure investment was by the exposed sector.

25. Without this assumption most off-diagonal elements of both matrices do not significantly differ from zero. As expected, the long-run elasticities are therefore hardly affected by this assumption.

26. Procedures for computing standard errors that are consistent even in the presence of unkown heteroscedasticity were developed by White (1980).

27. Note that substitutability between the private inputs and infrastructure is calculated for a given output level. Therefore, the negative effect of infrastructure on private factor demand might be

counteracted by additional output which is also generated by more infrastructure investment.

28. See, e.g. Judge *et al.* (1985) for an introduction in estimation methods using stochastic prior information.

29. In 1993 the cost elasticity of public infrastructure is approximately -0.25. Given the public infrastructure stock and the production costs of the private sector, this implies that an increase of the public infrastructure stock by 1 billion guilders would have decreased the production costs of the private sector by approximately 625 million guilders.

30. Roughly 20 per cent of the cost benefits as computed in note 29 of a 1 billion increase in the stock of public infrastructure in 1993 accrues to the exposed sector. The remaining 80 per cent are cost reductions of the sheltered sector.

7. Output Effects of Infrastructure Investment[*]

7.1 INTRODUCTION

As noted in the previous chapters, recent years have witnessed a remarkable swell of interest in public infrastructure spending as a strategy to promote economic development. While specialists in regional and local economic development have long recognized higher infrastructure investment as a possible growth policy,[1] the genesis of this new attention is David Aschauer's (1989a) research on the impact of government investment on private sector productivity. Unlike several previous studies, Aschauer's results lead to the conclusion that public capital is productive, and not just a possible inducement to business location.

When summarizing the economic literature, we have seen in Chapter 4 that initially, various economists found output elasticities with respect to public capital of around 0.3. These high elasticities have in turn generated a raft of criticisms. As discussed in Chapter 4, the work of Aschauer (1989a) and his followers has been criticized on several grounds. One problem associated with the results of Aschauer (1989a) and many other previous studies is that they do not test for stationarity and obliviously use their data to analyze the effect of infrastructure on production. As reported in Chapter 5, correcting for the non-stationarity of the data often leads to rather implausible estimates of the output elasticity of public capital.

Another problem, which cannot easily be solved in the production function (or behavioural) approach, is raised by the causality issue. Many authors question whether smaller increases of public capital have indeed reduced productivity growth; alternatively, reduced productivity growth may have diminished the demand for public capital.

Besides influencing the productivity of the private sector, public capital investment has many more effects, such as interregional, intersectoral and intertemporal allocation and distribution effects, as well as trade, agglomeration,

---

[*]This chapter draws on Sturm *et al.* (1995), Groote *et al.* (1995) and Jacobs *et al.* (1996).

consequences for the public budget, employment, direct consumption and welfare effects. These, and others are normally disregarded in macroeconomic literature. It is very difficult to capture all such effects in one general framework, but the presence of one or more of them might contaminate the elasticity estimates presented in macroeconomic studies.

These considerations lead us to opt for an econometric approach which differs from that taken in most previous studies. Most authors derive single-equation regressions from first principles, run these regressions and base their conclusions on the elasticity estimates. Because of the lack of theory and the empirical controversy over the effect of infrastructure on the private sector, we choose to use as little economic theory as possible. In order to reach conclusions concerning the causal relationship between the variables, we apply Granger-causality tests in a multi-equation setting. Granger-causality tests are typically carried out within the framework of Vector AutoRegression (VAR) models as propagated by Sims (1980). In a VAR model a limited number of variables is distinguished that are explained by their owns lags and lags of the other variables, meaning that all variables are treated as jointly determined. This implies that *a priori* no causality directions are imposed. For instance, the causality might run from output to infrastructure; the opposite of what is usually assumed. An additional advantage is that infrastructure might indirectly influence output by raising the return of, e.g. machinery capital.

Apart from applying Granger-causality tests, we furthermore examine the mutual effects of different variables, using innovation accounting. Impulse-response functions and variance decompositions allow us to analyze the effect of infrastructure investment over time. How long does it take before output reacts to additional infrastructure investment?

As has been discussed in Chapter 4, only Clarida (1993), McMillin and Smyth (1994) and Otto and Voss (1996) have used a VAR framework to examine the effect of government capital on the private economy. This might stem from the fact that standard VAR methodology is not undisputed. For instance Cooley and LeRoy (1985) and more recently Duggal *et al.* (1995) note that in order to calculate impulse-response functions and variance decompositions, restrictions with regard to ordering are needed. These restrictions can be derived from theoretical considerations only, thereby nullifying one of the advantages of VAR analysis. However, the ordering of the variables is of minor importance in our model, since the variance-covariance matrix is practically diagonal.

Another innovation of this chapter is the exploitation of a new long run dataset on infrastructural capital formation in the Netherlands in the nineteenth century. So far, only the post-World War II period has been explored to any extent in the literature. Mayer (1980) argues that in applied econometrics one should seek to replicate previous results using a different dataset. Groote's (1996) book on capital formation in the form of infrastructure in the Netherlands allows us to study the relation for the second half of the last century, when the Netherlands went through the industrial revolution and large infrastructure projects were carried out. For example, the construction of a national railway network started in 1860, and the existing system of natural and artificial water-ways was enlarged, integrated, and modernized after 1850. It seems plausible then, that these infrastructural investments induced, or at least enabled, the integration of markets that were regionally and functionally separated before and thereby stimulated economic growth. To test this hypothesis, we will di-vide infrastructure investment into transport infrastructure and all remaining infrastructure investment.

It should be noted that unlike post-World War II infrastructure capital forma-tion, most of the investments in our dataset concern infrastructure which previ-ously did not exist at all. It is our belief that—due to, e.g. network effects—the construction of a new two-lane road has a larger effect on the economy than its expansion into a four-lane road.

In the econometric analysis of this chapter, we use capital formation figures instead of capital stocks because of the inherent problems of making capital stock estimates for infrastructural works using the standard perpetual inven-tory method. Although widely applied in literature—including this book—Feinstein (1968) has argued that the 'awkward' life cycle of infrastructural works, often without a clear date of 'birth' and nearly always without a clear moment of retirement, makes them less suited for application of the perpetual inventory method. Chapter 5 has also showed that assumptions concerning the lifespan of capital stocks can be crucial for the results. As we do not explic-itly estimate a production function, we are not forced to use capital stocks in our analysis. Furthermore, the time-series properties of the investment series facilitate the econometrical analysis considerably.

Gramlich (1994) has noticed that data limitations force economists to use public investment expenditures as a proxy for total infrastructure outlays. This may not be optimal. First of all, in many countries part of the infrastructure is financed and constructed by the private sector.[2] Secondly, public investment often consists of much more than infrastructure investment alone. For instance, many governments are responsible for residential investments and spend on public buildings. Our dataset solves both problems by capturing public as well as private infrastructure investment spending.

This chapter gives a quantitative underpinning of the belief that investments in transport infrastructures, such as roads and canals and in particular railways infrastructure, have in the previous century had large positive effects on the production level of the Dutch economy. The effect of non-transport infrastruc-ture investment is more of a short-run nature.

The chapter is structured as follows. The next section gives a brief descrip-tion of the Dutch economy in the previous century. Section 7.3 describes the data and their time-series properties, whereas the fourth section presents our estimation results based on these properties for the Netherlands. That section consists of three subsections, each discussing a step in our estimation procedure. Finally, the chapter provides a discussion of our findings.

7.2   THE NETHERLANDS IN THE 19TH CENTURY

During the first half of the nineteenth century the foundations of Dutch national wealth came under increasing pressure from foreign competition, which serves to explain why the Netherlands were continuously losing ground on neighbouring countries (Maddison, 1995). Infrastructural deficiencies hold a key position in explaining this slackness of Dutch relative economic performance. For instance, Griffiths (1979) argues that the impact of the high costs of raw materials, especially coal and iron, was aggravated by high costs of transport and communications due to the lack of a modern infrastructure.[3] Therefore, the main breakthrough in the Netherlands took place after the 1860s when transport costs could be reduced thanks to a large scale rehabilitation of the country's infrastructure.

In 1860 the first Railway Act was passed by parliament. As a consequence, the central government started to construct a national railway network. Before, Dutch railways consisted of four separate lines with a total length of only 350 kilometres. By 1885 the Netherlands had 1250 kilometres of public railway lines. As government construction induced several private railway companies to participate as well, the total length rose to 2280 kilometres of well-integrated railway lines.

At the same time, the existing system of natural and artificial waterways was enlarged, integrated, and modernized. Until the 1820s, the country still relied on its natural and historical endowment with rivers, barge canals dating from the seventeenth century, and coastal and estuary waters (De Vries, 1981; De Jong, 1992). Unfortunately, these became unsuited for increasing demands on the scale and reliability of transport. For instance, the country's main rivers, which linked the Amsterdam and Rotterdam harbours with the German hinterland, were improved after 1850. At the same time, these main harbours got new direct links to the North Sea.

Transaction costs in the Dutch economy were further reduced by the construction of a national telegraph network. Relative to other forms of infrastructure, however, this did not require large sums of money. As Field (1992) argues, its macroeconomic impact may be regarded as much greater than shown by the sums spent. This is exemplified by the 6.4 million telegrams being sent in 1913 against a mere 6,000 in 1850.

It seems plausible that these infrastructural investments have induced, or at least enabled, the integration of regionally and functionally separated markets, thereby stimulating economic growth. Indeed, historically this has often been implicitly assumed, without any qualitative or quantitative testing (De Jonge, 1968). After 1890 the main characteristics of the Dutch economy began to differ fundamentally. Sectors that are generally regarded as modern came to the forefront: metal working, machinery construction, chemicals. Investments in machinery and equipment became of greater importance over time. Therefore, and in order to investigate its relationship to infrastructure investments, we opted to include, besides Gross Domestic Product (GDP) and of course infrastructure investment, capital formation in machinery and equipment into our VAR analysis.

7.3 DATA

7.3.1 Description

This chapter builds on three relatively new datasets regarding Dutch economic development in the nineteenth century. These are the results of research by participants in the project on '*The Reconstruction of Dutch National Accounts, and the Analysis of the Development of the Dutch Economy, 1800–1940*', which has been under way since 1989 at the universities of Utrecht and Groningen.

Our VAR model includes GDP, infrastructure capital formation and capital formation in machinery and equipment. For the series on GDP and on investment in machinery and equipment, we refer to Smits *et al.* (1997). Both series are displayed in constant prices in figure 7.1. Because series for machinery investment are only available for the second half of the previous century, we consider the sample period 1853–1913 throughout this chapter.[4]

Data on infrastructural investments are taken from Groote (1996). He gives annual time series on capital formation in current and constant prices, and subdivided by sector or type of asset. Only the truly infrastructural aspects of these sectors are included. Thus, the permanent ways and works of railways are included, but rolling stock is not.

Because the definition of machinery and equipment is based on the definition of infrastructure, both series are complementary: the aggregation of investments in infrastructure and in machinery and equipment gives total capital formation, excluding residential and non-residential buildings.[5] Agricultural capital formation, including livestock, changes in stock and work in progress are all included in the category of machinery investment.

For analytical purposes, we will divide infrastructure investments into transport infrastructure and other remaining infrastructure. Transport infrastructure investments consist of main railways, light railways, (urban) tramways, canals

Figure 7.1   GDP and investment in machinery and equipment

Source: Smits *et al.* (1997).

and navigable rivers, harbours and docks, and (paved) roads. The other infrastructural sectors include: gas, electricity, water supply, the electromagnetic
telegraph, (local) telephone networks, drainage, dikes, and land reclamation.

Figure 7.2 displays these two series and their sum, i.e. total infrastructural
investments, at constant 1913 prices. As can be seen from this figure, except for
1860, transport infrastructure investments always exceeded other infrastructure
investments.

Prior to the analysis, natural logarithms are taken from all series.

7.3.2   Stationarity

The asymptotic distributions of causality tests are sensitive to unit roots and
time trends in the data series (Sims *et al.* 1990). The finite sample distribution
of these tests will also depend on these time-series properties (Stock and Watson, 1989). The rewriting of our original model, necessary to conduct impulse-
response analysis and variance decomposition analysis, assumes stability of
the model. A necessary condition to achieve stability is that the time series
are (trend) stationary. This condition prevails in the case of stationary series.
Therefore, non-stationary variables must be transformed into stationary ones

Figure 7.2 Investment in infrastructure

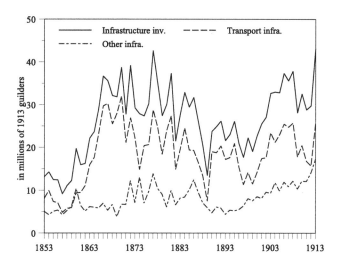

Source: Groote (1996).

before using them in our regression analysis.

To determine whether series are stationary, we use the augmented Dickey–Fuller (ADF) test and follow the testing strategy suggested by Dolado *et al.* (1990). Furthermore, we also apply the unit root test developed by Kwiatkowski *et al.* (1992) which has stationarity as its null hypothesis. Appendix A discusses both tests in greater detail.

Table 7.1 reports the outcomes of both tests.[6] Comparison of the *t*-statistics resulting from the ADF test, and the corresponding critical values show that all our time series are trend stationary. As both τ_μ's for GDP and machinery investment are insignificant, these two series are, according to the ADF test, only stationary around a deterministic trend. As only for the GDP and machinery investment series the null hypothesis of stationarity (η_μ) is rejected when using the test of Kwiatkowski *et al.* (1992), the findings of the ADF test are confirmed by that test.

In our estimations we will therefore include a trend variable. Filtering the trend from the individual series instead of including a trend in the regressions does not change the qualitative outcomes presented below.

As post-World War II economic time series are almost without exception non-stationary, the finding that the time series under consideration are trend

Table 7.1   Stationarity testing[a]

	AUGMENTED DICKEY–FULLER TEST				KWIATKOWSKI et al. TEST[d]	
	Trend		Constant		Trend	Constant
Series	Lags	τ_τ[b]	Lags	τ_μ[c]	η_τ[e]	η_μ[f]
GDP	0	−4.95**	0	0.28	0.120	1.231**
Mach.inv.	1	−4.79**	0	−1.13	0.051	1.107**
Infra.inv.	0	−3.68*	0	−3.73**	0.142	0.246
Transp.infra.	0	−3.88*	0	−3.32*	0.123	0.443
Other infra.	0	−3.62*	0	−3.76**	0.131	0.177

Sample: the Netherlands, 1853–1913.
[a] See main text for variable definitions.
[b] At a 5 (1) per cent significance level the MacKinnon (1991) critical values are −3.49 (−4.13) when a trend and a constant are included (τ_τ).
[c] At a 5 (1) per cent significance level the MacKinnon (1991) critical values are −2.91 (−3.55) when only a constant is included (τ_μ).
[d] The number of autoregressive lags is set at four.
[e] The asymptotic critical values for the significance levels of 5 (1) per cent are respectively 0.146 (0.216).
[f] The asymptotic critical values for the significance levels of 5 (1) per cent are respectively 0.463 (0.739).
* Significant at a five per cent level.
**Significant at a one per cent level.

stationary is in itself a remarkable result.[7] Nelson and Plosser (1982) conclude that most post-World War II macroeconomic variables are difference stationary, implying that a temporary shock has permanent effects and makes first-differencing, or the use of complex cointegration techniques necessary.[8]

Our results for the second half of the nineteenth century, however, clearly indicate that GDP and the investment series are trend stationary. At first sight, the trend-stationarity character of our series facilitates the mathematics. Unfortunately, trend stationarity also implies that changes in one variable cannot have a permanent effect on the other variables, because by definition all series ultimately return to their long-run trend paths. Therefore, the fact that our series are trend stationary is not only rather puzzling but also frustrates long-run effects of infrastructure investment, i.e. shocks on a trend-stationary variable cannot have permanent effects. For this reason, we limit our attention in this chapter to modelling the medium- and short-run effects.

7.4 VAR ANALYSIS

7.4.1 Granger-causality analysis

In order to test whether infrastructure influences GDP we first perform Granger-causality analysis. We have to restate our main hypothesis to make it testable: infrastructural capital formation is said to 'Granger cause' a rise in GDP, if the time-series prediction of GDP from its own past improves when lags of infrastructural capital formation are added to the equation. This interpretation of causality is, of course, intuitively attractive. It has therefore become widely accepted, although some of its implications are still under debate.[9]

As noted in Chapter 2, simple Granger-causality analysis may be obstructed by simultaneity effects: infrastructural capital formation may Granger cause GDP, while at the same time GDP Granger causes infrastructural capital formation. To avoid this problem, we analyze Granger causality in a so-called 'Vector AutoRegression' (VAR) model. VAR methodology resembles simultaneous-equation modelling in that several endogenous variables are considered together. In a VAR, only endogenous variables enter: each variable is explained only by its own lagged values and the lagged values of the other endogenous variables. If necessary, deterministic variables, such as a constant or a trend, are included. As no *a priori* identifying conditions concerning the causal relationship of the variables are needed, this solves the simultaneity problem. As we are also interested in the direction of causality, this is a clear advantage. Initially, we only have to decide which variables to include in our model.

We have opted to include, apart from GDP (y) and infrastructure capital formation (i), capital formation in machinery and equipment (m).[10] The reason for this approach is obvious: investments in machinery and equipment are made to stimulate profits by increasing output or higher productivity. Furthermore, as the series are trend stationary we include a deterministic trend. This gives the following VAR(p) model:

$$\begin{pmatrix} y_t \\ m_t \\ i_t \end{pmatrix} = \begin{pmatrix} a_{10} \\ a_{20} \\ a_{30} \end{pmatrix} + \begin{bmatrix} A_{11}(L) & A_{12}(L) & A_{13}(L) \\ A_{21}(L) & A_{22}(L) & A_{23}(L) \\ A_{31}(L) & A_{32}(L) & A_{33}(L) \end{bmatrix} \begin{pmatrix} y_{t-1} \\ m_{t-1} \\ i_{t-1} \end{pmatrix} + \begin{pmatrix} e_{1t} \\ e_{2t} \\ e_{3t} \end{pmatrix},$$

$$(7.1)$$

where, for $j,k = 1,\ldots,3$, a_{j0} are the 1×2 vectors containing a constant and a time trend, A_{jk} are polynomials of order p in the lag operator L, and e_{jt} are independent and identically distributed disturbance terms such that the covariance matrix $\Sigma = E(e_{jt}e_{kt})$ is not necessarily zero for $j \neq k$.

Where the order p is known, each equation in the system can be estimated by Ordinary Least Squares (OLS). Moreover, OLS estimates are consistent and asymptotically efficient. Even though the errors are correlated across equations, system estimators do not add to the efficiency of the estimation procedure since the regressions have identical right-hand-side variables (Denton, 1978).

A practical disadvantage of VAR is that the number of parameters to be estimated can easily become large. In our case—with three endogenous variables—each extra lag that is incorporated in the model brings in nine extra parameters. This quickly eats up degrees of freedom in the estimation procedure. Often, however, a substantial number of parameters hardly differ from zero. Moreover, Ahking and Miller (1985) and Thornton and Batten (1985) have shown that imposing common lag lengths has no basis in theory and can distort the estimates and lead to misleading inferences concerning causality, if lag structures differ across variables. To overcome this problem Hsiao (1981) suggests an approach that starts from univariate autoregression and sequentially adds lags and variables using Akaike's (1969, 1970) Final Prediction Error (FPE) criterion (Canova, 1995, pp. 62–63). Therefore, we will—besides reporting the outcomes of VAR models with common lag lengths imposed (VAR(p) model)—also discuss VAR models using the FPE criterion to select the appropriate lag specification for the individual variables in each equation (VAR-FPE model).[11]

Two drawbacks to using the FPE criterion approach should be mentioned. First, the sequential nature of the procedure may bias the joint nature of the process and the single equation approach is equivalent to ignoring the effect of possible correlation between the residuals. Therefore, we have carried out diagnostic checks to examine the adequacy of our VAR-FPE model specifications. This is done by deliberately underfitting and overfitting the system. The presented results are very robust.

Second, application of the FPE criterion reduces the complexity of the model itself, but increases the complexity of its estimation. As the right-hand-side variables in the equations may now differ, a gain in efficiency can occur by using a system estimator. We will therefore apply the Seemingly Unrelated Regression (SUR) estimator of Zellner (1962).

Hsiao (1981) has shown that under fairly general conditions the inclusion of a variable based on the FPE criterion is evidence for a weak Granger-causal ordering. If the lagged values of the explanatory variable further exert a statistically significant effect, then the Granger-causal impact can be identified as a strong form (Kawai, 1980).

As discussed in Chapter 2, the Granger-causality testing procedure does not generally give us an estimate of the sign of the overall effect. In order to test whether there exists a positive or negative effect of one variable on another, we apply the neutrality test in which we calculate the sum of the lagged values of an explanatory variable and test whether it significantly differs from zero (Zarnowitz, 1992, pp. 365–379).

Therefore, in this setting the analysis of a Granger-causal relation from infrastructure on GDP boils down to testing whether each of the A_{13}-elements in equation (7.1) differs from zero. If furthermore the sum of these A_{13}-elements is significantly positive, we know that infrastructure positively influences GDP. We cannot use ordinary F-tests, which apply to the individual equations, because the error terms may be correlated over the equations, and i may affect y through these correlated error terms. We estimate both the constrained and unconstrained systems as a whole and apply likelihood ratio tests.

Table 7.2 displays our results. The upper panel of the table gives the outcome for a model in which likelihood ratio tests are used to determine the order p of the model. We applied a 10 per cent significance level for the last lags. This results in a VAR(2) model. The lower panel of the table displays the results where the FPE criterion is used. For each equation we first report the number of lags that are included for each variable. Next, the χ^2-statistic reports whether all lags are significantly different from zero, i.e. the test results whether or not a strong Granger-causal relationship exists. Thirdly, we give the sum of the parameters of these lags, and finally the table displays the outcomes of the likelihood ratio test and whether these sums are significant. Links between the equations hamper interpretation of individual coefficients. Therefore, we do not report the individual coefficients. Of course the same holds for the sums, but the signs reveal whether there is a positive or a negative relationship between the variables.

As the table shows, there are differences between the VAR(2) and the VAR-FPE model. These differences mainly emerge in the GDP equation. It is our impression that such differences are the result of imposing common lag lengths. For instance, the VAR-FPE model shows that infrastructure investment should be included with a lag length of five in the GDP equation. Imposing common lag lengths underfits the lag specification of infrastructure investment in that equation. In turn, this underfitting might explain why the GDP's own lags become significant in the VAR(2) model. Despite the fact that according to the likelihood ratio tests, only 2 lags should be included in the VAR(p) model, we also estimated a VAR(4) model (not shown). The results of the VAR(4) model more closely resemble those of the VAR-FPE model, strengthening our preference for the VAR-FPE model.

Still, regardless of the model, the combined coefficient of lagged machinery investment in the GDP equation is not significant, whereas the individual coefficients are. Looking at the individual coefficient estimates reveals that the first coefficient is significantly negative and the second significantly positive. Apparently, the two effects cancel out.

The effect of infrastructure investment on GDP is positive and significant at the one per cent level in the VAR-FPE model. Including only two lags of infrastructure investment lowers the significance level. However, at a 10 per

Table 7.2 *VAR(2) and VAR-FPE model*[a]

	GDP eq.				Machinery inv. eq.				Infra.inv. eq.			
	lags	χ^2	sum	χ^2	lags	χ^2	sum	χ^2	lags	χ^2	sum	χ^2
VAR(2) MODEL												
GDP	2	11.17**	0.42	10.46**	2	1.30	0.36	0.26	2	7.66*	−1.32	6.47*
Mach.inv.	2	12.28**	0.02	0.68	2	32.48**	0.53	20.39**	2	0.60	0.01	0.03
Infra.inv.	2	5.20†	0.05	4.74*	2	1.15	−0.13	1.14	2	56.09**	0.83	55.52**
R^2 (adj.)				0.99				0.86				0.67
VAR-FPE MODEL												
GDP	1	2.17	0.17	2.17	0				4	6.74	−0.59	0.95
Mach.inv.	2	14.31**	−0.01	0.12	2	24.95**	0.43	12.56**	0			
Infra.inv.	5	15.35**	0.09	13.32**	0				1	39.71**	0.67	39.71**
R^2 (adj.)				0.99				0.87				0.58

Sample: the Netherlands, 1853–1913.
[a] See main text for variable definitions.
† Significant at a 10 per cent level.
* Significant at a 5 per cent level.
** Significant at a 1 per cent level.

136

cent level the effect is still significant. So our main hypothesis is confirmed: infrastructure investment is a significant explicand of GDP.

According to the FPE criterion, besides infrastructure only GDP enters the infrastructure equation. The negative sign of GDP indicates that a rise in GDP lowers infrastructure investment. As GDP is included with four lags in the VAR-FPE model, there is at least a weak Granger-causal relationship from GDP to infrastructure investment. Neither individual GDP coefficients, nor their sum, are significant in the VAR-FPE model. Taking only two lags in the VAR(2) model raises the significance level considerably and makes the χ^2-statistics of the Granger-causality and the neutrality test significant at the 5 per cent level. Therefore, we have to conclude that there is feedback between infrastructure and GDP. It should be noted, however, that infrastructure positively Granger causes GDP whereas GDP negatively Granger causes infrastructure.[12]

The most striking fact from the investment in machinery equation is that no relationship seems to exist between investment in machinery and equipment, and infrastructural investment. This does not confirm the hypothesis that infrastructure positively influences GDP indirectly through machinery outlays. Also business cycles, as indicated by changes in GDP, do not influence investment decisions in machinery and equipment. Only machinery investments in previous years affect this year's investments.

To summarize, we find evidence of only three Granger-causal relationships in table 7.2: infrastructure positively Granger causes GDP, machinery investment neutrally Granger causes GDP, and GDP negatively Granger causes infrastructure.

Splitting up the infrastructure series into transport and 'other' infrastructural capital spending allows some further conclusions. As table 7.3 shows, this time the VAR(p) model includes 4 lags and therefore resembles the VAR model using the FPE criterion more closely. The effect of transport infrastructure on GDP is more significant than the effect of other infrastructure investments. Furthermore, a longer lag length is necessary to capture the effect of transport infrastructure compared to the other infrastructure. This might indicate a longer-lasting effect of the former on GDP. Mainly, transport infrastructure is negatively affected by GDP.

This time, investment in machinery and equipment is not solely explained by its own lags. Mostly, other infrastructural investment positively influenced machinery investment. Therefore, we find some evidence that other infrastructure investment might indirectly influence GDP through machinery investment.

As previously noted, the values of the coefficients cannot be interpreted as indicators of the size of the effects. Sims (1980) therefore proposed the 'impulse-response' analysis, which will be discussed in the next section.

Table 7.3 VAR(4) and VAR-FPE model using transport and other infrastructure[a]

	GDP eq.				Machinery inv. eq.				Other infra. eq.				Transport infra. eq.			
	lags	χ^2	sum	χ^2	lags	χ^2	sum	χ^2	lags	χ^2	sum	χ^2	lags	χ^2	sum	χ^2
VAR(4) MODEL																
GDP	4	4.78	0.14	0.65	4	9.12†	−0.71	0.56	4	6.27	−0.57	0.43	4	10.58*	−2.39	6.22*
Mach.inv.	4	18.06**	0.03	1.79	4	37.12**	0.34	6.47*	4	6.79	0.15	1.63	4	3.36	−0.19	2.15
Other infra.	4	8.21†	0.04	1.64	4	9.95*	0.35	4.71*	4	32.42**	0.66	17.47**	4	11.10*	0.38	5.76*
Transp.infra.	4	14.03**	0.06	11.73**	4	10.33*	−0.15	2.21	4	12.46*	0.15	2.65	4	35.13**	0.62	30.35**
R^2 (adj.)		0.99				0.88				0.52				0.63		
VAR-FPE MODEL																
GDP	1	0.49	0.08	0.49	3	7.62†	−1.10	1.52	0				2	4.64†	−0.79	1.43
Mach.inv.	2	13.41**	−0.02	0.86	2	26.06**	0.33	8.36**	0				0			
Other infra.	1	5.21*	0.05	5.21*	2	7.49*	0.41	7.19**	2	28.25**	0.72	28.19**	0			
Transp.infra.	5	12.43*	0.06	10.99**	0				0				1	49.74**	0.70	49.74**
R^2 (adj.)		0.99				0.89				0.48				0.59		

Sample: the Netherlands, 1853–1913.
[a] See main text for variable definitions.
† Significant at a 10 per cent level.
* Significant at a 5 per cent level.
** Significant at a 1 per cent level.

7.4.2 Impulse-response analysis

Sims (1980) proposed to analyze a VAR model by observing the reactions over time of different shocks on the estimated system. Just as an autoregression has a moving average representation, a VAR can be written as a Vector Moving Average (VMA). The VMA representation is an essential part of Sims' (1980) methodology in that it allows us to trace the time path of various shocks on the variables contained in the VAR system. To get the VMA of equation (7.1) we have to iterate it backwards to obtain:

$$x_t = b_0 + \sum_{j=0}^{\infty} B_j e_{t-j}, \tag{7.2}$$

where $x_t = (y_t, m_t, i_t)'$, b_0 is the matrix containing constants and a trend, B_j are matrices filled with parameters, and e_t is the vector of residuals. A necessary condition to make this conversion possible is that the series are stationary.[13] As section 7.3 has shown, this condition prevails.

Many equivalent representations exist for model (7.2): for any non-singular matrix G, B_j can be replaced by $B_j G$ and e by $G^{-1}e$. A particular version is obtained by choosing some normalization. Without the use of such a G-matrix, i.e. $B_0 = I$, each component of e_t is the error that results from the one-step forecast of the corresponding component of x_t. These are the *non-orthogonal innovations* in the components of x. They are non-orthogonal because, in general, the covariance matrix $\Sigma = E(e_t e_t')$ is not diagonal.

There are two principal advantages of orthogonalized innovations over non-orthogonal ones. First, because orthogonalized innovations are uncorrelated, it is very simple to compute the variances of their linear combinations. Second, and more importantly, it can be rather misleading to examine a shock to a single variable in isolation, when historically it has always moved together with other variables. Since the equations in the VAR contain only lagged values of the system's variables, any contemporaneous relations among the variables are reflected in the correlation of the residuals across equations. The cross-equation residual correlation is removed by orthogonalization.

If we choose matrix G so that $G^{-1}\Sigma G'^{-1} = I$, then the new innovations $\varepsilon_t = G^{-1}e_t$ satisfy $E(\varepsilon_t \varepsilon_t') = I$. These *orthogonalized innovations* have the convenient property of being uncorrelated both across time *and* across equations. Matrix G can be any solution of $GG' = \Sigma$. There are many such factorizations of the positive definite Σ matrix. We use those based on the Choleski factorization, where G is chosen to be lower triangular with positive elements on the diagonal (Graybill, 1969, p. 299).

The Choleski decomposition implies an ordering of the variables from the most pervasive—a shock to this variable affects all the others in the current period—to the least pervasive—a shock does not affect any other variable in the current period. In this manner some economic structure is imposed on the computation of the impulse-response functions. Unfortunately, there are many ways to order the variables, and, e.g. as noted by Cooley and LeRoy (1985) and Duggal et al. (1995), the choice of one particular ordering might not be innocuous.[14] The key point is that the factorization forces a potentially important asymmetry on the system. We have to decide which factorization is appropriate.

The importance of the ordering depends on the magnitude of the correlation coefficient between the e_{jt}'s. Where the estimated correlations are almost zero, the ordering is immaterial. However, if a correlation coefficient is almost unity then a single shock in the system contemporarily affects two variables. In that case, the usual procedure is first to obtain the impulse-response functions using a particular ordering. Subsequently, these results are compared to the impulse-response functions obtained by reversing the ordering of the two variables. If the implications are quite different, additional investigation into the relationships between the variables is necessary. Fortunately, the largest absolute correlation in our three-variable model, which is between total infrastructure and GDP, equals only 0.15, implying that the ordering of the variables is of minor importance.[15]

The ordering we will employ is *infrastructure, machinery, output*. Placing GDP last is consistent with the single-equation studies cited earlier. As in single-equation studies, the other variables in the model directly affect GDP. Thus, placement of GDP last facilitates comparison of our results to single-equation studies. Placing *infrastructure* first is based on the assumption that contemporaneous shocks to infrastructure investment stem mostly from government decisions, which we see as less endogenous than the other variables.

Orthogonalization allows us to rewrite equation (7.2) to the following VMA:

$$
\begin{pmatrix} y_t \\ m_t \\ i_t \end{pmatrix} = \begin{pmatrix} b_{10} \\ b_{20} \\ b_{30} \end{pmatrix} + \sum_{j=0}^{\infty} \begin{bmatrix} \Phi_{11}(j) & \Phi_{12}(j) & \Phi_{13}(j) \\ \Phi_{21}(j) & \Phi_{22}(j) & \Phi_{23}(j) \\ \Phi_{31}(j) & \Phi_{32}(j) & \Phi_{33}(j) \end{bmatrix} \begin{pmatrix} \varepsilon_{1,t-j} \\ \varepsilon_{2,t-j} \\ \varepsilon_{3,t-j} \end{pmatrix},
$$
(7.3)

where $\Phi_j = B_j G$ and $\varepsilon_t = G^{-1} e_t$. The coefficients $\Phi_{kl}(j)$ of Φ_j can be used to generate the effects of ε_{jt} shocks on the entire time paths of y_t, m_t and i_t. The four elements $\Phi_{kl}(0)$ are instantaneous impact multipliers. For example, the coefficient $\Phi_{13}(0)$ is the instantaneous impact of a one-unit change in ε_{3t} on y_t. The imposed ordering of the variables implies $\Phi_{21}(0) = \Phi_{31}(0) = \Phi_{32}(0) = 0$. In the same way, the element $\Phi_{13}(1)$ is the one period response of unit changes in ε_{3t} on y_{t+1}.

The nine sets of $\Phi_{kl}(j)$-coefficients are called the impulse-response func-

Figure 7.3 Impulse responses of the VAR(2) model[a]

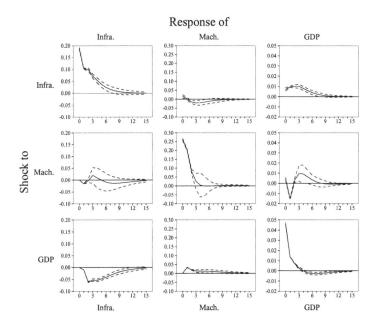

^aIncluding their 95 per cent confidence intervals.

tions. Plotting the impulse-response functions, i.e. plotting the coefficients of $\Phi_{kl}(j)$ against j, is a practical way to represent the behaviour of the series in response to the various shocks. In order to give an indication of statistical reliability, we report these responses along with a 95 per cent confidence interval, computed using a procedure developed by Giannini (1992). Giannini (1992) has developed a method to generate error bands for impulse responses based on asymptotic Gaussian approximations of the distribution of the responses.

Figures 7.3 and 7.4 display these impulse-response functions and their error bands for the estimated equations in table 7.2. In interpreting the graphs it may be helpful to remember that the variables are all in logarithms, so that in each case a 0.01 movement corresponds to a one per cent change. In addition, reading across any column, the scale on the vertical axis is the same for all of the shocks. These graphs allow several conclusions.

As the upper-right panel of both figures shows, the responses of the GDP-equation to a shock in infrastructure investment are highly significant. The size of the shock is such that it adds somewhat more than 18 per cent to infrastructure investments. The maximum response of GDP is somewhat above 1 per cent

Figure 7.4   Impulse responses of the VAR-FPE model[a]

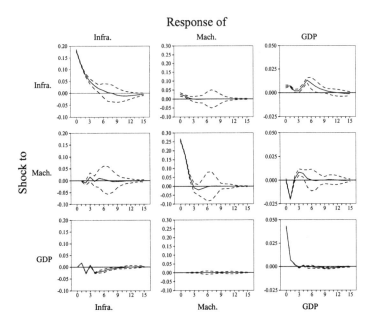

[a]Including their 95 per cent confidence intervals.

and is reached after three and five years in the VAR(2) and VAR-FPE model, respectively. This might be interpreted as evidence that it takes the system some time to adapt to changes in the infrastructural environment. The initial small positive effect in figure 7.4 may be caused by backward linkages, or direct impulses on the economy through the demand for labour, raw materials and other capital goods when infrastructural works are constructed. In this interpretation, the real effects of infrastructural investment on the economy, or the forward linkages, would pay off only in the medium term. Due to the inclusion of only two lags, the response of GDP in the VAR(2) model is already maximized after two years and does not show the two-peak feature. Apparently, the two effects displayed in figure 7.4 are encapsulated in one in figure 7.3.

Evidently, infrastructural investments cause changes in the economic system to which economic agents need time to adapt. Large technical systems, such as railways and the telephone networks, have other relationships with the rest of the economy. Externality effects of these large technical systems set in motion an incremental trajectory of technological and organizational improvements in other sectors of the economy. Before economic agents are able to join in on this trajectory, they need time to adapt both their behavioural strategies, and their durable physical assets.[16] In several studies, infrastructural improvements, especially railways, canals and port facilities, are shown to have had a gradual, but eventually no less profound, effect on the locus of, e.g. ship building, brewing and dairy industries in the Netherlands (Clement, 1994, pp. 204–206; Van der Knaap, 1978; Passchier and Knippenberg, 1978).

The responses of y_t to shocks in infrastructure and machinery, respectively, differ in three ways. First, a growth impulse of machinery investment dies out much faster than an infrastructure impulse. After six years, machinery investment ceases to be effective. It takes approximately eleven years before a shock in infrastructure investment dies out. Obviously, the economy adapts more easily to changes in machinery capital. Second, the point estimates of the responses of machinery investments are on average lower than those of infrastructure. As furthermore the size of the shock to the machinery and equipment equation is much larger (approximately 26 per cent) compared to the infrastructure equation (approximately 18 per cent), and since machinery investment exceeds infrastructure investment most of the time, this suggests that the aggregate effect of infrastructure investment on GDP in the period under study has been much larger. From this it is tempting to conclude that investing in infrastructure was a rational decision in the nineteenth century. Third, GDP decreases remarkably in the first period after a machinery shock. Apparently, the economy needs one period to adapt to the altered stock of machines.

As can be seen from the lower-left panel of especially figure 7.3, growth of GDP has on average a negative effect on investment in infrastructure. This again supports the view of infrastructure as a prerequisite for growth, and as a large technical system, characterized by indivisibilities. When, after heavy initial investment, a certain threshold in the level of infrastructure is attained, the economy starts to grow. By then, indivisibilities will have generated an overcapacity in infrastructural services. Infrastructural investment needs are thus much smaller and will taper off, whereas GDP can continue to grow.

These results fortify the previous Granger-causality results. Mainly infrastructure investment has a large effect on GDP and it takes some time for GDP to react to changes in infrastructure.

Figures 7.5 and 7.6 display the corresponding impulse responses where infrastructure investment is subdivided. The ordering employed here is *transport infrastructure, other infrastructure, machinery, output*. As might be expected from the causality analysis before, transport infrastructure causes a large rise in GDP and peaks after five years. The instantaneous impact of total infrastructure can largely be attributed to other infrastructure. Of course, this is exactly what was to be expected beforehand.

One of the important differences between the VAR(4) and VAR-FPE model

Figure 7.5   Impulse responses of the VAR(4) model using transport and other
infrastructure investment[a]

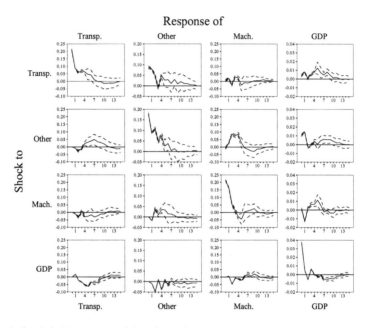

[a]Including their 95 per cent confidence intervals.

is that in the former, other infrastructure has a long-lasting positive effect on
transport infrastructure outlays. The response peaks after seven years. Apparently, investment in other infrastructure increases the need for transport
infrastructure over a long time. As the FPE criterion did not allow the other
infrastructure variable in the transport infrastructure equation, this effect is not
present in the VAR-FPE model.

As expected from table 7.3, machinery investment is largely influenced
by other infrastructure. Transport infrastructure, on the other hand, does not
significantly alter the course of machinery investment.

In the VAR-FPE model in which infrastructure investment is subdivided, the
largest absolute correlation of 0.35 is between GDP and other infrastructure
investment. Therefore, the relative ordering of GDP and other infrastructure
investment might have a significant effect on our results. However, interchang-
ing other infrastructure and GDP in the ordering hardly alters figure 7.6. Of
course, the instantaneous effect of other infrastructure on GDP disappears by
assumption. However, after one period, the responses are approximately the

Figure 7.6 Impulse responses of the VAR-FPE model using transport and other infrastructure[a]

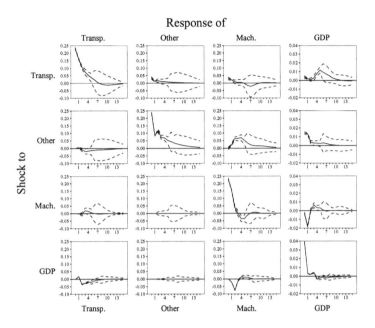

[a]Including their 95 per cent confidence intervals.

same as in figure 7.6. For the same reason, GDP now has a large positive instantaneous effect on other infrastructure investments. But again, the effects are similar after the first period.

7.4.3 Variance decomposition

In this subsection we will decompose the forecast error variance due to each one of the shocks. The forecast error variance decomposition tells us the proportion of the movements in a sequence due to its 'own' shocks versus shocks which may be ascribed to the other variables. If, for example, ε_{3t} shocks explain none of the forecast error variance of y_t at all forecast horizons, we can say that GDP is exogenous to infrastructure investment. In that case, y_t evolves independently of the ε_{3t} shocks and the i_t sequence. At the other extreme, ε_{3t} shocks could explain all the forecast error variance in y_t at all forecast horizons, so that GDP would be entirely endogenous. It is typical for a variable to explain almost all its forecast error variance at short horizons and smaller

Table 7.4   Forecast error variance decompositions[a]

EQUATION	INNOVATION	0	1	3	5	10	15
GDP	GDP	97.6	78.2	75.7	68.2	64.1	64.1
		(0.5)	(0.7)	(1.2)	(1.6)	(3.1)	(3.0)
	Mach.inv.	0.0	17.7	20.1	20.0	18.7	18.7
		(0.0)	(0.6)	(1.2)	(1.9)	(2.1)	(2.1)
	Infra.inv.	2.4	4.1	4.2	11.8	17.1	17.2
		(0.5)	(0.5)	(0.6)	(1.9)	(4.3)	(4.3)
Mach.inv.	GDP	0.0	0.0	0.0	0.0	0.0	0.0
		(0.0)	(0.0)	(0.0)	(0.0)	(0.0)	(0.0)
	Mach.inv.	99.1	99.1	99.1	99.1	99.1	99.1
		(0.3)	(0.3)	(0.3)	(0.3)	(0.4)	(0.4)
	Infra.inv.	0.9	0.9	0.9	0.9	0.9	0.9
		(0.3)	(0.3)	(0.3)	(0.3)	(0.4)	(0.4)
Infra.inv.	GDP	0.0	0.7	01.9	3.5	4.1	4.1
		(0.0)	(0.0)	(0.1)	(0.2)	(0.4)	(0.4)
	Mach.inv.	0.0	0.0	0.5	0.7	0.8	0.8
		(0.0)	(0.0)	(0.3)	(0.7)	(0.9)	(0.9)
	Infra.inv.	100.0	99.3	97.6	95.9	95.1	95.1
		(0.0)	(0.0)	(0.4)	(0.8)	(1.1)	(1.1)

Sample: the Netherlands, 1853–1913.
[a]The forecast error variance decompositions are in percentages of the VAR-FPE model. Standard errors are shown in parentheses.

proportions at longer horizons. We would expect this pattern if ε_{3t} shocks had little contemporaneous effect on y_t, but acted to affect y_t with a lag.

Note that the variance decomposition analysis contains the same problem inherent in impulse-response function analysis. In order to identify the ε_{jt}, it is necessary to impose some restrictions. The Choleski decomposition used in the previous subsection requires that all the one-period forecast error variance of i_t is due to ε_{3t}. If we use the reverse ordering, all the one-period forecast error variance of y_t would be due to ε_{1t}. The effects of these alternative assumptions are reduced at longer forecasting horizons. In practice, it is therefore useful to examine the variance decomposition at various forecast horizons. As the horizon is extended, the variance decompositions should converge.

To decompose the standard error of forecast we assume that the coefficients of the model are known, so the standard error of forecast is lower than the true uncertainty with estimated coefficients. We ignore this sampling error term, which depends upon the squares of the coefficients and becomes extremely complicated as the size of the model and the number of forecast steps increases. Instead, we concentrate upon those due to the effects of the innovations. Again we use the procedure suggested by Giannini (1992) to calculate standard errors.

Table 7.5   Forecast error variance decompositions using transport and other infrastructure[a]

EQUATION	INNOVATION	0	1	3	5	10	15
GDP	GDP	87.0	67.2	65.5	59.9	55.9	55.8
		(1.1)	(1.0)	(1.1)	(1.8)	(4.7)	(4.7)
	Mach.inv.	0.6	15.1	16.2	15.5	14.4	14.4
		(0.2)	(0.5)	(0.8)	(1.2)	(1.8)	(1.8)
	Other infra.	11.6	16.8	17.0	15.9	15.3	15.3
		(1.1)	(1.0)	(1.1)	(1.4)	(3.1)	(3.1)
	Transp.infra.	0.8	0.8	1.2	8.8	14.4	14.4
		(0.3)	(0.3)	(0.5)	(2.4)	(7.9)	(7.9)
Mach.inv.	GDP	0.0	0.6	6.3	6.1	6.0	6.0
		(0.0)	(0.0)	(0.3)	(0.3)	(0.6)	(0.6)
	Mach.inv.	98.3	97.1	83.2	77.4	74.9	74.6
		(0.5)	(0.5)	(1.4)	(2.5)	(6.3)	(6.9)
	Other infra.	0.0	0.6	8.9	15.1	16.8	17.2
		(0.0)	(0.1)	(1.5)	(2.9)	(5.7)	(6.3)
	Transp.infra.	1.7	1.8	1.6	1.5	2.2	2.3
		(0.5)	(0.5)	(0.4)	(0.4)	(3.2)	(3.2)
Other infra.	GDP	0.0	0.0	0.0	0.0	0.0	0.0
		(0.0)	(0.0)	(0.0)	(0.0)	(0.0)	(0.0)
	Mach.inv.	0.0	0.0	0.0	0.0	0.0	0.0
		(0.0)	(0.0)	(0.0)	(0.0)	(0.0)	(0.0)
	Other infra.	97.9	97.9	97.9	97.9	97.9	97.9
		(0.5)	(0.5)	(0.6)	(0.9)	(1.9)	(2.1)
	Transp.infra.	2.1	2.1	2.1	2.1	2.1	2.1
		(0.5)	(0.5)	(0.6)	(0.9)	(1.9)	(2.1)
Transp.infra.	GDP	0.0	0.4	2.2	2.8	2.9	2.9
		(0.0)	(0.0)	(0.2)	(0.4)	(0.5)	(0.5)
	Mach.inv.	0.0	0.0	0.4	0.6	0.6	0.6
		(0.0)	(0.0)	(0.3)	(0.7)	(0.8)	(0.8)
	Other infra.	0.0	0.0	0.5	0.9	1.3	1.4
		(0.0)	(0.0)	(0.4)	(0.9)	(3.5)	(4.1)
	Transp.infra.	100.0	99.6	97.0	95.7	95.1	95.1
		(0.0)	(0.0)	(1.1)	(2.5)	(6.3)	(7.5)

Sample: the Netherlands, 1853–1913.

[a]The forecast error variance decompositions are in percentages of the VAR-FPE model using infrastructure divided into transport and other infrastructure. Standard errors are shown in parentheses.

As the conclusions are virtually the same, we only present the results for the models in which the FPE criterion is used.

As can been seen in table 7.4, the forecast errors of infrastructure in our three-variable model and machinery investment both are mainly due to their own shocks. In the long-run, GDP shocks can explain only 4 per cent of the forecast error of infrastructure, whereas shocks in infrastructure investment capture hardly 1 per cent of the forecast error of machinery investment.

On the other hand, the decompositions of the GDP forecast error as tabulated in table 7.4 show that a comparatively large part is accounted for by machinery and infrastructure investment shocks. In the long run almost 40 per cent of the variance is explained by machinery and infrastructure investments shocks, both capturing approximately 18 per cent. Conspicuously, machinery investment shocks already explain a large part after the first period, whereas infrastructure only significantly starts to contribute to explaining the forecast error after five periods. Again, infrastructural investments take almost five periods to have an effect.

In table 7.5, the variance decomposition for our four-variable model shows that both types of infrastructure combined explain almost 30 per cent of the forecast errors of GDP. The differences of the effect of transport and other infrastructure investment on GDP are large. While other infrastructure shocks already reaches its maximum in explaining GDP variance after two years (17.3 per cent), transport infrastructure really starts to play a role in explaining GDP variance after only five years.

Both the forecast errors of other and of transport infrastructure are mainly explained by their own shocks. Only a minor 3 per cent of the forecast error of transport infrastructure is explained by movements in GDP. This time, however, the variance in machinery investment is for more than 17 per cent ultimately explained by shocks in other infrastructure investment, and around 6 per cent of its movements are due to shocks in GDP.

7.5 DISCUSSION

In this chapter we have exploited a new dataset covering the second half of the nineteenth century of the Netherlands. After having determined that our series are trend stationary, we have estimated several VAR models in levels. Using Granger-causality test and innovation accounting, we were able to give a firm quantitative and statistical basis to intuitive conclusions drawn earlier from the description of the infrastructural system in the Netherlands in the nineteenth century. From all models tested here, we conclude that infrastructural investments have positively influenced output in the Netherlands in the second half of the nineteenth century.

Splitting up infrastructure investment shows that both transport investment and other infrastructural projects as well, have contributed to the Dutch industrial revolution. Whereas transport infrastructure affects GDP after five years, other infrastructure seems to induce short-run demand effects. As transport infrastructure has a larger and longer-lasting effect on GDP, these infrastructure projects in particular seem to have induced, or at least enabled, the integration of markets which were regionally and functionally separated before.

Transport infrastructure does not significantly influence machinery investment. Only other infrastructure investments seem to be related to machinery investment. Therefore, the thesis that transport infrastructure positively influences GDP indirectly, through machinery outlays, is not confirmed.

GDP is the only variable in our model that has an effect on the level of infrastructure outlays. Investments in transport infrastructure are especially negatively affected by increases in GDP.

Of course, one has to be careful translating these findings from the past into policy recommendations. For instance, most of the investments in our dataset concern infrastructure which previously did not exist at all. The effect on the economy of expansion of an already existing infrastructure network— as is common nowadays—might differ from that of the development of a new network. However, this study has made it clear that different types of infrastructure can have different effects on the economy. As especially shocks in non-transport infrastructure investment have shown, aggregate demand impulses cannot be ruled out beforehand. Many macroeconomic studies concentrate solely on the productivity effects of additional infrastructure investment. Therefore, it is highly likely that these productivity effects tend to be overestimated.

NOTES

1. See, e.g. Hirschman (1958), Mera (1973), Blum (1982), Helms (1985), Eberts (1986), Nijkamp (1986), and Costa *et al.* (1987).
2. In the previous chapter this serves as a possible explanation why the exposed sector of the Dutch economy—which holds a significant part of the infrastructure stock—is less dependent upon the publicly provided part of that stock than is the sheltered sector, which hardly owns any infrastructure at all.
3. Other growth-retarding factors mentioned are the high and sticky real wages, the national government wrestling to pay off an enormous debt (Mokyr, 1976), and institutional rigidities on the local level squeezing entrepreneurial initiatives (Olson, 1982).
4. Data on machinery investment are available as from 1850. However, in order to exclude the outlying peak in infrastructural investment in 1852 caused by the reclamation of the 'Haarlemmermeer', our sample period starts in 1853.
5. Residential and non-residential investments of neither the public nor the private sector are captured in our dataset.
6. We also used the modifications to the Dickey–Fuller unit root tests as suggested by Phillips (1987) and Phillips and Perron (1988). The conclusions are virtually the same as compared to the ADF tests.
7. Time series over the nineteenth century for the United Kingdom prove to be trend stationary as well (Feinstein, 1972, 1988).
8. It is generally held that time series covering a longer time span are only stationary if one allows for one or more structural breaks in the series concerned (De Haan and Zelhorst, 1993; Zelhorst and De Haan, 1995; Crafts and Mills, 1997).
9. For an early overview of pros and cons of Granger causality, see Granger (1980).
10. The model in which total infrastructure investment is taken up will be described. By subdivid-

ing infrastructure the model can be expanded in a trivial way.

11. See, e.g. Hsiao (1981, 1982), Caines *et al.* (1981), Fackler (1985), Darrat (1988), Erenburg and Wohar (1995) or Sturm *et al.* (1995) for description and application of the procedure we followed.

12. Using post-World War II data, in Chapter 2, we have already reported a negative effect of production on public investment in the Netherlands in Chapter 2.

13. The VAR model needs to be stable in order to make the conversion. Formally, our VAR(p) model is stable if $\det[I_3 - A(1)z - \ldots - A(p)z^p] \neq 0$ for $|z| \leq 1$. A stable VAR(p) model is stationary (Lütkepohl, 1991, pp. 9–21). By calculating the the spectral radius of the supermatrix we find that all our VAR models are in fact stable (Schoonbeek, 1989).

14. In the case of k variables, there are $k!$ ways of ordering them.

15. Nevertheless, we changed the ordering in several ways. As expected, the outcomes stay roughly the same.

16. For an elaboration on this see, e.g. David (1985, 1990).

8. Conclusions

8.1 INTRODUCTION

The purpose of this book is twofold. In the first part, we test several hypotheses explaining the development of public capital spending in the OECD area, and the Netherlands in particular. The main question we try to answer in the first part is why public capital outlays decreased so dramatically after the early seventies. We analyze the effects of the decline in public capital outlays on the private sector of the economy in the second part. Can decreased public capital spending explain the productivity slowdown after the early seventies? To answer this question we have mainly focused on the Netherlands. However, some results for the United States (US) are also presented.

In recent years public investment has become an important topic in many OECD countries. Aschauer (1989a) initiated the scientific debate on the effect of public investment on the economy. He claimed that the decrease in public capital spending can explain the decline in productivity growth which occurred in the US after the early seventies. His results not only sparked scientific research into the impact of public sector capital spending on private sector output, but also attracted much attention outside the scientific world. Higher infrastructure spending soon formed a major part of President Clinton's economic plans. Of late, the issue of public investment has also been high on the political agenda in the European Union (EU). In the past few years, many important new infrastructure projects have been developed in Europe: the Channel Tunnel, the high speed rail network, new transAlpine basetunnels and EU-funded infrastructure projects in the poorest regions (financed from the Cohesion Fund). One cannot fail to notice that this new interest of European governments in infrastructure coincides with a further step towards integration, marked, e.g. by the completion of the internal market and the Maastricht treaty.

In this concluding chapter, we will summarize our findings and offer some discussion. Section 8.2 summarizes the results presented in the first part of this book concerning the development of public capital spending. Section 8.3 discusses the main conclusions of the second part, regarding the impact of public capital spending. Finally, the last section offers some general observations and suggestions for further research.

8.2 DEVELOPMENT

The first part of this book consists of two chapters. Using Dutch data, in Chapter 2 we test several hypotheses which have been put forward in the economic literature explaining dwindling public capital spending. In Chapter 3 we take a panel of 22 OECD countries to test various politico-institutional explanations.

Chapter 2 describes the development of Dutch public investment after World War II. Different investment categories are considered. In particular, public expenditure on infrastructure decreased considerably after the seventies. We have formulated several hypothesis which we test by applying so-called bivariate Granger-causality tests.

Our first hypothesis concerns the relationship between private and public investment. Both investment categories are related. In Chapter 3 we find a positive relationship; apparently, private and public investment are complements. For the Netherlands the direction of causation is clear: public investment positively influences private investment. Or to put it another way, the development of private investment does not help in explaining the development of public investment. The same goes for the production of the private sector. Like private investment, private production of (in particular) the (construction) sector is influenced by public investment (in infrastructure), there being hardly any evidence of reverse causation.

Demographic factors seem to have played an important role in explaining the development of public capital spending. The hypothesis that a declining rate of population growth caused the decrease in public investment is confirmed by the Dutch data. Also the expected growth in the number of schoolchildren positively affected public investment in school buildings. The future number of civil servants has positively influenced investment in public buildings. Finally, an increase in the number of cars leads to an increase in infrastructure spending (and not the other way around).

As often stated, an important reason for the decline in public investment might be that it is easier to cut back on public capital spending compared to other public expenditures as this would not directly hurt any particular interest group. Furthermore, the consequences will only become apparent in the long run. However, in Chapter 2 we do not find any relationship between budgetary problems of the government and public investment levels in the Netherlands. Neither the increased interest burden nor the rise in the public deficit crowded public investment out of the government budget.

In Chapter 3 we again test several hypotheses in order to explain the development of public capital spending. This time, however, we use a panel of 22 OECD countries covering the period 1980–92. As previous studies concerning the development of total public spending have shown that institutional and political factors are very important, we concentrate in Chapter 3 on politico-institutional determinants.

We do not find any support for most of the politico-institutional hypotheses. The hypothesis that politically weak governments, e.g. minority governments, more easily cut the public capital spending budget than do strong governments is not confirmed by our empirical results. Nor do we find any relationship between the political colour of the government and the development of public investment. Furthermore, the degree of government centralization does not influence the size of the public capital spending budget. The political business cycle hypothesis states that public spending, and therefore also public capital spending, increases in election years. No evidence supporting this hypothesis is found either. We find that governments with a short policy horizon more easily postpone public investment than do governments with a longer policy horizon.

In contrast to the findings in Chapter 2, Chapter 3 reports that during periods of fiscal contraction, governments cut relatively more from the public investment budget as compared to other spending categories. This confirms the hypothesis that in hard budget times public investment is a politically easier target than are other types of government spending.

As in Chapter 2, we find a positive relationship between private investment and public investment. However, this time the causal relationship seems to go in the opposite direction: private investment affects the size of the public capital spending budget.[1]

To summarize, we produce evidence that most politico-institutional hypotheses do not play an important role in explaining the development of public capital spending in the OECD in the eighties. Only the policy horizon of the government, periods of fiscal contraction, and private investment can provide a partial explanation of the decrease in public investment in the OECD area.

8.3 IMPACT

In the second part, we try to estimate empirically the effect of declining public capital spending on the private sector. The simple fact that public investment has declined in most OECD countries in itself is no evidence that public capital is currently undersupplied. Chapter 4 gives an extensive summary of the methods and techniques used so far to estimate these effects. We distinguish five different ways to derive the impact of public capital on a macroeconomic level. Each of these methods has its advantages and disadvantages. Chapters 5 to 7 expand three of these methods and apply them to the Dutch situation. In Chapter 5 we also present new results for the US.

The method which has been used most widely is called the production function approach. By adding the stock of public capital as an additional production

factor to a (Cobb–Douglas) production function, initially high output elasticities of public capital were found. However, nowadays most economists would
agree that this production function approach has several drawbacks. The most
important objections concerning this approach are (1) doubt as to the implied
causal ordering, (2) restrictions connected with the use of a Cobb–Douglas
functional form, and (3) the time-series properties of the data which upset the
interpretation of the outcomes.

Chapter 5, where we apply the production function approach to both US and
Dutch post-World War II data, concludes that in particular the last point renders
normal interpretation of the estimated coefficients impossible. As the time
series are both non-stationary and not cointegrated if the production function is
estimated in levels, we have to estimate it in first differences. Besides the fact
that the estimated coefficients no longer take economically meaningful values,
it is doubtful whether we are still estimating a long-run production function.
By using first differences, we implicitly assume that a change in the capital
stock affects the level of production in the same year.

A second approach is dubbed the behavioural approach. By looking at a
dual profit or cost function and deriving factor-demand or factor-share equations from it, this approach aims to model the economic behaviour of firms.
These studies usually take flexible functional forms to specify the profit or
cost function. In that way they assure that hardly any restrictions are placed on
the underlying production function. Therefore, at least one of the major objections raised by the production function approach is solved. However, several
problems remain. Problems concerning non-stationarity of the time series are
hardly considered in these studies. The issue of causality is also ignored. The
use of flexible functional forms, and therefore the estimation of a large number
of parameters, requires that the database contains a lot of information. For
this reason many of these studies use panel data. In general, such studies find
significant effects of public capital. However, these effects are almost always
smaller than those found in production function studies.

In Chapter 6 we apply the behavioural approach using a so-called symmetric
generalized McFadden cost function which we extend with public capital.
The model is estimated using post-World War II data for the economy of the
Netherlands. The results indicate that infrastructure has a significant effect on
cost and output of the private economy. A 10 per cent increase in infrastructure
on average decreases the cost of the private economy by 3 per cent. The effect
of infrastructure on the demand for labour and private capital is unclear.

Sectoral data reveal that there are great differences between the exposed
and sheltered sectors of the Dutch economy. Unlike the sheltered sector (trade,
banking, and other private market services), the exposed consists of branches
which compete on the foreign market (agriculture, manufacturing, and transport). A high rate of substitutability between the private production factors and

infrastructure in the sheltered sector leads to a large negative effect of infra-structure on the production cost of that sector. For the exposed sector these substitutability effects are considerably less and often outweighed by comple-mentary effects of one of the private production factors with infrastructure. This results in a statistically insignificant cost elasticity of public infrastructure in that sector. Therefore, the sheltered sector in particular has benefited from the stock of infrastructure.

A third way to analyze the impact of public investment on economic growth is by using Vector AutoRegression (VAR) models. This VAR approach en-forces hardly any restrictions on the data and in particular allows us to solve the causality issue. When the time-series properties are taken into account properly, this approach solves all three important objections raised by the pro-duction function approach. However, as no explicit production function is esti-mated, it is hard to guess at the output elasticity of public capital. So far only a few studies have used this approach; they have produced rather mixed results.

Chapter 7 presents our VAR study of the Dutch economy in the previous century. We use a new and unique database which is the outcome of research by participants in the project on '*The Reconstruction of Dutch National Accounts, and the Analysis of the Development of the Dutch Economy, 1800–1940*' con-ducted at the universities of Utrecht and Groningen. We estimate a VAR model using output, investment in machinery and equipment, and infrastructure in-vestment covering the period 1853–1913. The results of the Granger-causality tests show that an improvement in infrastructure had a positive effect on pro-duction. Because the time series for infrastructure are built up from the micro level, we can divide them into investment in transport infrastructure and other infrastructure investment. Both types of investment have positively affected the level of output.

Subsequently, we apply innovation analysis to the estimated models to see how output reacts particularly to a shock in infrastructure investment. After an initial demand effect, it takes a while before an improvement in infrastructure has a capacity effect on output. Splitting up infrastructure reveals that the short-run effect is mainly due to other infrastructure, whereas transport infrastructure is effective after five years. Apparently, it takes time for economic agents to adjust their behaviour.

The hypothesis that investment in infrastructure has been important for the output growth which took place at the end of the previous century has domi-nated historical descriptions. Chapter 7 presents for the first time quantitative results which support this hypothesis. However, the results only cover the short and medium run. As all time series used are (trend) stationary, we are not able to estimate long-run effects using VAR analysis. Subsequent research is needed to determine whether improvements in infrastructure resulted in a higher long-run growth path.

Chapter 4 discusses two other methods which, given their disadvantages, are not applied in the remaining chapters of this book. Some studies have tried to estimate the impact of public investment using cross-section growth regressions. The main objections against this approach are the biased estimation results when several variables are omitted and again, reverse causation. So far, hardly any conclusions based upon these cross-section growth regressions— especially if applied to a group of heterogeneous countries—are robust.

A final method which is discussed in Chapter 4 is to incorporate public capital in a structural model. The problem with this approach is that in studies implementing it, model builders simply impose an effect of public capital on productivity. The imposed production and substitution elasticities are crucial for the forecast results. Given the wide variability of these elasticities found in other studies, we are a long way from obtaining estimates which are sufficiently precise to enable us to plug in values for new infrastructure stock and other variables in a structural model and to obtain reliable estimates of future economic benefits.

In the second part of this book we conclude that public capital probably stimulates economic growth, but that we are still unsure about the size of this effect. Given the large number of studies in this area this is a rather disappointing conclusion.

8.4 DISCUSSION

Infrastructure issues have moved to the top of the policy agenda in many OECD countries. Whether this trend will actually lead to higher spending levels remains to be seen. Indeed, as we show in Chapter 3, there is evidence that public capital spending is a relatively easy target during periods of fiscal contraction. As many countries still have to redress their public finances, the lip-service many politicians pay in favour of higher public investment should be interpreted with some scepticism.

At the end of this book, a word of caution pertains to extrapolating its findings into the future. Even if infrastructure has been productive in the past— which is what our results, reported in Chapters 6 and 7, suggest—this does not imply that future investment will also be productive. Economic advantages associated with future infrastructure may be different from those of the past. For instance, it could be very beneficial to build a network of motorways, while expanding this network may yield substantially fewer additional benefits. Simply looking at patterns in the past may tell very little about future effects of public investment.

The enthusiasm among policymakers for higher infrastructure spending has been matched, if not surpassed, by scepticism on the part of many economists

(Munnell, 1993). This book only adds to this scepticism by showing that the methodology of the early production function studies is flawed, and that it is hard to get precise estimates of the productivity effect of public capital spending.

As it is still unclear to what extent additional public investments affect the private economy, decisions concerning public investment should not be motivated by alleged growth-stimulating effects of public investment. Therefore, the aggregated regression results presented in the second part of this book cannot be used to guide future investments. Possibly, cost-benefit analysis can generate more reliable estimates of the net benefits of specific infrastructure projects or may be helpful to determine which among a variety of possible investments should be undertaken.

Most macroeconomic studies, including this one, concentrate on the alleged productivity effects of public capital spending. However, as the VAR results presented in Chapter 7 suggest, public capital spending might also induce other effects, such as spillovers and short-run effects. This might be one of the reasons why production function studies using macro data come up with rather disappointing results; they concentrate on the capacity effects of improvements in public infrastructure, without taking into account these other effects.

Infrastructure does not only affect the economy within a single region as is assumed in the approaches applied in this book. Interregional effects are probably also very important. In terms of the production function approach, an increase in infrastructure will lead to higher output levels, which implies a generative growth effect in the regions concerned. Maybe, by looking at a geographically smaller area, it is possible to get—besides insights into these additional effects—better estimates of the productivity effect of public capital.

NOTES

1. The differences between the results in Chapter 2 versus Chapter 3 might stem from both the sample period and the countries under consideration. Whereas Chapter 2 concentrates on the Netherlands between 1953 and 1990, Chapter 3 looks at almost the entire OECD over a much shorter time period, i.e. 1980–92. Without further investigation, it is difficult to pinpoint the exact reasons for the diverging outcomes.

A. Stationarity

A.1 INTRODUCTION

Important differences lie between stationary and non-stationary time series.[1] Unlike non-stationary series, (trend) *stationary* series fluctuate around a constant long-run mean (trend) and have a finite variance which is time-invariant.[2]

The assumptions of the classical regression model often necessitate that the regression variables are (trend) stationary. In the presence of non-stationary variables, there might be what Granger and Newbold (1974) call a *spurious regression*. A spurious regression has a high R^2, t-statistic that appears to be significant, but the results are without any economic meaning. The regression output 'looks good' because the least-squares estimates are not consistent and the customary tests of statistical inference do not hold.

To determine whether the series are stationary, we use four different testing procedures in this book: the augmented Dickey–Fuller (ADF) test, a test developed by Harris (1992), which we will call the bootstrapped unit root (BUR) test, a test developed by Kwiatkowski *et al.* (1992) and one by Leybourne and McCabe (1994). The latter two have stationarity as their null hypothesis. This chapter briefly discusses the main ideas behind these tests.

In both the ADF and the BUR tests non-stationarity is the null hypothesis. The way in which these tests are carried out ensures that the null hypothesis is accepted unless there is strong evidence against it. Several studies have argued that these tests have little power to discriminate between a *unit root*, i.e. a non-stationary process, and a near unit root process. Equivalently, most time series are not very informative about whether or not there is a unit root (DeJong *et al.* 1989; Diebold and Rudebusch, 1991). Several authors have shown that the ADF test tends to reject the non-stationary hypothesis far too often, when the series have large moving average processes (Molinas, 1986). The Kwiatkowski *et al.* (1992) and Leybourne and McCabe (1994) tests include, besides autoregressive processes as in the ADF and BUR tests, also a first-order moving average process. Because macroeconomic series with fairly large, positive first-order moving average components seem to be a common feature, and because the null and alternative hypothesis are switched, these new tests might be good supplements especially to the ADF and BUR tests.

Figure A.1   The ADF testing strategy of Dolado et al.[a]

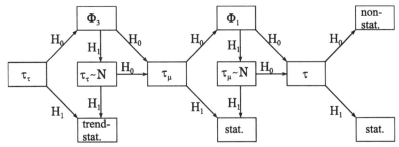

[a]N stands for the normal distribution. All other abbreviations and variables are described in the text.

A.2   AUGMENTED DICKEY–FULLER TEST

The test which we apply to all our time series is the augmented Dickey–Fuller (ADF) test developed by Dickey and Fuller (1979, 1981). They consider three different regression equations that can be used to test for the presence of a unit root:

$$\Delta x_t \;=\; \eta_0 + \eta_1 t + \eta_2 x_{t-1} + \sum_{i=1}^{p} \eta_{2+i} \Delta x_{t-i} + \varepsilon_t, \qquad (A.1)$$

$$\Delta x_t \;=\; \eta_0 + \eta_2 x_{t-1} + \sum_{i=1}^{p} \eta_{2+i} \Delta x_{t-i} + \varepsilon_t, \qquad (A.2)$$

$$\Delta x_t \;=\; \eta_2 x_{t-1} + \sum_{i=1}^{p} \eta_{2+i} \Delta x_{t-i} + \varepsilon_t. \qquad (A.3)$$

where x_t is the series being tested, t represents the trend variable, p is the number of lags included, and ε_t is an independent identically distributed residual term.

The difference between the three regressions concerns the presence of the deterministic elements η_0 and $\eta_1 t$. The first equation includes both an intercept (or drift term) and a linear time trend. In this equation, rejecting the null hypothesis of a unit root, i.e. when η_2 is significantly smaller than zero, implies that x_t is trend stationary. In the other two equations this would mean that x_t is stationary (around a drift term).

The testing strategy we follow is based on Dolado *et al.* (1990) and is outlined in figure A.1.

In the first step we estimate equation (A.1) using ordinary least squares. The test is implemented through the usual t-statistic of $\hat{\eta}_2$, denoted as τ_τ. Under the null hypothesis τ_τ will not follow the standard t-distribution; adjusted critical values are computed by MacKinnon (1991). If τ_τ is significantly negative, the null of non-stationarity is rejected, and the series are trend stationary. In this case there is no need to proceed any further.

However, if τ_τ is insignificant, we test the joint null hypothesis that $\eta_1 = \eta_2 = 0$ using the F-statistic denoted as Φ_3, and using the relevant critical values from Dickey and Fuller (1981). If Φ_3 is significant, we again test for a unit root now using the critical values of the standard t-distribution.

If η_1 and η_2 are jointly insignificant in the maintained model, we set $\eta_1 \equiv 0$ and estimate equation (A.2). Again we test for the unit root, now denoting the t-statistic of $\hat{\eta}_2$ as τ_μ and using the relevant critical values from MacKinnon (1991). If the null hypothesis is rejected, again there is no need to proceed any further.

If it is not rejected, the joint null hypothesis $\eta_0 = \eta_2 = 0$ with use of the F-statistic, denoted as Φ_1, is tested, employing the critical values reported by Dickey and Fuller (1981). Again, if it is significant, we test for a unit root using the standardized normal distribution.

If η_0 and η_2 are jointly insignificant, we remove the constant from the testing equation as well ($\eta_0 \equiv \eta_1 \equiv 0$) and estimate equation (A.3). The new t-statistic is called τ. Again for this t-statistic MacKinnon (1991) reports relevant critical values. The last step is to examine whether the null hypothesis is rejected or not, i.e. whether the series are stationary or not.

The number of lags used in the estimated equations, were determined in a similar way as applied by Perron (1989). We start with a fixed number of lags. If the last lag is insignificant at a 10 per cent level (using the standard normal distribution), it is omitted. Now we include one lag less. Again it is tested whether the last lag is significant or not. This procedure is repeated until the last lag is significant (or there are no lags left, in which case the test is called the Dickey–Fuller (DF) test). We took this high significance level because, as Perron (1989, p. 1384) pointed out:[3]

"...including too many extra regressors of lagged first-differences does not affect the size of the test but only decreases its power. Including too few lags may have a substantial effect on the size of the test."

A.3   BOOTSTRAPPED UNIT ROOT TEST

The reason why the ADF test alone cannot entirely serve our purposes is easily explained. As Harris (1992, p. 616) noticed:

"When only a small sample size is available there is a concern with the *a priori* size of the (ADF test). Given this problem a restricted version of (equations (A.1) to (A.3)) can be estimated for each of the variables under consideration and then bootstrapped. On the basis of Monte–Carlo replications, it is possible to compute the size of the test."

By bootstrapping the ADF test, this new test is in effect undertaking the same type of Monte–Carlo work that generated the tables of critical values, but now calculates critical values relevant to our own specific dataset. We refer to Harris (1992) for a formal description of the bootstrapping technique.

A.4   KWIATKOWSKI *et al.* TEST

Kwiatkowski *et al.* (1992) provide a straightforward test of the null hypothesis of stationarity against the alternative of a unit root. They use a parameterization which provides a plausible representation of both stationary and non-stationary variables and which leads to a test of the hypothesis of stationarity.

Specifically, they choose a components representation in which the time series under study is written as the sum of two (three) parts: (a deterministic trend), a random walk, and a stationary residual. The null hypothesis of (trend) stationarity corresponds to the hypothesis that the variance of the random walk equals zero. Kwiatkowski *et al.* (1992) show that this hypothesis can be tested in the following way:

- Calculate the residuals from the least squares regression of x_t on an intercept (and time trend). Denote these residuals $\hat{\varepsilon}_t$.
- Define the partial sum process of the residuals:

$$S_t = \sum_{i=1}^{t} \hat{\varepsilon}_i, t = 1, \ldots, T, \tag{A.4}$$

where T is the number of observations.

- Construct a consistent estimator of what Kwiatkowski *et al.* (1992) call the 'long-run variance':

$$s^2(l) = \frac{1}{T} \sum_{t=1}^{T} \hat{\varepsilon}_t^2 + \frac{2}{T} \sum_{i=1}^{l} \left(w(i,l) \sum_{t=i}^{T} \hat{\varepsilon}_t^2 \hat{\varepsilon}_{t-i}^2 \right), \tag{A.5}$$

where $w(i,l)$ is the Barlett window $w(i,l) = 1 - s/(l+1)$ as in Newey and West (1987). The autocorrelation lag truncation number l is set by the researcher and captures possible error autocorrelation.

- Finally, construct the following statistic:

$$\hat{\eta} = \frac{\sum_{t=1}^{T} S_t^2}{s^2(l)}. \tag{A.6}$$

Kwiatkowski *et al.* (1992) derive the asymptotic distribution of this statistics under general conditions on the stationary error. Furthermore, the asymptotic distribution is valid under the null hypothesis as well as under the alternative that the series is non-stationary.

A.5 LEYBOURNE AND MCCABE TEST

The last test we use has recently been suggested by Leybourne and McCabe (1994). Once more, this test has stationarity as its null hypothesis. Despite the fact that it is derived along similar lines as the test of Kwiatkowski *et al.* (1992), there is one important difference between the two: they differ in their treatment of autocorrelation. The test of Kwiatkowski *et al.* (1992) depends on an autocorrelation lag truncation number l. Unfortunately, the value of that statistic can be very sensitive to the value l and hence also the test inference. In contrast, the value of the Leybourne and McCabe (1994) statistic is not heavily influenced by choosing too many lags to correct for potential autocorrelation, and therefore tends to be more robust.

The model behind this last test assumes that the variable x_t can be split into three (four) parts: (a part described by a trend,) an autoregressive part, a stationary residual, and a random walk process. If the variance of the last part equals zero, x_t is (trend) stationary. Leybourne and McCabe (1994) show that this hypothesis can be tested in the following way:

- Estimate the following ARIMA$(p,1,1)$ model with maximum likelihood:

$$\Delta x_t = (\beta +) \sum_{i=1}^{p} \phi_i \Delta x_{t-i} + \zeta_t - \theta \zeta_{t-1}, \tag{A.7}$$

where ζ_t is normally distributed with mean zero and variance σ^2/θ.
- Use the estimated coefficients ϕ_i^* to construct the series x_t^*:

$$x_t^* = x_t - \sum_{i=1}^{p} \phi_i^* x_{t-i}. \tag{A.8}$$

- Calculate the residuals from the least squares regression of x_t^* on an intercept (and time trend). Denote these $\hat{\varepsilon}_t$.
- Construct the following statistic:

$$\hat{s} = \frac{1}{T} \frac{\hat{\varepsilon}' V \hat{\varepsilon}}{\hat{\varepsilon}' \hat{\varepsilon}}, \tag{A.9}$$

where $[V]_{ij} \equiv \min[i, j]$ and T is the number of observations.

Kwiatkowski *et al.* (1992) tabulated the asymptotic critical values of this statistic.

NOTES

1. For an introduction into the concept of stationarity we refer to Enders (1995).
2. Formally, a time series x_t having a finite mean and variance is *covariance* stationary if, for all t, i and j, $E(x_t) = E(x_i)$, $Var(x_t) = Var(x_i)$ and $Cov(x_t, x_i) = Cov(x_{t-j}, x_{i-j})$. A so-called *strongly* stationary process need not have a finite mean and/or variance. As we only consider covariance stationary series in this book, there is no ambiguity in using the term stationary.
3. Furthermore, Molinas (1986, p. 281) noticed that "...a rather large number of lags has to be taken in (the ADF test) in order to capture the essential dynamics of the residuals."

Bibliography

Aaron, H.J. (1990), 'Why is infrastructure important? Discussion', in A.H. Munnell (ed.), *Is there a shortfall in public capital investment?*, Vol. 34 of *Conference Series*, Boston: Federal Reserve Bank of Boston, pp. 51–63.

Ahking, F.W. and S.M. Miller (1985), 'The relationship between government deficits, money growth and inflation', *Journal of Macroeconomics*, 7(4), 447–467.

Ai, C. and S.P. Cassou (1995), 'A normative analysis of public capital', *Applied Economics*, **27**, 1201–1209.

Akaike, H. (1969), 'Fitting autoregressive models for prediction', *Annals of the Institute of Statistical Mathematics*, **21**, 243–247.

Akaike, H. (1970), 'Statistical predictor identification', *Annals of the Institute of Statistical Mathematics*, **22**, 203–217.

Allen, C. (1997), 'A survey of flexible functional forms applied to production analysis', in C. Allen and S. Hall (eds), *Macroeconomic modelling in a changing world: towards a common approach*, Wiley Series in Financial Economics and Quantitative Analysis, Chichester: Wiley, Chapter 1, pp. 17–40.

Arrow, K.J. and M. Kurz (1970), *Public investment, the rate of return and optimal fiscal policy*, Baltimore: Johns Hopkins University Press.

Aschauer, D.A. (1989a), 'Is public expenditure productive?', *Journal of Monetary Economics*, **23**, 177–200.

Aschauer, D.A. (1989b), 'Does public capital crowd out private capital?', *Journal of Monetary Economics*, **24**, 171–188.

Aschauer, D.A. (1989c), 'Public investment and productivity growth in the Group of Seven', *Economic Perspective*, **13**, 17–25.

Aschauer, D.A. (1990), 'Why is infrastructure important?', in A.H. Munnell (ed.), *Is there a shortfall in public capital investment?*, Vol. 34 of *Conference Series*, Boston: Federal Reserve Bank of Boston, pp. 21–50.

Aubin, C., J.-P. Berdot, D. Goyeau and J.-D. Lafay (1988), 'The growth of public expenditure in France', in J.A. Lybeck and M. Henrekson (eds), *Explaining the growth of government*, Amsterdam: Elsevier Science Publishers B.V., North-Holland, Chapter 10, pp. 201–230.

Bajo-Rubio, O. and S. Sosvilla-Rivero (1993), 'Does public capital affect private sector performance? An analysis of the Spanish case, 1964–88', *Economic Modelling*, **10**(3), 179–184.

Baltagi, B.H. and N. Pinnoi (1995), 'Public capital stock and state productivity growth: further evidence from an error components model', *Empirical Economics*, **20**(2), 351–359.

Banerjee, A., J.J. Dolado, J.W. Galbraith and D.F. Hendry (1993), *Co-integration, error-correction, and the econometric analysis of non-stationary data*, New York: Oxford University Press.

Barro, R.J. (1989), 'A cross-country study of growth, saving, and government', NBER Working Paper 2855, Cambridge: National Bureau of Economic Research.

Barro, R.J. (1990), 'Government spending in a simple model of endogenous growth', *Journal of Political Economy*, **98**(5), S103–S125.

Barro, R.J. (1991), 'Economic growth in a cross section of countries', *Quarterly Journal of Economics*, **106**, 407–443.

Barro, R.J. and J.-W. Lee (1994), 'Sources of economic growth', *Carnegie-Rochester Conference Series on Public Policy*, **40**, 1–46.

Barro, R.J. and S. Wolf (1989), 'Data appendix for economic growth in a cross-section of countries', unpublished manuscript.

Barro, R.J. and X. Sala-I-Martin (1992), 'Public finance in models of economic growth', *Review of Economic Studies*, **59**(201), 645–661.

Baumol, W.J. (1967), 'Macroeconomics of unbalanced growth: the anatomy of urban crisis', *American Economic Review*, **57**, 415–426.

Baumol, W.J. (1986), 'Productivity growth, convergence and welfare: what the long-run data show', *American Economic Review*, **76**, 1072–1085.

Berg, M. van den and J.-E. Sturm (1997), 'The empirical relevance of the location factors modelled by Krugman', SOM Research Report No. 97C01, Groningen: SOM.

Berndt, E.R. and B. Hansson (1991), 'Measuring the contribution of public infrastructure capital in Sweden', NBER Working Paper 3842, Cambridge: National Bureau of Economic Research.

Bijl, M. (1983), 'Infrastructuur en economisch herstel', *Economisch Statistische Berichten*, **68**, 928–931.

Blanchard, P. (1992), 'Software review', in L. Mátyás and P. Sevestre (eds), *The econometrics of panel data. Handbook of theory and applications*, Dordrecht: Kluwer Academic Publishers, Chapter 22, pp. 521–546.

Blum, U. (1982), 'Effects of transportation investments on regional growth', *Papers of the Regional Science Association*, **53**, 151–168.

Boarnet, M.G. (1997), 'Infrastructure and the productivity of public capital: the case of streets and highways', *National Tax Journal*, **50**(1), 39–58.

Boorsma, P.B., J.H.M. Donders, M. Meeles and P. de Vries (1987), 'Economische infrastructuur', *Economisch Statistische Berichten*, **72**, 300–304.

Boot, P.A. (1986), 'Overheidsinvesteringen en structuurbeleid. Van terugploegen naar vooruitzien?', *Openbare Uitgaven*, **18**(4), 149–159.

Broer, D.P. and W.J. Jansen (1989), 'Employment, schooling and productivity growth', *De Economist*, **137**(4), 425–453.

Buiter, W.H. (1977), '"Crowding out" and the effectiveness of fiscal policy', *Journal of Public Economics*, **7**, 309–328.

Caines, P.E., K.C.W. Keng and S.P. Sethi (1981), 'Causality analysis and multivariate autoregressive modelling with an application to supermarket sales analysis', *Journal of Economic Dynamics and Control*, **3**, 267–298.

Cameron, D.R. (1978), 'The expansion of the public economy: a comparative analysis', *American Political Science Review*, **72**, 1243–1261.

Cameron, D.R. (1985), 'Does government cause inflation? Taxes, spending and deficits', in L. Lindberg and C. Maier (eds), *The politics of inflation and economic stagnation*, Washington, D.C.: Brookings Institution, Chapter 9, pp. 224–279.

Canova, F. (1995), 'The economics of VAR models', in K.D. Hoover (ed.), *Macroeconometrics: developments, tensions and prospects*, Dordrecht: Kluwer Academic Publishers, Chapter 3, pp. 57–97.

Caves, D.W., L.R. Christensen and W.E. Diewert (1982), 'The economic theory of index numbers and the measurement of input, output, and productivity', *Econometrica*, **50**(6), 1393–1414.

Clarida, R.H. (1993), 'International capital mobility, public investment and economic growth', NBER Working Paper 4506, Cambridge: National Bureau of Economic Research.

Clement, M. (1994), 'Transport en economische ontwikkeling: analyse van de modernisering van het transportsysteem in de provincie Groningen (1800–1914)', Ph.D. dissertation, Groningen: University of Groningen.

Coelli, T.J. (1996), 'Measurement of total factor productivity growth and biases in technological change in Western Australian agriculture', *Journal of Applied Econometrics*, **11**, 77–91.

Conrad, K. and H. Seitz (1992), 'The "public capital hypothesis": the case of Germany', *Recherches Economiques de Louvain*, **58**(3–4), 309–327.

Conrad, K. and H. Seitz (1994), 'The economic benefits of public infrastructure', *Applied Economics*, **26**, 303–311.

Cooley, T.F. and S.F. LeRoy (1985), 'Atheoretical macroeconometrics: a critique', *Journal of Monetary Economics*, **16**, 283–308.

Costa, J. da Silva, R.W. Ellson and R.C. Martin (1987), 'Public capital, regional output, and developments: some empirical evidence', *Journal of Regional Science*, **27**(3), 419–437.

CPB Netherlands Bureau for Economic Policy Analysis (1985), 'Het beleid inzake (overheids-)investeringen. Brief van de minister van EZ. Bijlage 1:

overheidsinvesteringen in samenhang met de economie. Bijlage 2: nadere beschouwing van de overheidsinvesteringen in de GWW-sector in samenhang met de economie', *Tweede Kamer*, **18869**(1), 15–24.

Crafts, N.F.R. and T.C. Mills (1997), 'Europe's golden age: an econometric investigation of changing trend rates of growth', in B. van Ark and N.F.R. Crafts (eds), *Quantitative aspects of post-war European economic growth*, Cambridge: Cambridge University Press, Chapter 11.

Crihfield, J.B. and M.P.H. Panggabean (1995), 'Is public infrastructure productive? A metropolitan perspective using new capital stock estimates', *Regional Science and Urban Economics*, **25**, 607–630.

Dalamagas, B. (1995), 'A reconsideration of the public sector's contribution to growth', *Empirical Economics*, **20**(3), 385–414.

Dalen, H.P. van and O.H. Swank (1996), 'Government spending cycles: ideological or opportunistic?', *Public Choice*, **89**, 183–200.

Darrat, A.F. (1988), 'Have large budget deficits caused rising trade deficits?', *Southern Economic Journal*, **54**(4), 879–887.

David, P.A. (1985), 'Clio and the economics of QWERTY', *American Economic Review*, **75**, 332–337.

David, P.A. (1990), 'The dynamo and the computer: an historical perspective on the modern productivity paradox', *American Economic Review*, **80**, 355–361.

Davidson, R. and J.G. MacKinnon (1993), *Estimation and inference in econometrics*, Oxford: Oxford University Press.

DeJong, D.N., J.C. Nankervis, N.E. Savin and C.H. Whiteman (1989), 'Integration versus trend stationarity in macroeconomic time series', Working Paper 89–99, Iowa City: University of Iowa, Department of Economics.

Deno, K.T. (1988), 'The effect of public capital on U.S. manufacturing activity: 1970 to 1978', *Southern Economic Journal*, **55**(1), 400–411.

Denton, F.T. (1978), 'Single equation estimators and aggregation restrictions when equations have the same set of regressors', *Journal of Econometrics*, **8**, 173–179.

Devarajan, S., V. Swaroop and H. Zou (1996), 'The composition of public expenditure and economic growth', *Journal of Monetary Economics*, **37**, 313–344.

Dickey, D.A. and W.A. Fuller (1979), 'Distribution of the estimates for autoregressive time series with a unit root', *Journal of the American Statistical Association*, **74**, 427–431.

Dickey, D.A. and W.A. Fuller (1981), 'Likelihood ratio statistics for autoregressive time series with a unit root', *Econometrica*, **49**(4), 1057–1072.

Diebold, F.X. and G.D. Rudebusch (1991), 'On the power of Dickey-Fuller tests against fractional alternatives', *Economics Letters*, **35**, 155–160.

Diewert, W.E. (1974), 'Applications of duality theory', in M.D. Intriligator and D.A. Kendrick (eds), *Frontiers of quantitative economics. Volume II*, Amsterdam: Elsevier Science Publishers B.V., North-Holland, pp. 106–120.

Diewert, W.E. (1976), 'Exact and superlative index numbers', *Journal of Econometrics*, **4**(4), 115–145.

Diewert, W.E. and T.J. Wales (1987), 'Flexible functional forms and global curvature conditions', *Econometrica*, **55**(1), 43–68.

Diewert, W.E. and T.J. Wales (1995), 'Flexible functional forms and tests of homogeneous separability', *Journal of Econometrics*, **67**(2), 259–302.

Dolado, J.J., T. Jenkinson and S. Sosvilla-Rivero (1990), 'Cointegration and unit roots', *Journal of Economic Surveys*, **4**(3), 249–273.

Dowrick, S. (1992), 'Technological catch up and diverging incomes: patterns of economic growth 1960–88', *The Economic Journal*, **102**, 600–610.

Draper, N. and T. Manders (1996a), 'Structural changes in the demand for labor', CPB Research Memorandum 128, The Hague: CPB Netherlands Bureau for Economic Policy Analysis.

Draper, N. and T. Manders (1996b), 'Why did the demand for Dutch low-skilled workers decline?', *CPB Report, Quarterly Review of CPB Netherlands Bureau for Economic Policy Analysis*, **1**, 29–32.

Duggal, V.G., C. Saltzman and L.R. Klein (1995), 'Infrastructure and productivity: a nonlinear approach', paper presented at the 7th World Congress of the Econometric Society in Tokyo, Japan, 22–29 August.

Easterly, W. and S. Rebelo (1993), 'Fiscal policy and economic growth', *Journal of Monetary Economics*, **32**, 417–458.

Eberts, R.W. (1986), 'Estimating the contribution of urban public infrastructure to regional growth', Working Paper 8610, Cleveland: Federal Reserve Bank of Cleveland.

Eberts, R.W. (1990), 'Cross-sectional analysis of public infrastructure and regional productivity growth', Working Paper 9004: Federal Reserve Bank of Cleveland.

Edin, P. and H. Ohlsson (1991), 'Political determinants of budget deficits: coalition effects versus minority effects', *European Economic Review*, **35**(8), 1597–1603.

Eisner, R. (1991), 'Infrastructure and regional economic performance: comment', *New England Economic Review*, pp. 47–58.

Eisner, R. (1994), 'Real government saving and the future', *Journal of Economic Behavior and Organization*, **23**(2), 111–126.

Enders, W. (1995), *Applied econometric time series*, Wiley Series in Probability and Mathematical Statistics, New York: Wiley.

Engle, R.F. and C.W.J. Granger (1987), 'Co-integration and error correction: representation, estimation, and testing', *Econometrica*, **55**(2), 251–276.

Erenburg, S.J. (1993), 'The real effects of public investment on private investment', *Applied Economics*, **25**, 831–837.

Erenburg, S.J. and M.E. Wohar (1995), 'Public and private investment. Are there causal linkages?', *Journal of Macroeconomics*, **17**(1), 1–30.

Evans, P. and G. Karras (1994a), 'Are government activities productive? Evidence from a panel of U.S. states', *Review of Economics and Statistics*, **76**(1), 1–11.

Evans, P. and G. Karras (1994b), 'Is government capital productive? Evidence from a panel of seven countries', *Journal of Macroeconomics*, **16**(2), 271–279.

Fackler, J.S. (1985), 'An empirical analysis of the market for goods, money, and credit', *Journal of Money, Credit, and Banking*, **17**(1), 28–42.

Feinstein, C.H. (1968), *Domestic capital formation in the United Kingdom, 1920–1936*, Cambridge: Cambridge University Press.

Feinstein, C.H. (1972), *National income, expenditure, and output of the United Kingdom, 1855–1965*, Cambridge: Cambridge University Press.

Feinstein, C.H. (1988), 'National statistics, 1760–1920, sources and methods of estimation for domestic reproducible fixed assets and work in progress, overseas assets, and land', in C.H. Feinstein and S. Pollard (eds), *Studies in capital formation in the United Kingdom, 1750–1920*, Oxford: Clarendon Press, pp. 258–471.

Field, A.J. (1992), 'The magnetic telegraph, price and quantity data, and the management of capital', *Journal of Economic History*, **52**(2), 401–413.

Finn, M. (1993), 'Is all government capital productive?', *Federal Reserve Bank of Richmond, Economic Quarterly*, **79**(4), 53–80.

Ford, R. and P. Poret (1991), 'Infrastructure and private-sector productivity', *OECD Economic Studies*, **17**, 63–89.

Futagami, K. and K. Mino (1995), 'Public capital and patterns of growth in the presence of threshold externalities', *Zeitschrift für Nationalökonomie*, **61**(2), 123–146.

Futagami, K., Y. Morita and A. Shibata (1993), 'Dynamic analysis of an endogenous growth model with public capital', *Scandinavian Journal of Economics*, **95**(4), 607–625. (Also published in T.M. Andersen and K.O. Moene (eds) (1993), *Endogenous Growth*, Cambridge: Blackwell Publishers, pp. 217–235.)

Garcia-Milà, T. and T.J. McGuire (1992), 'The contribution of publicly provided inputs to states' economies', *Regional Science and Urban Economics*, **22**, 229–241.

Garcia-Milà, T., T.J. McGuire and R.H. Porter (1996), 'The effects of public capital in state-level production functions reconsidered', *Review of Economics and Statistics*, **78**(1), 177–180.

Geweke, J., R. Meese and W. Dent (1983), 'Comparing alternative tests of causality in temporal systems. Analytic results and experimental evidence', *Journal of Econometrics*, **21**(1), 161–194.

Giannini, C. (1992), *Topics in structural VAR econometrics*, Berlin: Springer Verlag.

Glomm, G. and B. Ravikumar (1994), 'Public investment in infrastructure in a simple growth model', *Journal of Economic Dynamics and Control*, **18**, 1173–1187.

Gonzalo, J. (1994), 'Five alternative methods of estimating long run equilibrium relationships', *Journal of Econometrics*, **60**(1–2), 203–233.

Gramlich, E.M. (1994), 'Infrastructure investment: a review essay', *Journal of Economic Literature*, **32**, 1176–1196.

Granger, C.W.J. (1969), 'Investigating causal relations by econometric models and cross-spectral methods', *Econometrica*, **37**(3), 424–438.

Granger, C.W.J. (1980), 'Testing for causality. A personal viewpoint', *Journal of Economic Dynamics and Control*, **2**, 329–352.

Granger, C.W.J. and P. Newbold (1974), 'Spurious regressions in econometrics', *Journal of Econometrics*, **2**(2), 111–120.

Graybill, F.A. (1969), *Introduction to Matrices with Applications in Statistics*, Belmont: Wadsworth.

Griffiths, R.T. (1979), *Industrial retardation in the Netherlands 1830–1850*, The Hague: Martinus Nijhoff Publishers.

Grilli, V., D. Masciandaro and G. Tabellini (1991), 'Political and monetary institutions and public financial policies in the industrial countries', *Economic Policy*, **13**, 341–392.

Groote, P.D. (1996), *Infrastructure and Dutch economic development: a new long run data set for the Netherlands 1800–1913*, Vol. 211 of *Nederlandse Geografische Studies / Netherlands Geographical Studies*, Groningen.

Groote, P.D., J.P.A.M. Jacobs and J.-E. Sturm (1995), 'Output responses to infrastructure investment in the Netherlands 1853–1913', GGDC Research Memorandum GD-24, Groningen: Groningen Growth and Development Centre.

Guilkey, D.K. and M.K. Salemi (1982), 'Small sample properties of three tests for Granger-causal ordering in a bivariate stochastic system', *Review of Economics and Statistics*, **64**(4), 668–680.

Haan, J. de and C.A. de Kam (1991), 'Personeelsvermindering rijksoverheid', in C.A. de Kam and J. de Haan (eds), *Terugtredende overheid. Realiteit of retoriek? Een evaluatie van de grote operaties*, Schoonhoven: Academic Service, Chapter 3, pp. 39–54.

Haan, J. de and D. Zelhorst (1993), 'Does output have a unit root? New international evidence', *Applied Economics*, **25**, 953–960.

Haan, J. de and J.-E. Sturm (1994), 'Political and institutional determinants of fiscal policy in the European Community', *Public Choice*, **80**, 157–172.

Haan, J. de and J.-E. Sturm (1996), 'Politiek-institutionele verklaringen voor de daling van overheidsinvesteringen', *Openbare Uitgaven*, **28**(2), 71–77.

Haan, J. de and J.-E. Sturm (1997), 'Political and economic determinants of OECD budget deficits and government expenditures: a reinvestigation', *European Journal of Political Economy*, **13**(4), 739–750.

Haan, J. de, J.-E. Sturm and B.J. Sikken (1996), 'Government capital formation: explaining the decline', *Weltwirtschaftliches Archiv*, **132**(1), 55–74.

Hackl, F., F. Schneider and G. Withers (1993), 'The public sector in Australia: a quantitative analysis', in N. Gemmell (ed.), *The growth of the public sector: theories and international evidence*, Aldershot: Edward Elgar, Chapter 14, pp. 212–231.

Hagen, G.H.A. van, R.C.G Haffner and P.M. Waasdorp (1995), 'How strong is the case for public investments in human capital? Assessments with an AGE model', paper presented at the 51st Congress of the International Institute of Public Finance, Lisbon, Portugal, 21–24 August.

Harris, R.I.D. (1992), 'Small sample testing for unit roots', *Oxford Bulletin of Economics and Statistics*, **54**(4), 615–625.

Hausman, J.A. (1978), 'Specification tests in econometrics', *Econometrica*, **46**(6), 1251–1271.

Helms, L.J. (1985), 'The effect of state and local taxes on economic growth: a time series-cross section approach', *Review of Economics and Statistics*, **67**(4), 574–582.

Henrekson, M. (1988), 'Swedish government growth. A disequilibrium analysis', in J.A. Lybeck and M. Henrekson (eds), *Explaining the growth of government*, Amsterdam: Elsevier Science Publishers B.V., North-Holland, Chapter 6, pp. 93–132.

Hirschman, A.O. (1958), *The strategy of economic development*, New Haven: Yale University Press.

Holtz-Eakin, D. (1992), 'Public-sector capital and the productivity puzzle', NBER Working Paper 4122, Cambridge: National Bureau of Economic Research. (Also published in *Review of Economics and Statistics*, **76**(1), 1994, 12–21.)

Holtz-Eakin, D. and A.E. Schwartz (1994), 'Infrastructure in a structural model of economic growth', NBER Working Paper 4824, Cambridge: National Bureau of Economic Research. (Also published in *Regional Science and Urban Economics*, **25**, 1995, 131–151.)

Holtz-Eakin, D. and A.E. Schwartz (1995), 'Spatial productivity spillovers from public infrastructure evidence from state highways', NBER Working Paper 5004, Cambridge: National Bureau of Economic Research. (Also published in *International Tax and Public Finance*, **2**, 1995, 459–468.)

Hsiao, C. (1981), 'Autoregressive modelling and money-income causality detection', *Journal of Monetary Economics*, **7**, 85–106.

Hsiao, C. (1982), 'Time series modeling and causal ordering of Canadian money, income and interest rates', in O.D. Anderson (ed.), *Time series analysis: theory and practice*, Amsterdam: Elsevier Science Publishers B.V., North-Holland.

Hulten, C.R. (1996), 'Infrastructure capital and economic growth: how well you use it may be more important than how much you have', NBER Working Paper 5847, Cambridge: National Bureau of Economic Research.

Hulten, C.R. and R.M. Schwab (1991a), 'Is there too little public capital?', paper presented at the conference on Infrastructure Needs and Policy Options for the 1990s, American Enterprise Institute of Public Policy Research.

Hulten, C.R. and R.M. Schwab (1991b), 'Public capital formation and the growth of regional manufacturing industries', *National Tax Journal*, **44**(4), 121–134.

Hulten, C.R. and R.M. Schwab (1993), 'Endogenous growth, public capital, and the convergence of regional manufacturing industries', NBER Working Paper 4538, Cambridge: National Bureau of Economic Research.

Jacobs, J.P.A.M., P.D. Groote and J.-E. Sturm (1996), 'Waren investeringen in infrastructuur produktief in Nederland (1850-1913)?', in *NEHA-jaarboek voor economische, bedrijfs- en techniekgeschiedenis*, Vol. 59, Amsterdam: Nederlandsch Economisch-Historisch Archief, Chapter XII, pp. 238–257.

Johansen, S. (1988), 'Statistical analysis of cointegration vectors', *Journal of Economic Dynamics and Control*, **12**, 231–254.

Johansen, S. (1991), 'Estimation and hypothesis testing of cointegration vectors in Gaussian vector autoregressive models', *Econometrica*, **59**(6), 1551–1580.

Jong, H.J. de (1992), 'Dutch inland transport in the nineteenth century; a bibliographical review', *Journal of Transport History*, **13**(1), 1–22.

Jongbloed, B.W.A., D.J.P. Kerstens, G.H. Kuper and E. Sterken (1991), 'The CCSO database of annual data. Description and listing of data (version '91)', CCSO Series 13, Groningen: CCSO Centre for Economic Research.

Jonge, J.A. de (1968), 'De industrialisatie in Nederland tussen 1840 en 1914', Ph.D. dissertation, Amsterdam: Vrije Universiteit.

Jorgenson, D.W. (1986), 'Econometric methods for modelling producer behavior', in Z. Grilliches and M.D. Intriligator (eds), *Handbook of econometrics, volume III*, Amsterdam: North-Holland, Chapter 31, pp. 1841–1915.

Jorgenson, D.W. (1991), 'Fragile statistical foundations', paper presented at the conference on Infrastructure Needs and Policy Options for the 1990s, American Enterprise Institute of Public Policy Research.

Judge, G.G., W.E. Griffiths, R.C. Hill, H. Lütkepohl and T.-C. Lee (1985), *The theory and practice of econometrics*, 2nd edn, New York: Wiley.

Kamps, H. (1985), 'Overheidsinvesteringen', *Economisch Statistische Berichten*, **70**, 189–189.

Kavanagh, C. (1997), 'Public capital and private sector productivity in Ireland, 1958-1990', *Journal of Economic Studies*, **24**(1-2), 72–94.

Kawai, M. (1980), 'Exchange rate-price causality in the recent floating period', in C. Bigman and C. Taya (eds), *The functioning of floating exchange rates. Theory, evidence, and policy implications*, Cambridge: Ballinger, pp. 189–211.

Keeler, T.E. and J.S. Ying (1988), 'Measuring the benefits of a large public investment. The case of the U.S. federal-aid highway system', *Journal of Public Economics*, **36**, 69–85.

Kelly, T. (1997), 'Public investment and growth: testing the non-linearity hypothesis', *International Review of Applied Economics*, **11**(2), 249–262.

Khan, M.S. and C.M. Reinhart (1990), 'Private investment and economic growth in developing countries', *World Development*, **18**(1), 19–27.

Khan, M.S. and M.S. Kumar (1997), 'Public and private investment and the growth process in developing countries', *Oxford Bulletin of Economics and Statistics*, **59**(1), 69–88.

Kirchgässner, G. and W.W. Pommerehne (1988), 'Government spending in federal systems: a comparison between Switzerland and Germany', in J.A. Lybeck and M. Henrekson (eds), *Explaining the growth of government*, Amsterdam: Elsevier Science Publishers B.V., North-Holland, Chapter 14, pp. 327–356.

Kitterer, W. and C.-H. Schlag (1995), 'Sind öffentliche Investitionen produktiv? Eine empirische Analyse für die Bundesrepublik Deutschland', *Finanzarchiv*, **52**(4), 460–477.

Klundert, T. van de (1993), 'Crowding out of private and public capital accumulation in an international context', *Economic Modelling*, **10**(3), 273–284.

Knaap, G.A. van der (1978), 'A spatial analysis of the evolution of an urban system: the case of the Netherlands', Ph.D. dissertation, Rotterdam: Erasmus Universiteit Rotterdam.

Kwiatkowski, D., P.C.B. Phillips, P. Schmidt and Y. Shin (1992), 'Testing the null hypothesis of stationarity against the alternative of a unit root: how sure are we that economic time series have a unit root?', *Journal of Econometrics*, **54**(1), 159–178.

Lau, S.-H.P. and C.-Y. Sin (1997), 'Public infrastructure and economic growth: time-series properties and evidence', , **73**(221), 125–135.

Lee, J. (1992), 'Optimal size and composition of government spending', *Journal of Japanese and International Economies*, **6**, 423–439.

Levine, R. and D. Renelt (1992), 'A sensitivity analysis of cross-country growth regressions', *American Economic Review*, **82**, 942–963.

Levine, R. and S.-J. Zervos (1993), 'Looking at the facts: what we know about policy and growth from cross-country analysis', Working Paper 1115, Washington, D.C.: World Bank.

Leybourne, S.J. and B.P.M. McCabe (1994), 'A consistent test for a unit root', *Journal of Business and Economic Statistics*, **12**(2), 157–166.

Long, J.B. de (1988), 'Productivity growth, convergence and welfare: comment', *American Economic Review*, **78**, 1138–1154.

Lucas, R.E. (1988), 'On the mechanics of development planning', *Journal of Monetary Economics*, **22**, 3–42.

Lütkepohl, H. (1991), *Introduction to multiple time series analysis*, Berlin: Springer Verlag.

Lybeck, J.A. (1988), 'Comparing government growth rates: the non-institutional vs the institutional approach', in J.A. Lybeck and M. Henrekson (eds), *Explaining the growth of government*, Amsterdam: Elsevier Science Publishers B.V., North-Holland, Chapter 3, pp. 29–47.

Lynde, C. (1992), 'Private profit and public capital', *Journal of Macroeconomics*, **14**(1), 125–142.

Lynde, C. and J. Richmond (1992), 'The role of public capital in production', *Review of Economics and Statistics*, **74**(1), 37–45.

Lynde, C. and J. Richmond (1993a), 'Public capital and long-run costs in U.K. manufacturing', *The Economic Journal*, **103**, 880–893.

Lynde, C. and J. Richmond (1993b), 'Public capital and total factor productivity', *International Economic Review*, **34**(2), 401–414.

MacKinnon, J.G. (1991), 'Critical values for cointegration tests', in R.F. Engle and C.W.J. Granger (eds), *Long-Run Economic Relationships. Readings in Cointegration*, New York: Oxford University Press, Chapter 13, pp. 267–276.

Maddison, A. (1992), 'Standardised estimates of fixed investment and capital stock at constant prices: a long run survey for 6 countries', unpublished manuscript.

Maddison, A. (1993), 'Standardised estimates of fixed capital stock: a six country comparison', *Innovazione E Materie Prime*, pp. 3–29.

Maddison, A. (1995), *Monitoring the world economy 1820–1992*, Paris: Organisation for Economic Co-operation and Development.

Mankiw, N.G., D. Romer and D.N. Weil (1992), 'A contribution to the empirics of economic growth', *Quarterly Journal of Economics*, **107**, 407–437.

Mas, M., J. Maudos, F. Pérez and E. Uriel (1993), 'Competitividad, productividad industrial y dotaciones de capital público', *Papeles de Economía Española*, **57**, 144–160.

Mas, M., J. Maudos, F. Pérez and E. Uriel (1994a), 'Capital público y crecimiento regional español', *Moneda y Crédito*, **198**, 163–193.

Mas, M., J. Maudos, F. Pérez and E. Uriel (1996), 'Infrastructures and productivity in the Spanish regions', *Regional Studies*, **30**(7), 641–650.

Mas, M., J. Maudos, F. Pérez and E. Uriel (1994b), 'Disparidades regionales y convergencia en las comunidades autónomas', *Revista de Economía Aplicada*, **2**(4), 129–148.

Mas, M., J. Maudos, F. Pérez and E. Uriel (1995a), 'Public capital and convergence in the Spanish regions', *Entrepreneurship and Regional Development*, **7**, 309–327.

Mas, M., J. Maudos, F. Pérez and E. Uriel (1995b), 'Growth and convergence in the Spanish provinces', in H.W. Armstrong and R.W. Vickerman (eds), *Convergence and Divergence Among European Regions*, European Research in Regional Science, London: Pion Limited, Chapter 13, pp. 66–88.

Mayer, T. (1980), 'Economics as a hard science: realistic goal or wishful thinking', *Economic Inquiry*, **18**, 165–178.

McFadden, D. (1978), 'The general linear profit function', in M. Fuss and D. McFadden (eds), *Production economics: a dual approach to theory and applications. Volume 1*, Amsterdam: North-Holland, pp. 219–268.

McMillin, W.D. and D.J. Smyth (1994), 'A multivariate time series analysis of the United States aggregate production function', *Empirical Economics*, **19**(4), 659–674.

Mera, K. (1973), 'Regional production functions and social overhead capital: an analysis of the Japanese case', *Regional and Urban Economics*, **3**(2), 157–186.

Merriman, D. (1990), 'Public capital and regional output: another look at some Japanese and American data', *Regional Science and Urban Economics*, **20**, 437–458.

Mokyr, J. (1976), *Industrialization in the Low Countries 1795–1850*, New Haven: Yale University Press.

Molinas, C. (1986), 'A note on spurious regressions with integrated moving average errors', *Oxford Bulletin of Economics and Statistics*, **48**(3), 279–282.

Mooij, R.A. de, J. van Sinderen and M.W. Toen-Gout (1996), 'Welfare effects of different public expenditures and taxes in the Netherlands', Research Memorandum 9602, Rotterdam: Research Centre for Economic Policy, Erasmus University Rotterdam.

Morrison, C.J. and A.E. Schwartz (1992), 'State infrastructure and productive performance', NBER Working Paper 3981, Cambridge: National Bureau of Economic Research. (Also published in *American Economic Review*, **86**, 1996, 1095–1111.)

Morrison, C.J. and A.E. Schwartz (1996), 'Public infrastructure, private input demand, and economic performance in New England manufacturing', *Journal of Business and Economic Statistics*, **14**(1), 91–101.

Munnell, A.H. (1990), 'Why has productivity growth declined? Productivity and public investment', *New England Economic Review*, pp. 2–22.

Munnell, A.H. (1992), 'Infrastructure investment and economic growth', *Journal of Economic Perspectives*, **6**(4), 189–198.

Munnell, A.H. (1993), 'An assessment of trends in and economic impacts of infrastructure investment', in *Infrastructure Policies for the 1990s*, Paris: Organisation for Economic Co-operation and Development, Chapter 2, pp. 21–54.

Munnell, A.H. and L.M. Cook (1990), 'How does public infrastructure affect regional economic performance?', *New England Economic Review*, pp. 11–32. (Also published in A.H. Munnell (ed.) (1990), *Is there a shortfall in public capital investment*, Volume 34 of *Conference Series*, Boston: Federal Reserve Bank of Boston, pp. 69–103.)

Nadiri, M.I. and T.P. Mamuneas (1994a), 'Infrastructure and public R&D investments, and the growth of factor productivity in US manufacturing industries', NBER Working Paper 4845, New York: National Bureau of Economic Research.

Nadiri, M.I. and T.P. Mamuneas (1994b), 'The effects of public infrastructure and R&D capital on the cost structure and performance of U.S. manufacturing industries', *Review of Economics and Statistics*, **76**(1), 22–37.

Nazmi, N. and M.D. Ramirez (1997), 'Public and private investment and economic growth in Mexico', *Contemporary Economic Policy*, **15**(1), 65–75.

Nelson, C.R. and C.I. Plosser (1982), 'Trends and random walks in macroeconomic time series: some evidence and implications', *Journal of Monetary Economics*, **10**, 139–167.

Newey, W.K. and K.D. West (1987), 'A simple, positive semi-definite, heteroskedasticity and autocorrelation consistent covariance matrix', *Econometrica*, **55**(3), 703–708.

Nijkamp, P. (1986), 'Infrastructure and regional development: a multidimensional policy analysis', *Empirical Economics*, **11**(1), 1–21.

OECD (1994), *OECD Annual National Accounts (volume 2): detailed tables*, Paris: Organisation for Economic Co-operation and Development. (Floppy disk)

OECD (1995), *OECD Economic Outlook*, Vol. 57, Paris: Organisation for Economic Co-operation and Development.

Olson, M. (1982), *The rise and decline of nations*, Yale.

Otto, G. and G.M. Voss (1994), 'Public capital and private sector productivity', *The Economic Record*, **70**(209), 121–132.

Otto, G. and G.M. Voss (1996), 'Public capital and private production in Australia', *Southern Economic Journal*, **62**(3), 723–738.

Oxley, H. and J.P. Martin (1991), 'Controlling government spending and deficits: trends in the 1980s and prospects for the 1990s', *OECD Economic Studies*, **17**, 145–189.

Pack, H. (1994), 'Endogenous growth theory: intellectual appeal and empirical shortcomings', *Journal of Economic Perspectives*, **8**(1), 55–72.

Park, J.Y. and P.C.B. Phillips (1989), 'Statistical inference in regressions with integrated processes: part 2', *Econometric Theory*, **5**(1), 95–132.

Passchier, N. and H. Knippenberg (1978), 'Spoorwegen en industrialisatie in

Nederland', *Geografisch Tijdschrift*, **12**(5), 381–395.

Perron, P. (1989), 'The great crash, the oil price shock, and the unit root hypothesis', *Econometrica*, **57**(6), 1361–1401.

Phillips, P.C.B. (1987), 'Time series regressions with a unit root', *Econometrica*, **55**(2), 277–301.

Phillips, P.C.B. and B.E. Hansen (1990), 'Statistical inference in instrument variables regression with I(1) processes', *Review of Economic Studies*, **57**(189), 99–125.

Phillips, P.C.B. and P. Perron (1988), 'Testing for a unit root in time series regressions', *Biometrika*, **65**, 335–346.

Pinnoi, N. (1994), 'Public infrastructure and private production: measuring relative contributions', *Journal of Economic Behavior and Organization*, **23**(2), 127–148.

Ram, R. (1996), 'Productivity of public and private investment in developing countries: a broad international perspective', *World Development*, **24**(8), 1373–1378.

Ram, R. and D.D. Ramsey (1989), 'Government capital and private output in the United States', *Economics Letters*, **30**, 223–226.

Rask, K. (1995), 'The structure of technology in Brazilian sugarcan production, 1975–87. An application of a modified symmetric generalized McFadden cost function', *Journal of Applied Econometrics*, **10**, 221–232.

Ratner, J.B. (1983), 'Government capital and the production function for U.S. private output', *Economics Letters*, **13**, 213–217.

Rebelo, S. (1991), 'Long run policy analysis and long run growth', *Journal of Political Economy*, **99**(3), 500–521.

Reimers, H.-E. (1992), 'Comparisons of tests for multivariate cointegration', *Statistical Papers*, **33**, 335–359.

Rietveld, P. (1989), 'Infrastructure and regional development. A survey of multiregional economic models', *The Annals of Regional Science*, **23**, 255–274.

Roemers, R.J.J. and H.J. Roodenburg (1986), 'Overheidsinvesteringen', in H. den Hartog, K.A. Heineken, B. Minne, R.J.J. Roemers and H.J. Roodenburg (eds), *Investeren in Nederland*, Vol. 17 of *CPB Research Memorandum*, The Hague: CPB Netherlands Bureau for Economic Policy Analysis.

Romer, P.M. (1986), 'Increasing returns and long-run growth', *Journal of Political Economy*, **94**(5), 1002–1037.

Romer, P.M. (1989), 'Human capital and growth: theory and evidence', NBER Working Paper 3173, Cambridge: National Bureau of Economic Research.

Roodenburg, H.J. (1984), 'Overheidsinvesteringen en economische groei', CPB Research Memorandum 10, The Hague: CPB Netherlands Bureau for Economic Policy Analysis.

Roubini, N. and J. Sachs (1989a), 'Political and economic determinants of budget deficits in the industrial democracies', *European Economic Review*, **33**(5), 903–938.

Roubini, N. and J. Sachs (1989b), 'Government spending and budget deficits in the industrial countries', *Economic Policy*, **8**, 99–132.

Sargent, T.J. (1976), 'A classical macroeconomic model for the United States', *Journal of Political Economy*, **84**(2), 207–238.

Saunders, P. (1993), 'Recent trends in the size and growth of government in OECD countries', in N. Gemmell (ed.), *The growth of the public sector: theories and international evidence*, Aldershot: Edward Elgar, Chapter 2, pp. 17–33.

Saunders, P. and F. Klau (1985), 'The role of the public sector: causes and consequences of the growth of government', *OECD Economic Studies*.

Schoonbeek, L. (1989), 'Eigenvalues and eigenvectors of macroeconometric models', Ph.D. dissertation, Groningen: University of Groningen.

Seitz, H. (1993), 'A dual economic analysis of the benefits of the public road network', *The Annals of Regional Science*, **27**, 223–239.

Seitz, H. (1994), 'Public capital and the demand for private inputs', *Journal of Public Economics*, **54**, 287–307.

Seitz, H. and G. Licht (1995), 'The impact of public infrastructure capital on regional manufacturing production cost', *Regional Studies*, **29**(3), 231–240.

Shah, A. (1992), 'Dynamics of public infrastructure, industrial productivity and profitability', *Review of Economics and Statistics*, **74**(1), 28–36.

Sims, C.A. (1972), 'Money, income, and causality', *American Economic Review*, **62**, 540–552.

Sims, C.A. (1980), 'Macroeconomics and reality', *Econometrica*, **48**(1), 1–48.

Sims, C.A., J.H. Stock and M.W. Watson (1990), 'Inference in linear time series models with some unit roots', *Econometrica*, **58**(1), 113–144.

Smits, J.P.H., E. Horlings and J.L. van Zanden (1997), 'The measurement of gross national product and its components: the Netherlands, 1800–1913', Research Memorandum 1, Utrecht: N.W. Posthumus Institute.

Solano, P.L. (1983), 'Institutional explanations of public expenditures among high income democracies', *Public Finance*, **38**, 440–458.

Solow, R.M. (1956), 'A contribution to the theory of economic growth', *Quarterly Journal of Economics*, **70**, 65–94.

Solow, R.M. (1994), 'Perspectives on growth theory', *Journal of Economic Perspectives*, **8**(1), 45–54.

Sørensen, R.J. (1988), 'The growth of public spending in Norway 1865–1985', in J.A. Lybeck and M. Henrekson (eds), *Explaining the growth of government*, Amsterdam: Elsevier Science Publishers B.V., North-Holland, Chapter 12, pp. 265–298.

Statistics Netherlands (1988), *Miljoenennota 1988*, The Hague: SDU Publishers.

Statistics Netherlands (1989), *Negentig jaren statistiek in tijdreeksen. (Historical series of the Netherlands 1899–1989)*, The Hague: SDU Publishers.

Statistics Netherlands (1995), *Nationale rekeningen 1994. (National accounts 1994)*, The Hague: SDU Publishers.

Statistics Netherlands (1996), *Time series labour accounts 1969–1993: estimations by educational level, provisional data (*in Dutch: *Tijdreeksen arbeidsrekeningen 1969–1993: ramingen van het opleidingsniveau, een tussenstand)*, Voorburg: Statistics Netherlands.

Stock, J.H. and M.W. Watson (1989), 'Interpreting the evidence on money-income causality', *Journal of Econometrics*, **40**(1), 161–181.

Sturm, J.-E. (1994), 'Beloop en determinanten van overheidsinvesteringen, 1959–1990', paper presented at the NVOF/IOO 'Workshop voor jonge onderzoekers'.

Sturm, J.-E. (1997), 'The impact of public infrastructure capital on the private sector of the Netherlands: an application of the symmetric generalized McFadden cost function', CPB Research Memorandum 133, The Hague: CPB Netherlands Bureau for Economic Policy Analysis.

Sturm, J.-E. and G.H. Kuper (1996), 'The dual approach to the public capital hypothesis: the case of the Netherlands', CCSO Series 26, Groningen: CCSO Centre for Economic Research.

Sturm, J.-E. and J. de Haan (1995a), 'Is public expenditure really productive? New evidence from the USA and the Netherlands', *Economic Modelling*, **12**(1), 60–72.

Sturm, J.-E. and J. de Haan (1995b), 'Oorzaken en gevolgen van afnemende overheidsinvesteringen', *Tijdschrift voor Politieke Economie*, **17**(4), 10–29.

Sturm, J.-E. and J. de Haan (1998), 'Public capital spending in the Netherlands: developments and explanations', *Applied Economics Letters*, **5**, 5–10.

Sturm, J.-E., G.H. Kuper and J. de Haan (1996), 'Modelling government investment and economic growth on a macro level: a review', CCSO Series 29, Groningen: CCSO Centre for Economic Research. (Forthcoming in S. Brakman, H. van Ees and S.K. Kuipers, editors, *Market behaviour and macroeconomic modelling*, London: MacMillan.)

Sturm, J.-E., J.P.A.M. Jacobs and P.D. Groote (1995), 'Productivity impacts of infrastructure investments in the Netherlands 1853–1913', SOM Research Report No. 95D30, Groningen: SOM.

Summers, R. and A. Heston (1988), 'A new set of international comparisons of real product and price levels: estimates for 130 countries, 1950–1985', *Review of Income and Wealth*, **34**, 1–25.

Summers, R. and A. Heston (1991), 'The Penn world table (mark 5): an expanded set on international comparisons, 1950–1988', *Quarterly Journal of Economics*, **106**, 327–368.

Swan, T. (1956), 'Economic growth and capital accumulation', *Economic*

Record, **32**, 334–361.

Tatom, J.A. (1991), 'Public capital and private sector performance', *Federal Reserve Bank of St Louis Review*, **73**(3), 3–15.

Terrell, D. (1996), 'Incorporating monotonicity and concavity conditions in flexible functional forms', *Journal of Applied Econometrics*, **11**, 179–194.

Thornton, D.L. and D.S. Batten (1985), 'Lag-length selection and tests of Granger causality between money and income', *Journal of Money, Credit, and Banking*, **17**(2), 164–178.

Toda, H.Y. (1995), 'Finite sample performance of likelihood ratio tests for cointegration ranks in vector autoregressions', *Econometric Theory*, **11**(5), 1015–1032.

Toda, H.Y. and T. Yamamoto (1995), 'Statistical inference in vector autoregressions with possibly integrated processes', *Journal of Econometrics*, **66**(1–2), 225–250.

Toen-Gout, M.W. and J. van Sinderen (1995), 'The impact of investment in infrastructure on economic growth', Research Memorandum 9503, Rotterdam: Research Centre for Economic Policy, Erasmus University Rotterdam.

Toen-Gout, M.W. and M.M. Jongeling (1994), 'Investment in infrastructure and economic growth', OC*f*EB Research Memorandum 9404, Rotterdam: OC*f*EB.

Turnovsky, S.J. (1996), 'Optimal tax, debt, and expenditure policies in a growing economy', *Journal of Public Economics*, **60**, 21–44.

Vereniging Nederlandse Gemeenten (1994), 'Geld voor gemeenten', in *VNG congresbundel 1994*, The Hague, VNG Publishers.

Vries, J. de (1981), *Barges and capitalism, passenger transport in the Dutch economy 1632–1839*, Utrecht.

Wagner, A. (1877), *Finanzwissenschaft, Teil 1: Allgemeine oder theoretische Volkswirtschaftslehre*, Lehr- und Handbuch der politischen Ökonomie, Leipzig: Winter.

Wagner, A. (1890), *Finanzwissenschaft, Teil 2: Theorie der Bestcucrung, Gebührenlehre und allgemeine Steuerlehre*, Lehr- und Handbuch der politischen Ökonomie, Leipzig: Winter.

Westerhout, E.W.M.T. and J. van Sinderen (1994), 'The influence of tax and expenditure policies on economic growth in the Netherlands: an empirical analysis', *De Economist*, **142**(1), 43–61.

White, H.L. (1980), 'A heteroskedasticity-consistent covariance matrix and a direct test for heteroskedasticity', *Econometrica*, **48**(4), 817–838.

Wiley, D.E., W.H. Schmidt and W.J. Bramble (1973), 'Studies of a class of covariance structure models', *Journal of the American Statistical Association*, **68**, 317–323.

Wylie, P.J. (1996), 'Infrastructure and Canadian economic growth 1946–1991', *Canadian Journal of Economics*, **29**, S350–S355.

Zalm, G. (1985), 'De mythe van de overheidsinvesteringen', *Bestuur*, **4**(11), 14–19.

Zanden, J.L. van and R.T. Griffiths (1989), *Economische geschiedenis van Nederland in de 20e eeuw*, Utrecht: Het Spectrum.

Zarnowitz, V. (1992), *Business Cycles: theory, history, indicators, and forecasting*, Vol. 27 of *Studies in Business Cycles*, Chicago: University of Chicago Press.

Zelhorst, D. and J. de Haan (1995), 'The nonstationarity of aggregate output: some additional international evidence', *Journal of Money, Credit, and Banking*, **26**(1), 23–33.

Zellner, A. (1962), 'An efficient method of estimating seemingly unrelated regressions, and tests for aggregation bias', *Journal of the American Statistical Association*, **57**, 348–368.

Author Index

Numbers followed by b refer to the bibliography.

183

Subject Index